Apocaly~~~

Apocalypse

From Antiquity to the Empire of Modernity

John R. Hall

polity

First published in 2009 by Polity Press

Polity Press
65 Bridge Street
Cambridge CB2 1UR, UK.

Polity Press
350 Main Street
Malden, MA 02148, USA

ISBN-13: 978-0-7456-4508-7
ISBN-13: 978-0-7456-4509-4(pb)

A catalogue record for this book is available from the British Library.

Typeset in 10.5 on 12 pt Palatino
by SNP Best-set Typesetter Ltd., Hong Kong
Printed and bound in The United States by Maple Vail.

The publisher has used its best endeavours to ensure that the URLs for external websites referred to in this book are correct and active at the time of going to press. However, the publisher has no responsibility for the websites and can make no guarantee that a site will remain live or that the content is or will remain appropriate.

Every effort has been made to trace all copyright holders, but if any have been inadvertently overlooked the publishers will be pleased to include any necessary credits in any subsequent reprint or edition.

For further information on Polity, visit our website:
www.politybooks.com

The former handling of this Historye, was a certaine preparation &
fitting of the parts as they were distinguished one from the other, but
this perpetuall narration compacteth all into one, & setteth the whole
building before our eyes, that we might see to what perfection that
singular frame doth at length come. Nowe it is reserved for this time,
because there could not be a full understanding of these things before
the last Trumpet. The events came forth by little and little, and point
by point, to the knowledge of which the world attained severally &
by leasure – like, as when hangings are unfolded, but nowe when al
things were at last accomplished, it was a fit time to see the whole
garment displaid at large, and to make up the whole frame of the
building together & at once. ...

Thomas Brightman, *A REVELATION of the Revelation* ...
(1615: 396–367 [*sic*])

Contents

Detailed Contents

Acknowledgements

The present book draws together themes that span three decades of my work. Indeed, it has origins in my interest in religion when I was growing up. Many people along the way have helped me in ways that do not lend themselves to bibliographic references, and I want to thank them. My parents, Edmund Kennard Hall and Marian Ross Hall, brought me along on their religious journeys, but they did not push any particular faith or practice upon me. My father, who died in 1961, was an embryologist and a kind and thoughtful man. When I was young, he wisely resisted trying to answer my questions about whether it is possible to reconcile predestination and free will. My mother, with her abiding interest in literature and criticism, cultivated my concern with hermeneutic issues in social inquiry throughout her life, until her death in 1998. H. Stith Bennett introduced me to phenomenology, and during my years in graduate school and thereafter, Guenther Roth encouraged the engagement between phenomenology and the sociology of Max Weber that is at the heart of the present volume. I also deeply appreciate the colleagueship and friendship of Michael Hechter and Philip Schuyler.

To undertake a phenomenological history of the apocalyptic and modernity in the long term inevitably is to write a synthesis that ranges far beyond the expertise of any single scholar, certainly my own. The scale of the project has confronted me with choices about what episodes and issues to examine, and in what ways. All those who write about history know that, even on much narrower topics, they usually could burrow down to deeper levels of detail than economy of exposition allows. Written history is, by its nature, telescoped interpretation. Here, that historiographic condition is doubled, or even tripled: I traffick not in archival data, but in other scholars' time- and discipline-bound studies. I often do so on the basis of an agenda different from those of scholars on whose analyses I have drawn (themselves not always the most well-known sources, but instead an incomplete and sometimes apocalyptically skewed selection of the scholarship on a topic). The result is necessarily a highly exploratory and provisional inquiry. The compensation, I hope, is that it brings into focus an otherwise unavailable understanding of the apocalyptic in relation to modernity.[1]

To try to make sense of humanity's historical legacies over the long term inevitably requires transgressing the borders of academic specializations. For these purposes, licenses for poaching are justifiable in principle, and they should be freely issued. I hope that the license taken here has not become excessive, for the present book is deeply indebted to the scholars who have studied and debated diverse issues linked to its analytic themes. Beyond those cited in endnotes, I wish to thank the people who have read, critiqued, and discussed with me various presentations, working papers, and chapter drafts that built toward and became incorporated into the present volume: Ari Adut, Mucahit Bilici, Anthony Blasi, Fred Block, Kenneth Broome, Sande Cohen, Jack Goldstone, Laura Grindstaff, William Hagen, Gary Hamilton, Naomi Janowitz, Michelle Kendall, Ming-cheng Lo, Reginald McGinnis, Rebecca Moore, Angela Moskow, Ben Orlove, Isaac Reed, Candace Rudmose, Philip D. Schuyler, David Simpson, Blake Stimson, Eddy U, Robin Wagner-Pacifici, Barbara Walters, and Fred Wherry. In addition, I much appreciate opportunities I have had to participate in the communities constituted through the University of California – Davis Center for History, Society, and Culture and the UC Davis Department of Sociology's Power and Inequalities Workshop. Beyond Davis, this project has benefited from exchanges on the New Religious Movements listserve, and from various occasions when I have presented material subsequently incorporated into the present study: the 2002 Conference on Religions and Violence organized by the Canadian Ministry of Foreign Affairs in cooperation with the University of California Institute for Global

[1] Perry Anderson, in *Passages from Antiquity to Feudalism* (1974: 7–9), confronted much the same array of challenges, and I have taken inspiration from how he addressed them.

Conflict and Cooperation; the 2006 conference, "Dying for Faith," at Kings College London; as well lectures and colloquia at the University of California – Los Angeles, Lancaster University, Stanford University, the University of Sussex, and Yale University. I am grateful to Penney Alldredge for her research assistance during an early phase of the project, and to Genevieve Payne for her editorial help during the last phases of completing the manuscript. Finally, my editor at Polity, Emma Longstaff, gave crucial early encouragement for writing this book, and Jonathan Skerrett and Justin Dyer shepherded it through important phases of production and copyediting. Those who so graciously offered all this help are not responsible for the shortcomings that remain.

In a more material way, UC Davis has supported this study through two Faculty Research Grants as well as a sabbatical year in which I drafted the book. I also wish to thank Routledge for permission to incorporated revised versions of text from John R. Hall, "Apocalypse 9/11," pp. 265–82 in Phillip C. Lucas and Thomas Robbins, eds., *New Religious Movements in the Twenty-First Century: Legal, Political, and Social Challenges in Global Perspective* (London: Routledge, 2004). In addition, portions of the book have been developed on the basis of a long working paper from which a shorter essay is also being published: John R. Hall, "Apocalypse, history, and the empire of modernity," pp. 3–16 in Madawi Al-Rasheed and Marat Shterin, eds., *Dying for Faith: Religiously Motivated Violence in the Contemporary World* (London: I.B. Tauris, 2009).

Writing a book depends on a considerable theft of time, stealing away from those you love, from the communities in which you live, seizing odd moments to write on the roof or elsewhere, living out part of your life in something of an other-worldly existence. My wife, Jenny Broome, our eight-year-old daughter Phoebe Cecile Hall, and three-year-old Nicola Ross Hall not only have tolerated this odd behavior, they have accommodated and facilitated it beyond any reasonable expectation. I am deeply appreciative of their patience, and hope I can redeem it in this-worldly life in the future. No, Phoebe, I didn't think the publisher would endorse your proposed title, *The Apocalypse Comes to Town*, but it has real poetic strength, and I'm glad you were interested enough to propose it. I dedicate this book to you and to Nicola, and the future that the two of you embody.

1

Seeing through the Apocalypse

In 2006, the American cable channel Comedy Central presented spliced-together clips from U.S. television news coverage of "the Apocalypse." Finally it had come to this, the Apocalypse as news. CNN's Paula Zahn posed the lead question: "Are we really at the end of the world? We asked CNN's faith-and-values correspondent Delia Gallagher to do some checking." Later in the segment, CNN anchor Kyra Phillips reported: "At least a couple of those four horsemen of the Apocalypse are saddling up as we speak." This prompted the Comedy Central anchor to ask, "Yo, Wolf? Can we get a live shot of that?" Comedy Central's send-up was amusing to watch, in part because it shows how sober, down-to-earth modern news has been displaced by breathless postmodern coverage. Nevertheless, it gave me pause. Comedy Central zeroed in on the *zeitgeist* of an epoch. But we need to do more than trivialize American news media's pseudo-earnest construction of the Apocalypse.

Apocalyptic dramas rarely sweep up significant numbers of people, but they do sometimes. If one measure of an era concerns how widely people embrace any of various apocalyptic meanings, surely we have been experiencing some serious end times, even if we are not agreed about the End of What. The apocalypse is no longer simply the grist of "end of the world" cartoons, "doomsday cults," or the potentially serious, but ultimately insignificant, Y2K anxieties about computers crashing when their software calendars rolled over to the year 2000. Numerous examples suggest that an apocalyptic mood is no longer confined to cultures of religious fundamentalism. 9/11, the globalized Islamicist movement, and the counterposed "War on Terror" triggered diverse mainstream apocalyptic references. In a 2002 *Time*/CNN poll, 59% of Americans surveyed believed that the events depicted in the Book of Revelation would come true. In 2005, Hurricane Katrina both fueled religious anticipation of the coming apocalypse and merited news consideration as an apocalyptic event in its own right. A serious non-fiction book entitled *The World without Us* projects a scenario in which human beings no longer survive on Earth. Only slightly less dismal is *The New Yorker* story about creating a global seed bank. Called "Sowing for Apocalypse," the article anticipates possible crop failures that raise the specter of "widespread starvation." In 2008, Russia's invasion of Georgia provoked rhetoric about an apocalyptic resurgence of the Cold War, and the *New York Times* described economic conditions as "sliding from grim to potentially apocalyptic."[1] We no longer just have an apocalyptic counterculture; there is an apocalyptic culture to boot.

Such apocalyptic invocations concerning imminent or ongoing catastrophes "of biblical proportions," as the rhetoric goes, signal the seriousness of crises, but they sometimes use the word "apocalypse" loosely, and they thereby blur meanings of the term. This is unfortunate. Yet how might we make sense of such a religiously charged term as "the Apocalypse"? One approach is to "translate" it for purposes of social inquiry.[2]

What I will call "the apocalyptic" encompasses a broad range of beliefs, events, and social processes centered on cultural disjunctures concerned with "the end of the world" and thereafter.[3] As the meaning of the ancient Greek word *apokalyptein* suggests, an apocalyptic crisis is marked by "disclosure." In ways that people often read the Bible's New Testament, disclosure means "revelation" of God's will, purpose, or plan, either through prophecy or in events themselves. However, apocalypse can be shifted out of its ordinary register by noting that prophecy is divinely inspired speech, and not inherently speech predicting future events. This suggests that even within religion, an apocalyptic text may be something other than an eschatology that describes the final and absolute end of the world. Such texts usually are not about the End, but about the Present Crisis. Theologies often address the question of eschatology, and are thus in some sense apocalyptic, but theologies – and actions – become more centrally apocalyptic when the *present* historical moment is experienced as the ending of the old order and the passage to a new beginning in a post-apocalyptic era. As the scholar of rhetoric Stephen O'Leary has observed, the central apocalyptic argument can be captured in the formula, "The world is coming to an end." Yet, he continues, the rhetorical possibilities that emerge from the formula are manifold. For this reason, it is important to give consideration to a range of apocalyptic meanings that are not exclusively religious in the conventional sense.[4]

"Disclosure" can entail not only prophecy but also the subject that prophecy addresses. Ordinarily, the culture of an established social order, especially its religious legitimations, screens off everyday life from the harsh light of ultimate reality.[5] However, sometimes the manifestation of powerful forces envelops collective social experience. Apocalypse as disclosure may unveil aspects of the human condition or present historical moment that pierce the protective screen, just as a loved one's death proves traumatic for those who survive, but on a wider scale. Previously taken-for-granted understandings of "how things are" break down. Historically new possibilities are revealed, so awesome as to foster collective belief that "life as we know it" has been transgressed, never to be the same again. Events or prophecies mark a collective crisis so striking that it undermines normal perceptions of reality for those involved, thereby leading people to act in unprecedented ways, outside their everyday routines. Sociologically, then, the time of the apocalypse encompasses more than the religious end time of God's final judgment, or some absolute and final battle of Armageddon. Rather than the actual end of the world, the apocalypse is typically "the end of the world as we know it," an extreme social and cultural disjuncture in which dramatic events reshape the relations of many individuals at once to history.

Life, civilization, and indeed the physical and biological conditions of planetary survival ultimately are precarious, and we live on a tiny planet in an unimaginably immense universe. However, most people would rather hold the awe and anxieties at bay and take the conditions of our everyday existence for granted, pretending them to be durable, even immutable. The apocalypse upsets this contrivance. Under its sign, unfolding history is interrupted. Thus, an apocalyptic episode is a special moment of *social time*. The German social critic Walter Benjamin alluded to this circumstance when he wrote about how a present historical moment could be shot through with "chips of messianic time."[6] Yet Benjamin's image of messianic time bears unpacking. How does the Messiah come? When, for whom, and to accomplish what? Sociologists like myself cannot answer such questions directly: we are researchers, not prophets. What we can do is to look to diverse historical situations in which apocalyptic times engulf social action, when people in various quarters act out one or another apocalyptic narrative. Such narratives, when they manifest, often arise on multiple fronts. Thus, a generalized climate of apocalyptic expectation sometimes takes hold when people confront natural disasters, social or economic dislocation, or calendrical shifts such as the passage to the third millennium or the end of the Mayan calendar in 2012. More intensely, revolutionary apocalyptic narratives call on people to transcend their everyday lives under special historical circumstances, to undergo a rebirth of self and act collectively in sectarian organizations of true believers. In turn, the actions of such groups can amplify a generalized apocalyptic mood.[7] In these dialectical processes, apocalyptic imaginaries can give rise to historical times that are themselves apocalyptic.

This, of course, is not the premise of either the apocalyptic news coverage or Comedy Central's send-up of it. They both invoked a particular religious understanding that treats the apocalypse as a preordained event, already prophesied in intricate detail. Though Comedy Central's satire may have disabused some among the U.S. public of this kind of apocalyptic thinking, it may also have reassured those who were not predisposed to apocalyptic thinking that there was no real crisis, thus helping sustain the seemingly limitless complacency of some Americans about civic issues and world affairs.

The present book is based on a different premise: if we leave to one side questions about God's will, thinking about the apocalyptic can move beyond either mystification or amusement. We can still laugh at the apocalyptic joke, but we need not allow historical encounters with "disclosures" to become overwhelmed by awe. Instead, we can consider the apocalyptic directly, in relation to wider social processes, by examining extreme events and the passionate meanings that envelop them. We can thus significantly shift how we make sense of history and the social conditions of our existence.

Although seemingly alien to modern life, the apocalyptic sometimes punctures history in decisive ways that lie beyond the purview of conventional social and historical research. In this book, I trace a history of the apocalyptic from ancient origins in Mesopotamia to increasingly complex manifestations in relation to emergent modern society. By way of this historical analysis, I argue that encounters with the apocalyptic, and ways of "containing" and "harnessing" it, have shifted dramatically at various historical junctures – for example, in early Jewish and Christian apocalyptic movements, in the emergence of Islam, in the Crusades and the Protestant Reformation, and in increasingly secular ways in the French Revolution, other revolutionary movements, and the consolidations of modern states. The latest apocalyptic eruption of world-historical significance is, of course, the globalized jihad of al-Qaida and its allies versus the Bush administration's counterposed "War on Terror" undertaken from within what I will call the *Empire of Modernity* – that historically emergent generalized global complex of governing projects and strategic power initiatives centered in the West, and militarily in the U.S.

Containing and harnessing the apocalyptic have not been one-directional initiatives: those confronting the apocalyptic, we will see, changed as well, in part by absorbing apocalyptic features that transform society itself. Most importantly, the violence of the state and of modern insurgent revolutionary movements, now increasingly played out in relation to the Empire of Modernity, has taken on apocalyptic trappings.

The apocalyptic thus has a history not because it is a single, coherent social force or reified "thing," but because the interactions between alternative kinds of apocalyptic manifestations and broader social developments have had relatively durable *configurational* consequences, both for subsequent apocalyptic eruptions and for society more broadly.

The history I trace here is only one of many narratives that could be offered.[8] It focuses predominantly, though not exclusively, on the West, where apocalyptic visions arose early, and with profound repercussions.[9] The apocalyptic has also surfaced outside the West, sometimes through diffusion from the West, sometimes through largely independent developments. Today, it has a global significance. The persistence and renewed importance of the apocalyptic in modern times confronts us with the puzzle of a phenomenon that seems neither modern nor non-modern, or perhaps a hybrid of both.[10] But we can go beyond simply acknowledging this heterogeneous complexity. Viewing history "in the long run" through the lens of the apocalypse allows us to reach new understandings of the character of modern society, the forces structuring our historical situation, and the prospects for our world. This book is dedicated to that end.

To understand modern society in a new way requires us to become agnostic about any teleology that assumes the movement of history as "progress" toward some end point of utopian perfection. Indeed, such an assumption is now empirically in doubt.

For much the same reason, we need to avoid any "totalizing" assumption that "Modernity" constitutes a coherent whole. As S. N. Eisenstadt has argued, there are "multiple modernities" rather than a single, overarching reality.[11] Under these historical circumstances, we can no longer rely on modern social theory as our interpretive guide. We need a fresh alternative strategy that avoids complacently employing any of the conventional modern lenses.

A "phenomenology of history" offers such a strategy. This strategy, daunting enough as a term, involves an even more challenging shift in how we think about history. Social phenomenology seeks to identify the most basic ways in which each of us is situated in the "lifeworld" – the everyday realm of the temporally unfolding here-and-now within which we live our lives, connecting to other people and media, social groups and institutions, culture and history.[12] By addressing how different kinds of social time become elaborated in the here-and-now, phenomenology moves away from the conventional modern assumption that there is one, objective world time. It thus disrupts any ordinary sense of "history" as a set of sequenced events located on a line of past objective time. Thus, a broader phenomenological "history of times" becomes integrated with the narrower "time of history."[13]

My central concern is with times that are *apocalyptic*. However, apocalyptic times, eruptions that they are, arise in relation to diverse other kinds of social time: the *synchronic* time centered in the here-and-now, the *diachronic* time of the calendar and clock, and other social elaborations of time – history (itself an invention of social self-understanding, as we will see), strategic time, social constructions of "eternity," and so forth. Thus, a history of multiple social times helps establish a level playing field in which the calendar and "clock time" so important to modern society are no longer privileged in relation to other kinds of social time with which they become intermingled. And different kinds of social time, as we will see, are mediums through which the organization of social life and the exercise of power take quite different forms. The time through which bureaucracy operates, for example, is radically different from the time experienced within a community, different again from the time of war. Piecing together how different kinds of social time emerge and become interrelated in different historical epochs yields a first pass at a phenomenology of history.

With this approach, we can consider how the apocalyptic, along with other seemingly alien, non-modern social forms, articulates with diverse modernizing developments. A phenomenology of history centered on the apocalyptic thus offers a new way of understanding society. With it, we can look to the world as it is becoming. Rather than looking backward to the twentieth-century theories of society developed when high modernity seemed more than just ideology, phenomenology promises a (but not "the") social theoretical description of historical reality.

The chapters that follow pursue a genealogical account of how and why possibilities of the apocalyptic have shifted over the long run, and with what consequences for modern society.

- Chapter 2 describes alternative ways that social time can be orchestrated, and then explores the dawn and historical emergences in the ancient world of both the modern sense of history and the apocalyptic.
- In chapter 3, I show how key transformations of the apocalyptic in Western Christendom from the Crusades through the initial phases of the Protestant Reformation of the sixteenth century reorganized sacred powers in relation to the powers of increasingly powerful "absolutist" states.
- Chapter 4 focuses first on the rise of objective, diachronic time, and then on the containment and harnessing of religious apocalypticism by both Protestant and Catholic European states from the sixteenth to the eighteenth century and, in a decisive new way, in the French Revolution.
- Chapter 5 explores nineteenth- and twentieth-century developments of both religious apocalypticism and secularization of the apocalyptic – in state-initiated war, revolutionary movements, and terrorism that played out in a world increasing structured as the Empire of Modernity.
- In chapter 6, the emergence of the global apocalyptic war of the early twenty-first century – framed on one side as jihad and on the other as the "War on Terror" – is traced in relation to the hybridic circumstances of modernity's empire.
- The history of the apocalyptic in relation to the emergence of modern society detailed in earlier chapters yields, in chapter 7, a radically recast understanding of modernity itself, and thus provides a novel and clear calculus by which to consider alternative pathways of history beyond apocalyptic struggle. In light of modernity's relationships to the apocalyptic, I ask, where do we stand? What are our prospects?

My hope is that bringing the long-run history of the apocalyptic into view within a single sociological analysis will yield understandings that build on the many specific studies to which the present inquiry refers. The scope of this historical survey may seem reminiscent of earlier and now discredited "grand theories" or "universal histories." But I make no universalistic claim to trace the history of humanity or the character of society from some "objective" vantage point. The present study has a sharply delimited focus on the apocalyptic in relation to modernity, and this means that a great deal else gets left out – even concerning the apocalyptic, much less historical developments more widely. Given the long time span considered in this short volume, it amounts to an exploratory inquiry rather than a grand theory or universal history. The stakes are quite different. Once we put into question the relation of the apocalyptic to the emergence of modern society, it is impossible to go back to modern theoretical projects of purification that claim to get at the "essential" character of either modernity or the apocalyptic. Since the eclipse of high modernity, with the rise of postmodern skepticism, and especially in the wake of 9/11, advanced societies have faced increasing cultural pessimism about the prospects of the modern vision, and defenders of that vision have offered increasingly beleaguered affirmations of it. The pessimism no doubt has real sources, and the affirmations are often heartfelt, but both partly derive from a myopic understanding of modernity that comes of misconstruing it on the basis of its (incompletely realized) program. Under these conditions, a pragmatic exploration borne of an altogether different viewpoint may prove useful.

2

The Ancient Origins of History and the Apocalypse

To understand either the apocalyptic or modernity in a new, phenomenological way depends on recognizing their forms of social temporality. But today we are so used to coordinating activities within the web of clock and calendar enveloping our lives that objective time seems "natural" to us. No one doubts that the week has seven days, the day, twenty-four hours, the hour, sixty minutes. Yet a moment's reflection will underscore what a series of social theorists and historians have observed about social time. Yes, in certain respects it is based on repetitive physical phenomena – the earth tilted in its axis in relation to the sun, around which it orbits, the rotation of the earth on its own axis yielding day and night – and human biochemical and neural processes. However, the units of time by which social life is temporally ordered are arbitrary. Hours might have a hundred minutes, and minutes, fifty seconds. Some social groups have "weeks" that last five or six days between weekly markets, and others fail to identify seasons or even years. In some societies in the past, the number of hours of day equaled the number of hours of night, even though in regions of the world with strong seasons, this meant that in the winter, night hours lasted longer than day hours. In short, despite how nearly ubiquitous measurement of time has become, people in different social settings organize and experience even objective temporality in highly divergent ways.[1]

As phenomenological sociologists emphasize, the possibilities of social life are diverse in how they are organized and experienced. Each of us experiences a "shock" when moving from one "finite province of meaning," where we gear into the world in a particular way, to another one where we gear in differently – from dream time to waking up in the world around us, from sitting around the house to working, from talking to making love, or watching television, a movie, or a play.[2] The most diverse social phenomena – bureaucracy, work, worship, play, war, and shopping, for example – are constituted by how people collectively orchestrate and negotiate the multiple horizons and always unfolding mix of temporally structured meaningful social actions – in the vivid present, in anticipation of the future, and in meaningful remembrance of past events. When we consider social life in these terms, phenomenology shifts our attention from events and processes "in" conventional, continuously unfolding "real" time toward sometimes intersecting, sometimes relatively autonomous *social* temporalities of life. By the same token, "history" no longer amounts to a web of events linked on an objective temporal grid; events themselves have to be considered in their temporally textured historicities.[3] This "phenomenological turn" provides a distinctive way to address social processes as diverse as class formation, economic activity, politics, and social movements. A phenomenology of modernity thus can aspire to provide a way of linking everyday life and history.[4]

To chart developments of the apocalyptic and modernity in phenomenological terms, I will proceed by way of reference to six types of social temporality:

1   The most straightforward situation we can imagine involves meanings that are completely contained in the *here-and-now*. Action does not reference events "outside" the horizon of the unfolding moment. But life is rarely, if ever, so simple.

2   *Collective synchronic time* ritually organizes "sacred" meanings designed to guide action. Traditions, memories, precedents, "the old ways" of doing things, habits – all these create the here-and-now – even when oriented to the future – as a presumed replication, reenactment, or commemoration of the past.

3   *Diachronic time* uses rational and objective unit durations of time – seconds, hours, days, weeks, and so on – to provide a constructed framework for coordinating social action and scheduling and commodifying activities, most notably, labor.

4   Historically oriented *strategic time* orients toward intercontingent sequences. People make meanings in relation to events prior to the

present that yield emergent conditions upon which they act in the vivid present to try to influence contingent outcomes and thus advance future attainment of goals. When action is oriented to anticipation of "the End," strategic time becomes *pre-apocalyptic*.

5   *Post-apocalyptic* temporality is strongly inflected with utopian meanings, for apocalypticists, centered on constructing a tableau of the social in a New Era, either a heavenly one or a *"timeless eternity"* on earth, which is approached from a different direction through tradition that seeks a "return" to a "golden age."

6   Finally, *transcendence* encompasses the various ways that the world of everyday experience and the conventional institutional structures of society may fall away or be "bracketed," making absolute present time available to be experienced as "infinite."

This ensemble of possibilities yields a typology that models alternative yet interconnected social temporalities (see figure 2.1). I will invoke these types of temporality as benchmark reference points in the remainder of this book. As we will see, the often nuanced, hybrid, and overlapping complexities of lived temporal enactments cannot be reduced to the six ideal types. Nevertheless, as figure 2.1 shows, alternative basic patterns of social interaction and organization are associated with the six types, suggesting a degree of face validity.[5] Moreover, the typology can be used to tease out the deep meaning structures of more elaborated temporal social forms – both in relation to a single type (e.g., different constructions of apocalyptic temporality) and as hybrids (e.g., tradition mapped in the objective time of a ritual calendar).

Among actual historical developments, both the apocalyptic and modernizing social forms entail distinctive social temporalities. These can be tracked in their historical emergence. However, we have to suspect that many of the developments important to either modernity or the apocalyptic are *discontinuous* with one another: they do not have sequential histories in their own right. Lacking any reason to assume other than this non-linear circumstance, we can trace a genealogy of apocalyptic developments in relation to modernity by pursuing a "configurational history" – one that zeroes in on the most salient and decisive "structural" shifts in apocalyptic circumstances over the long run.[6] This chapter initiates that configurational history in two steps: (1) engaging in a brief and necessarily speculative consideration of primordial social temporalities along what I will call the "synchronic" axis centered in

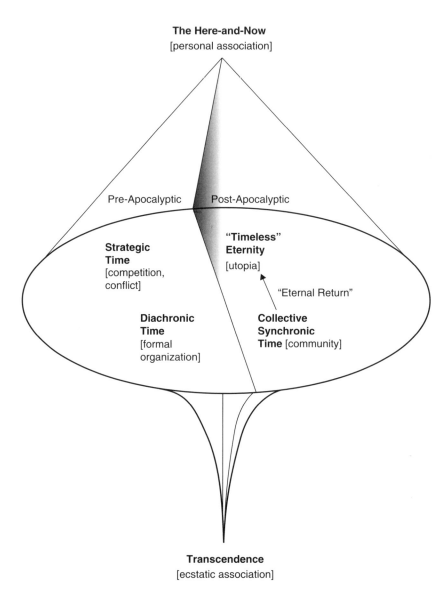

Figure 2.1. A general model of meaningful social temporalities that structure the vivid present, with associated typical forms of social interaction in brackets

the immediately present "here-and-now"; and (2) examining the deep origins of the temporal possibilities of "apocalypse" and "history" that first strongly emerge in ancient times – among the followers of Zarathustra, in ancient Israelite religion, in early Christianity, and in the religion of Islam.

Antecedents: time in its primordial and ancient enactments

The earliest forms of social temporality are those that arose in primordial hunting and gathering societies, and then, with the rise of agriculture and the domestication of animals, during the advent of the ancient cities and civilizations that began to emerge in the fourth millennium BCE. Sketching the basic structures of primordial and ancient times can help us determine whether and how they persist during later historical epochs, and what novel temporalities arose.

The social marking of the cycle of human life can be traced back as far as Neanderthals who buried their dead tens of thousands of years ago. Also, birth inherently is a central event, and early human societies began to mark the passage of their young to adulthood in puberty rites of passage. Moreover, hunting and gathering groups clearly had to orient to seasonal changes, for animal life cycles affected hunting, and plant cycles affected gathering. When agriculture emerged around 10,000 years ago, the seasonal cycle of social life became even more pronounced.[7]

Overall, we may surmise, the temporality of a social group orchestrated its daily rounds, years and seasons (including weather-shift seasons near the equator), festivals marking temporal passages, and the cycles of human birth, life, and death. Temporal experience was centered in the here-and-now, which referenced various objective events – days, lunar and solar cycles – and social rounds of time, but initially without formalizing their measurement. Life transpired in the sequenced ebb and flow of events, not within "time" as a medium or "thing." Here and more generally, as the philosopher Jean-François Lyotard observed, "we must not say time flows *in* consciousness – it is, on the contrary, consciousness which, on the basis of its now, deploys or constitutes time."[8] The challenge is to identify the alternative forms in which this constituting activity occurs in the social world.

In primordial social worlds, the here-and-now was not undifferentiated in its moments. Rather, we may posit a "synchronic axis" that encompasses all the forms of social time strongly centered in the here-and-now in and of itself. What primordial synchronic temporalities might there have been, apart from the everyday here-and-now? On the evidence from ethnographies of surviving groups, insofar as they can be read back, the here-and-now likely was structured in part by storytelling that created "taleworlds" about significant prior events.[9] There is also considerable archeological evidence that primordial human societies engaged in rituals. These rituals, which brought group members together in collectively experienced events, mark first steps in the institutionalization of social time, organized on the basis of tradition. Here, the French sociologist Émile Durkheim argued, is to be found religion in its most "elementary" form.[10] In Durkheim's 1912 account, religion ritually constitutes society's moral and normative imaginary. Importantly, the performance of rituals distinguishes whatever is considered holy – the "sacred" – from "profane" everyday things. Durkheim's theory is rightly critiqued as overly functionalist, ahistorical, and inattentive to religion's diverse meaningful and institutional manifestations. But his basic point about ritual is well taken: it brings the realm of the sacred into the immediacy of vivid present experience, and thereby orchestrates an episode of the here-and-now as a distinctive ecstatic experience of collective excitement that crystallizes social solidarity in the group.[11] Implicitly, Durkheim constructs the synchronic time of elementary societies as divided between the profane here-and-now and the here-and-now of ritual. The latter cordons off the sacred, and the sacred here-and-now potentially alters the collective experience of the here-and-now from what German philosopher Herman Schmalenbach described as people's experience of "communion" with each other to an ecstatic moment of transcendence.[12]

In the mid-twentieth century, the theorist of religion Mircea Eliade identified much the same range of temporalities, but he gave a different valence to ritual. Like Durkheim's account of elementary religion, Eliade's structuralist account of sacred time generalizes across diverse societies. The key difference from Durkheim centers on the relation of ritual to collective meanings. For Eliade, *all* meaningful action in early societies was ritualistic, and communally held archetypes organized such action in relation to mythic meanings. "[W]e might say," he wrote, "that the archaic world knows nothing of 'profane' activities: every act which has a definite meaning – hunting, fishing, agriculture; games, conflicts, sexuality, – in some way participates in the sacred." For Eliade, action in relation to myth obtains a distinctive temporal character: myths frame action as one or another "eternal return," an ahistorical reversion of events to archetypal "exemplary models." Life in its sacred aspects is thus constituted through re-creation of "eternal" traditional meanings, and the here-and-now is constituted in all meaningful respects – even war – in relation to the sacred. Thus, in this theory, ritual is not simply an occasioned collective event that transcends the profane here-and-now through sacred moments shared within the community, as Durkheim held, but rather, "the abolition of time through the imitation of archetypes and the repetition of paradigmatic gestures."[13]

Despite the striking differences between Durkheim and Eliade's theories, both are centered on the synchronic axis, in which temporality is organized via the relations between traditions and their reenactment, which constitute "a chain of memory."[14] Within a world in which objective diachronic time is at most subdominant, submerged by the relative unimportance of linear sequence compared to episodic repetition, both Durkheim and Eliade recognize three temporalities along the synchronic axis: (1) the everyday here-and-now, however much circumscribed by norms and traditions; (2) the performance of ritual in the here-and-now; which sometimes accesses (3) the ecstatic experience of the here-and-now as a transcendent link to the sacred. The differences between the theories have to do with the relation drawn between everyday life and ritual, and whether ritual is collective (Durkheim) or potentially a matter of individual conduct as well (Eliade).[15] On either account, primordial temporal experience may reference passages of objective time in the days, lunar and solar cycles, and seasons, but life is centered in the here-and-now. The differences between the two accounts do not pose a theoretical conflict to be adjudicated: they chart theoretical poles along which empirical variation in the temporal organization of social life can be charted.

A central question remains. Clearly, the advent of more complex early ancient civilizations is marked by both an increasing focus on the measurement of objective diachronic time – the time of the calendar and what would become the clock – and the development of highly complex cosmologies. Yet did these historically new forms of temporality mark a shift toward modern consciousness of "historical" time? It would seem not.

Beginning at least 4,800 years ago in Babylonian Sumer, in Egypt, and elsewhere, and later in the Incan and Mayan societies in the Americas, peoples developed lunar and solar calendars, as well as sundials that could chart the passage of the day.[16] However, it is the view of Eliade that the measurement of objective time initially did not shift the central constructions of temporality in the ancient world. To the contrary, he pointed to the persisting power of tradition and myth to frame cosmology in ways that would resist the ordering of life by way of objective temporality. Eliade acknowledged the gradual increase in the precision of measuring objective time. But he made two points. First, the possibility of measuring time objectively does not dictate who employs such measurement, and how. Both in ancient societies and thereafter, elites calculated times that other people neither used nor cared about.[17] Second, Eliade held that in various ancient societies, the use of objective time measurement met with resistance against what he called "the terror of history." Historical consciousness, he argued, threatened to insert human life into a matrix that was, from a traditional point of view, no longer meaningful, because events and activities would no longer be subject to organization in relation to eternal archetypes. Cosmology, though it might seem to evidence historical time, operates in the opposite way. "From the point of view of eternal repetition," Eliade asserted, "historical events are transformed into categories and thus regain the ontological order they possessed in the horizon of archaic spirituality."[18] Thus, India had its cycles of time, and ancient Greece had its mythic structures of meaning tied to the gods and demi-gods. Although ancient Greece developed complex and conflicting conceptualizations of time – including the existential moment and orientations toward strategy and historical action – as Aron Y. Gurevitch has noted, "The Greek perception of time was still strongly influenced by a mythic interpretation of reality."[19]

For Eliade, cultural and civilizational differences should not mask a basic unity that he claimed for both primordial peoples and the ancients – from the Sumerians and the Chinese to Indians, Egyptians, and the Greeks. History as an extended chronological sequence of events did not exist. This does not mean that there were no "historical" events. Nor does it mean that Herodotus and other ancient Greeks did not record and analyze events. Rather, the vision pursued by Herodotus and others failed to become institutionalized as a model of history.[20] Although history would be invoked, memory of events faded over a short number of generations to the point that events became detached from temporal sequences. In a process not so different from popular history today, historical events – a war, a famine – became reconstructed through processes of collective memory into mythic narratives that held "eternal" meanings. Thus, Eliade held, "the historic character of persons celebrated in epic poetry is not in question. But their historicity does not long resist the corrosive action of mythicization."[21] Rituals, even when they commemorated historic events, transubstantiated them into myths, and all the more so when they framed social events in relation to cosmic exemplary models (of birth, coming of age, death, the harvest, and so on).

Eliade's argument depicts an ancient era when history would have been "intolerable," something to be warded off. Here, we need not settle the question of whether he is correct concerning social *resistance* to history. The important point is that history as a strongly established conception of time did not exist. How then did historical temporality become central to structuring social existence? And whence the apocalypse?

History and apocalypse, connected at birth

No doubt history broke free of myth in multiple times and places. Eliade was simply wrong about one civilization. Ancient China differed from India: it embraced linear and historical as well as cyclical time.[22] However, the most historically significant post-synchronic constructions of temporality can be traced to the ancient part of the world we now call the Middle East. These developments took place, scholars are broadly agreed, through a complex interaction of peoples increasingly enveloped in broader Hellenist and then Roman cultural milieux – those embracing the prophet Zarathustra (called Zoroaster in Greek, hence Zoroastrianism as a religion); worshipers of Yahweh, the monotheistic god of the ancient Israelites; and the Christian religion that arose out of Judaism. Subsequently came the Muslim followers of Muhammad, worshiping the monotheistic god in the name of Allah. Both the dates and the lineages of cultural diffusion are disputed, especially for Zoroastrianism. However, as we will see in what follows, there is clear evidence that among both the followers of Zarathustra and the ancient Israelites, and subsequently the early Christians and Muslims, history could no longer be warded off by the deployment of cyclical cosmologies. The temporal structures of God's purposes became historical, and, in some cases, apocalyptic.

Cosmos become dualism: Zoroastrianism

Zoroastrianism is the transitional case away from the ancient synchronic ritualization of time, important for positing a cosmic conflict between a force of good and a force of evil. Because Zoroastrian oral traditions were not transcribed until the first millennium of the Common Era, its origins, connections to earlier traditions, subsequent revisions, and relationship to ancient Israelite religion are obscure. Nevertheless, many of its ideas have an ancient provenance, and scholars now suggest that the prophet Zarathustra lived sometime between 1500 and 1100 BCE.[23] Certain Zoroastrian motifs, literary motifs, and doctrines are shared with the oldest of India's religious texts, the Rig Veda, which dates to as early as 2000 BCE. Indeed, both religions derive from an Indo-Iranian culture that predated them.[24] Thus, sacred Zoroastrian texts spell out cycles of cosmological time that bear a striking resemblance to the cycles of time posited in ancient India. Yet in ways that seem to anticipate the apocalyptic literature of the Israelites, Zarathustra mapped cosmic time as the playing out of a struggle between opposed divine beings. Ahura Mazda, "Lord Wisdom," acted to sustain all that was good in the world, whereas the divine Angra Mainyu sought to advance *druj*, that is, falsehood and distortion, and their consequence, disorder.

Zoroastrianist scholar Mary Boyce argued that Zarathustra's prophecies mirror ancient Vedic combat myths, but with three differences. First, there is an emergent monotheism, albeit a dualistic one in which the good must fight against evil. Second, Zarathustra's cosmology becomes an eschatology that foresees the ultimate triumph of good over evil at the final battle terminating the cycles of cosmic time, whereupon the world is made "glorious." And, third, the people of the earth are not mere passive spectators in this eternal battle. Rather, people must make a choice between following the good and true, or the false and degenerate. Zarathustra mapped this eternal conflict in earthly terms, as a struggle between peaceful herding peoples and raiding bands of cattle rustlers who threatened herders.[25]

We cannot be sure whether Zoroastrian texts derive from Zarathustra's day or represent an *ex post facto* consolidation of oral traditions used to construct a coherent origin story for a later religion. Either way, Zarathustra's ideas offered a basic matrix for the interpretation of earthly history in relation to cosmic struggle. However, not only beleaguered herding peoples embraced the ideas concerning struggle: an empire did so as well. As the historian of religion Bruce Lincoln has shown, beginning in the sixth century BCE, Achaemenian rulers of Persia adapted dualist Zoroastrian ideas to show that the Wise Lord had chosen them to rule over an empire centered in Persia but ideally coterminous with the earth itself. It was the Wise Lord's plan to contain his dualistic divine adversary (known to the Achaemenians as "the Lie") by bringing the benefits of justice, tranquility, and order to the conquered peoples of the world/empire who would otherwise be subject to the Lie. Thus would the Wise Lord become restored to his full dominion over "primordial wholeness" at the end of history – the End of Time. Placing themselves in the redemptive role of the cosmic plan, the Achaemenian rulers engaged in torture of enemies in order to fight the Lie that dared to challenge empire. Zoroastrian ideas survived the conquest by the Macedonian Alexander the Great in 334–31 BCE, but messianic expectations faded. Eventually, a heretical theology, Zurvanism, reverted to a vast calendrical scheme of time that postponed any final reckoning by thousands of years.[26]

The apocalyptic expectation of the end of time and the post-apocalyptic heavenly reward for the faithful are clearly in evidence in Zarathustra's prophecies. Yet there is little to suggest that Zarathustra was promoting apocalyptic war; rather, he seems to have encouraged a more quietistic preparation.[27] And by far the most extensive portions of surviving Zoroastrian texts concern proper conduct of ritual and life, not anticipation of the eventual end of the world. There is no strong sense that a god intervenes in an eventful history in this world. Despite the tribulations of his people, Zarathustra advanced a cosmic theological dualism rather than an apocalyptic basis for charting a people's destiny. Yet at the hands of the Achaemenian rulers, this dualism spawned a ruthless apocalyptic justification of empire as the basis for divine restoration.

The ancient Israelites: covenant and apocalypse

The development of temporality beyond the here-and-now among the ancient Israelites differed from Zoroastrianism because the locus of the struggle of good versus evil shifted from the cosmic to the earthly plane. For the Israelites, history evidenced an emergent connection to their god, Yahweh. In the face of geopolitical set-backs, this sense of history as the destiny of a people in relation to

God eventually took on trappings of apocalyptic anticipation. The basic contours of these changes yielded radical developments of temporality, carried in the vessel of a religion that consolidated monotheism – the basis of Western religions.

Other ancient religions promoted supplication toward the gods, efforts to appease their anger, and attempts to gain their favor. But the gods do not seem to have talked back much; their benevolence, or lack thereof, would have to be judged by events. For the Israelites too, events were important signs, but they transpired within divine covenants forged through a direct "social" relationship with Yahweh. Yahweh was not a remote god. Rather, he had created humankind in his own image, and singled out the Israelites as his chosen people. Yet this special relationship did not give the Israelites some sort of divine free pass. Indeed, the promise of salvation did not center on heaven after individual death. It concerned the redemptive events that would affirm the destiny on earth of the Israelites as Yahweh's chosen people. Thus, as theologian Rudolf Bultmann observed, history for the Israelites was a unity "constituted by its meaning, the guidance or education of the people by God." Divine history would track the collective history of the Israelites in their struggles for political survival amidst the play of alien powers – Egypt, Babylon, Greece, Rome. If the conduct of the Israelites met with Yahweh's approval, the covenant would be fulfilled through redemptive events occurring *within* history – for example, the deliverance of Israel from the Egyptians. Conversely, the many trials and setbacks that the Israelites experienced came to be interpreted through a theodicy that explained their collective sufferings either as the wrath of Yahweh when they failed to fulfill the covenant or as a testing of their commitment to Yahweh. Insofar as the Israelites were faithful, their trials would thus perversely bind them all the more closely both to one another as a people and to Yahweh.[28] Increasingly, in the face of setbacks and political subjugation, covenantal narratives took the form of redemptive hope for a messiah – an earthly king who would fulfill Yahweh's promise – or for the final historical reckoning of an apocalypse.

Ancient Israelite religion developed in an historically emergent relationship with Yahweh, mediated through unfolding events on earth. The time of the "eternal return" achieved elsewhere through periodic ritual restoration was no doubt important among the ancient Israelites, but it became situated in relation to a new kind of religious time. Creation and eternity ultimately lie beyond human existence. History connected Yahweh with his chosen people in a series of events reaching from the past, through the present, and into the future.[29]

The source of the overall dynamic of ancient Israelite religion has been traced to the narrative of the writer called the Yahwist in the ninth century BCE. By linking the Genesis account of creation with the deliverance of the ancient Israelites from their bondage in Egypt, the Yahwist affirmed Yahweh's embrace of the Israelites as his chosen people and the lands of Canaan that they conquered as the place of their historical destiny. But scholarship now shows that this was, in the language of our day, an "invented tradition," meant to bring together the theretofore polytheistic "twelve tribes" of Israel by demonstrating their shared lineages in putative common ancestors, thereby legitimating a monotheistic religion under the war-god Yahweh, who had unified them militarily to undertake the conquest of Canaan. However, the alliance of the twelve tribes became much more than a military confederation. The northern kingdom of Israel and the southern kingdom of Judah were united by king David, and then Solomon. They became one people, under one god.[30]

Faith could be called upon to reinvigorate the military confederation. Historical setbacks were to be explained by an absence of devotion to Yahweh. So said the prophets. During the eighth and seventh centuries BCE, first the Neo-Assyrian empire, then the Babylonians, then the Persians led by the ruler Cyrus, dominated the lands of Canaan. The covenant basis of the ancient Israelites became further solidified on the basis of a decisive setback – the army of Nebuchadnezzar's destruction of Yahweh's temple in Jerusalem (which Solomon had had constructed in the tenth century), and the subsequent exile to Babylonia, in 586 BCE. It was under these conditions that the prophecy of Ezekiel provided the Israelites with what one scholar has called a "forward-looking" sense of destiny.[31] After Cyrus permitted the Israelite exiles to return to the land of Judah, they became an ever more distinct and separate community that remained powerless in the face of empires. As one religious historian observed, "Politically impotent, without an army or any means of defence, the population of Judah was forced to abandon all hope of regaining national independence in the foreseeable future."[32]

In the land of Judah, under centuries of struggle against domination, the ancient Israelites increasingly became the people of Judah, mostly ethnically Jews, and religiously Jews as practitioners of Judaic religion.[33] Earlier prophets had interpreted misfortunes of Yahweh's people in relation to their failures to maintain their past covenant with their god, failures that might be corrected in the present. But now, the locus of redemption increasingly shifted to the future. Under the duress of defeat and humiliation and exile, Ezekiel looked to a time yet to come when, somehow, Yahweh would redeem his chosen people. Later, writings attributed to the author whom scholars call the Second Isaiah foresaw the ultimate triumph of Yahweh's followers over their enemies, who would meet grisly ends, while Yahweh would establish something like a heaven-on-earth, a peaceable kingdom where, Isaiah prophesied, "the wolf shall lie down with the *lamb*" (Isaiah 11: 6–9).[34]

The sufferings of the Israelites under their covenant with Yahweh were translated into much stronger redemptive expectations in the centuries following Alexander the Great's 331 BCE conquest of the Persian Empire that included all of ancient Israel. First under Hellenistic rule, then with the Roman conquest of Jerusalem in 63 BCE, the Jews continued to be subject to the domination of external rulers who thwarted their worldly redemptive hopes.

With these developments came sectarian differentiation – among Pharisees, Sadducees, the Essenes, the Zealots, and others. There was an intensification of apocalyptic anticipations, not only that Yahweh's historical covenant with his chosen people would be fulfilled on earth, but in the Book of Daniel – completely alien to earlier Israelite traditions – that those who maintained faith might find salvation in life after death. Daniel spelled out the emergent apocalyptic expectations, and his writing demonstrates how historical time could become an object of social reconstruction. For Daniel was written *as though* from the historical moment of the Babylonian exile, but scholars now widely agree that the book was written around the time of the Maccabean revolt in the second century BCE, *after* many of the events that it purported to prophesy already had occurred. The obvious accuracy of retrospective prophecy presumably added weight to Daniel's prophesies about events yet to come, and in contrast to all other ancient Israelite literature, Daniel provided a numerical calculation of the end of time. In the end, if they stood firm under persecution, the Israelites would be redeemed, perhaps by a messiah, "one like a son of man." The writer continued, "There was given him dominion, and glory, and a kingdom, that all the peoples, nations, and languages should serve him: his dominion is an everlasting dominion, which shall not pass away" (Daniel 7: 13–14). Presumably, this was still the Israelite redemption in an earthly kingdom, yet Daniel 12: 2 also hinted at a possibility radical to Israelite theology: at the last troubles at the end of the world, "many of them that sleep in the dust of the earth shall awake, some to everlasting life, and some to shame and everlasting contempt."[35]

The Maccabean revolt against Hellenizing regulation of Judaic religion marked the onset of some two centuries of cultural crisis and conflict. It also marked the emergence of a kind of action approximating martyrdom, itself linked to the idea (novel in Israelite texts other than a brief allusion in Ezekiel 37) that resurrection could follow death. As one scholar commented, at the time of the Maccabean revolt in the middle of the second century BCE, those who martyr themselves in faith "are assured that they will be exalted to the stars. They can afford to lose their lives in this world, because they have a greater destiny beyond death."[36] For another scholar, "Hope of resurrection was intimately connected in the book of Daniel with martyrdom."[37]

From the time of the Maccabean revolt onward, faced with the prospect of enduring colonial rule that could only signify Yahweh's disfavor, parties and sects that followed Yahweh's covenant developed radically alternative stances toward their historical circumstances and what was increasingly viewed as their apocalyptic crisis. The Sadducees came to embrace Hellenism. The Essenes, possible keepers of the Dead Sea Scrolls discovered in the twentieth century at Qumran, adopted an extreme ascetic community rule and intense apocalyptic expectations. In the first century CE, the militant Zealots seem to have taken inspiration from the War Scroll (a copy of which was found at Qumran), in which military struggle is "placed within a firm apocalyptic framework." They launched a "holy war" against the Roman Empire.[38]

Though the Zealots are sometimes regarded as a proto-nationalist rather than a religious movement, they based their militant struggle on a "zeal for God." Here, as in other utopian movements, the modernist effort to differentiate the religious from the non-religious breaks down: *all* countercultural movements deal in a broad sense with the sacred, even if not formally so, for they seek to recast ultimate meanings of existence. The Zealots cast those meanings in relation to an apocalypse that they themselves would help precipitate, both through acts of war against Rome and by the assassination of moderate leaders of Yahweh's followers who might thwart their plans. The result, however, was a quite different apocalypse than they intended. The Jewish War against Rome ended in 73 CE, in the mass suicide of Zealots besieged by the Roman army at Masada, and in massacre, humiliating defeat, and enslavement for the Jewish people.[39]

For their parts, the Essenes retreated from society-at-large to sustain a community of the elect. For them, the War Scroll may have represented a manual for the final struggle of the Sons of Light against the Sons of Darkness, but there is little indication that they entertained any military plans to undertake a struggle against colonial rule. As the "congregation of the Sons of Heaven," more likely, they sought to "escape" the apocalypse, reaching the other side of time, the eternal – on earth, not in heaven. Yet their community probably did not survive the Jewish War against Rome.[40]

The developments of history and apocalypse in the traditions of the ancient Israelites were neither completely novel nor fully fixed. In the first place, especially in their later, more apocalyptic ideas, most notably, the War Scroll, the Jews may have been in dialogue with the Zoroastrian idea of cosmic historical struggle.[41] Secondly, notwithstanding Eliade's argument that historical consciousness among ancient elite Greek thinkers remained subject to popular mythic reduction, from Herodotus in the fifth century BCE onward, ancient Greek thinkers were strongly concerned with the documentation of historical events. Third, there is to be found a pronounced sense of historicity centered on the unfolding relationship with Yahweh, notably in the writings and editorial compilations of the author thought to have written the Hebrew Bible's Deuteronomistic history (Joshua, Judges, Samuel 1 and 2, Kings 1 and 2). Yet the Deuteronomist – in a way similar to compilers of ancient king lists that trace sometimes imaginary genealogical "descent" – invokes history in ways that make political and theological claims for the present and future, for example, by establishing the Israelite claim to land, and instituting a priesthood and kingship. An Israelite conception of specifically historical time – as opposed to the calendar of rituals and sacred holidays – was remarkably undeveloped in any *objective* temporal framework until the prophecy of Daniel spelled out the timing of the final judgment. Actual dates did not matter so much, and they were never mentioned in the Hebrew texts. Conflicts over calendars were animated by sectarian competitions concerning the schedule of rituals.[42]

However, the overall movements of ancient Israelite innovations in the construction of temporality are profound. "History" emerged as a dialectic of past and future realized by present action – all based on a covenantal relationship with Yahweh. Prophecies of apocalypse surfaced in the face of extreme setbacks under the alien rule of successive empires. Apocalyptic meanings became differentiated. They ranged from quietist anticipation that Yahweh would redeem his chosen people, to the holy war of the Zealots that would help precipitate the apocalypse, to the transcendence of apocalyptic chaos by the Essenes as a community of the elect who had embraced an "eternal" existence not in the afterlife, but on earth. These religious constructions of temporality all remain important today, in significant part because of how they became developed within Christianity.

The time of Jesus and the times of early Christianity

The sect that emerged with the ministry of Jesus of Nazareth was of course initially a Judaic one, but after the crucifixion of Jesus, Christianity eclipsed these origins, eventually to become legitimized within the Roman Empire. Closely bound up with these developments, early Christianity radically shifted historical time, apocalyptic time, and their relation to the transcendent time of eternity. These developments can be traced to the preaching of Jesus himself, to the apocalyptic expectations of his day, which intensified after his crucifixion, and to contending Christian responses to the failure of the final day of judgment to arrive as quickly as initially anticipated. The polysemic openness of the Christian religion to multiple interpretations attests its power. We can identify broad hermeneutic possibilities that arise in the ministry and crucifixion of Jesus and the early history of the Christian Church.

During the two centuries prior to the emergence of Jesus as a prophet, the Jews under imperial domination experienced political and religious subordination that fueled occasional rebellions as well as hopes for an earthly messiah (that is, a kingly leader) and apocalyptic expectations of a decisive event in which Yahweh would fulfill their promised earthly redemption. The synoptic gospels of Matthew, Mark, and Luke tell us that after his baptism by John, Jesus continued the apocalyptic vein of Judaic prophecy in his own ministry, sometimes incorporating emergent imageries of angels, demons, and Satan. Jesus told his disciples that the end of the current era and the beginning of the "kingdom" of God as an earthly reign were at hand, and he invoked the prophecy in Daniel to describe himself as the "son of man." Yet one historian of early Christianity has argued that the voicings of Jesus's claims to be the "anointed one" are "oblique and frequently ironic."[43] And although Jesus is said to have expected God's final judgment "before the people now living have all died" (Matthew 24: 34), he added, "no one knows, however, when that day and hour will come." In the gospels, Jesus was famously dismissive of ritualistic exactitude in religious worship, and he preached a transcendent love and forbearance in the face of hatred and persecution. But he also pointed to God's power and the "Awful Horror" that the prophet Daniel had foreseen, and he emphasized that salvation would come for the faithful, not for others.

The sermons and statements attributed to the historical Jesus involve different narrative voicings. From the subject position of a teacher and prophet, some offered strikingly new and heterodoxical ideas. Others drew on widely circulating religious ideas – such as the Sermon on the Mount with its elements found in the Hebrew Bible, Qumran scrolls, and the non-canonical Gospel of Thomas. Still others employed the transcendent voice of revelation from the subject position of divine inspiration. And others may be back-formations based on the early "Christianization" of Jesus. The biblical record of Jesus's teachings, then, is the object of a tremendous range of scholarly, religious, and spiritual interpretation. Yet the significance of this record was fixed by his crucifixion. According to the synoptic gospels, although Jesus would not himself so affirm to Roman governor Pontius Pilate, he was put to the cross as "king of the Jews," between two bandits (who may have been revolutionary Zealots[44]). The legacies of Jesus's life and crucifixion – and of Judaism – gradually consolidated over the next two centuries.

Judaism gravitated toward the Pharisees' rabbinic form, decisively after the disastrous religiously inspired rebellions that began with the Zealots' struggles and their defeat in the first Jewish–Roman War, and irreversibly after the Romans' brutal slaughter of thousands of Jews during the Bar Kokhba revolt, which ended in 135 CE. Yet rabbinic Judaism developed in part through what Daniel Boyarin calls a "production of difference" with early Christianity.[45] The Jewish diaspora in the wake of Roman suppression during the first and second centuries CE put to an end strong apocalyptic expectations that Yahweh would intervene any time soon to redeem the Jews' historic destiny as Yahweh's chosen people. Apocalyptic history would stretch out into historical time proper.[46]

For their parts, the early followers of Jesus contended with a different matrix of interpretive challenges. How could their messiah have died? When would he come again? What of the final judgment? How were the Jews to be redeemed? It is not for us to answer these questions. What is important is how different followers of Jesus came to answer them.[47] A split developed between the Jerusalem Church – which interpreted Jesus specifically as the messiah anticipated by the Israelite prophets – and the church outside Jerusalem as it developed under Paul of Tarsus. The Jerusalem followers of Jesus naturally saw their audience as Jews, they sought to fix Jesus's stature as the messiah of the Jews, and they located this messiahship within the apocalyptic narratives of Daniel and others. Jesus, for them, was the culmination of an historical relationship between the ancient Israelites and Yahweh. His crucifixion, initially disconcerting to his followers, became deemphasized in favor of fervent expectations of his prophesied return as the messiah of the Jews.

Paul, on the other hand, had a strong interest in universalizing the legacy of Jesus, and this interest led him to dissociate Jesus from the history of the Israelites. Jesus could not be their messiah as a chosen people, for that position would leave no space for gentiles as followers. At the hands of Paul, himself a Jew who became a follower after the crucifixion and never met Jesus, Jesus attained a new and decidedly mystical rather than historical significance – as Christ, the divine son of God whose death and resurrection offered the promise of a new and universal salvation of all humankind. As Rodney Stark has shown, Hellenized Jews of the diaspora represented a significant component of early Christian conversions.[48] But by converting, those Jews who became Christians assimilated to a non-ethnic "universal" identity. Even though Paul's dispensation was grounded in the universalistic extension of Yahweh's covenant with Israel, it had the perverse consequence of excluding the relevance of Judaic religious practice.[49] With Christ, believers – Jews or gentiles – were to die of their old selves and be reborn to an immediacy of fellowship whereby they could "live with him" (Romans 6: 8). One scholar observes, "Paul tells his followers that, because of this new mystical 'living in Christ,' they were no longer dependent on knowledge of the historical Jesus," but possessed the opportunity for knowledge of the "transcendental Christ."[50] Nor, then, would the personal memories of Jesus held within the Jerusalem Church bear any relevance to Christianity. Paul's transubstantiation of Jesus from the historical to the mystical simultaneously invented Christianity as universal salvation, discredited his Jerusalem competitors, and enhanced Paul's own hermeneutic authority. Yet this shift required other revisions. The salvation in question could not be the collective redemption that the followers of Yahweh sought as deliverance from their oppressors, sited as this redemptive need was in the historical struggles of a specific people. Writing some twenty years after Jesus's death, at a time before the four gospels had compiled accounts of the events surrounding Jesus's life, Paul did not characterize the crucifixion as the product of an episode involving Pontius Pilate and the Jews. Instead he employed a contemporary rhetoric of Gnostic mysticism, in which demonic "rulers of this age" (I Corinthians 2: 6–8) were tricked by God into putting Jesus to death so that he could fulfill God's plan for resurrection by offering a general opportunity for individuals to obtain God's forgiveness of sins and promise of salvation in their own lives.

Theologies of Jesus's crucifixion built upon an Israelite tradition of martyrdom, but in a radically new way. Previously, followers of Yahweh did not understand their acts of submission to death as bringing nearer the day of reckoning with history that Yahweh promised; their deaths were simply testaments symbolizing their faith in Yahweh, who one day would redeem his chosen people. The crucifixion of Jesus followed in the tradition of Israelite martyrdom. However, early Christians, probably influenced by Greek conceptions of heroism, interpreted the death of Jesus in ways that altered the meaning of martyrdom. In the archetypal Israelite pattern, Jesus could have avoided death by recanting faith but chose not to do so. In keeping with the frame of Israelite tradition, the martyrdom of Jesus could be seen as a sin-offering atoning for the acts of his opponents, the apostasy of doubters, and the failings of his followers.[51] But Paul's letter to the Romans (3: 19–26) interprets Jesus's death as something different: it becomes a shedding of blood through which God offers redemption from the guilt of sin to all humankind who testify to faith in Jesus. Hence, the formulation, "Christ died for our sins."[52] In Paul's account, martyrdom was transformed from the test of faith for Yahweh's people to the vessel of hope for those with faith in Christ – Jew and gentile alike. With universalization, salvation became individual and immediate. In the words of one analyst, Paul "conceived of the Christian as one who had died to his former self, becoming a new creation by his mystical integration with the transcendental Christ."[53] Through the rituals of baptism and communion, the Christian believer could ignore history or, as Eliade would have it, become inoculated from the "terror of history." But this would not transpire as an eternal return. Rather than looking back to a primordial earthly paradise, conversion – and then ritual – placed the Christian believer in an eternal present that does not really participate in history in this world.[54]

The legacy of Paul's novel interpretation itself depended on historical events. The Jerusalem Church, with its Judaic emphasis, initially was more effectively positioned to assert its legitimacy due to its participants' memories of Jesus himself. But the Jerusalem Church did not survive the Roman suppression of the Jews after their revolt that began in 66 CE. Instead, the revolt precipitated a broad gentile antagonism toward Jews. Followers would be well served by strongly dissociating Jesus from Jewish nationalism, even though he arguably was crucified "as a Jewish revolutionary."[55]

It was under these circumstances that the writer of the Gospel of Mark constructed a narrative of Jesus's trial and execution. Mark emphasized a mutual rejection by Jews and Jesus of one another, and claimed a decisive role of Jews in bringing Jesus to trial and crucifixion. He thus neatly conjoined a novel interpretation of the historical Jesus with a mystical account similar to Paul's, of the universal transcendent Christ as savior. Mark's synthesis left in play three elements, the dynamic among which would shape the emerging Christian Church – personal salvation, apocalypse, and history. Personal salvation might be both immediate and eternal, but believers still continued their earthly lives, and if their savior did not return soon, if the day of final reckoning foretold in the apocalyptic literature did not happen during their lifetimes, would death cheat them of eternal salvation? Alternative collective solutions to this puzzle fixed a new Christian hermeneutic matrix of temporality.

On the one hand, the Christian Church as it became institutionalized increasingly displaced any intense immediate expectation of the Second Coming (what the Christian Bible referred to, in Greek, as the *Parousia*) or the apocalypse more generally. At most, anxieties about the Day of Judgment might be employed to underscore the urgency of accepting Christ as savior. With Mark's synthesis, a division between the previous and the new life of the convert mirrored a pivotal event that marked a division of historical time, between the "old covenant" of the time before Christ and a new historical epoch, under a "new covenant." This was when the course of history changed. In turn, some Christians tried to calculate the dates of the *Parousia* and God's final judgment with exactitude. In the earliest known instance, Julius Africanus, in the first half of the third century, calculated that some 300 years remained.

However, temporal and historical precision did not make any substantial difference for Christianity as a philosophy of history, at least as it was consolidated by the North African bishop Augustine of Hippo. Early in the fifth century, Augustine forged a synthesis that still echoes in the twenty-first century. For Augustine, history continuously unfolds, but it has become divided by a dramatic, world-changing development – the life and death of Jesus Christ – that displaced the ancient Israelite emphasis on history as the narrative of shifts in Yahweh's favor or dissatisfaction toward his chosen people. Augustine proposed to track historical developments as the teleological unfolding of God's now universal plan, presumably until the end of time, whenever God should deem that day of judgment to arrive. World history had become sacred.[56]

Under this new temporalization of a history that begins anew, the institutionalized church came to assert what Max Weber called "office charisma," the embodiment of divine powers within the church as an organization, not dependent upon the personal charisma of its officials.[57] As theologian Rudolf Bultmann put it, "the church is changed from a community of the saved into an institution of salvation." In this reading, Christianity is founded on the paradox of a transcendental eternity of the end of history that is continuously anticipated and enacted within history, as an "eschatological present." The believer acts *in* the world, but on the basis of a vision not *of* the world.[58]

However, the trope of final judgment as incentive to conversion did not tamp down intense expectations about the Second Coming.[59] When and why the Apocalypse of John, or Book of Revelation, was written are questions still debated, as is the matter of how persecuted were the Christians of its day.[60] But there is no need to invoke social-science theories of "relative deprivation" in order to account for Revelation's contents. Ideology can build on memory, with or without the presence of extreme oppression. The main contours of the Apocalypse as text are clear enough. Its author, John, probably wrote from the Greek isle of Patmos in the eastern Mediterranean in the early 90s CE, when tradition has it that he was exiled by the Roman emperor Domitian.[61] John addressed his text to Christians in seven churches in Asia Minor, whom, in chapters 1 to 3, he rallied to the faith and against heresy and backsliding.

The apocalyptic scenario, which John abruptly began to depict in chapter 4, anticipated terrible events on earth that offered the hope of final redemption for those who believed, and violent suffering and destruction for everyone else. "A door was opened in heaven," and a trumpet spoke to John, telling him, "I will shew thee things which must be hereafter" (Revelation 4: 1).[62]

Thereupon John recounted symbolically saturated visions, of four beasts, the slain Lamb (Jesus) with seven horns and seven eyes, the famous four horsemen of the Apocalypse, the book with seven seals opened one by one, until the opening of the seventh seal leads to the seven angels sounding the seven trumpets, yielding torrents of hail and fire, pollution of the waters of the earth, the smiting of the sun, moon, and stars that spreads darkness in the world, and the furnace of the bottomless pit, from the smoke of which comes the plague of locusts that torment those lacking the seal of God on their foreheads, until the sixth angel unleashes an army of 200,000 horsemen who proceed to the slaughter of one-third of humankind by fire, smoke, and brimstone. Finally the seventh angel announces that "there should be time no longer" (Revelation 10: 6). This, then, is the beginning of the end. But only the beginning. Michael and his angels fight against a great red dragon. Then an angel announces, "Babylon [Rome] is fallen, is fallen, that great city, because she made all nations drink of the wine of the wrath of her fornication" (Revelation 14: 8). Thereupon those with 666, the mark of the beast, on their foreheads are "tormented with fire and brimstone in the presence of the holy angels, and in the presence of the Lamb" (Revelation 14: 10). With more wrath, plagues, and brimstone, and the terrible world-destructive earthquake at the battle of Armageddon, Babylon finally falls. But this is still not the end, for Satan has yet to be chained up while Christ and those put to death in his name rule as kings for a thousand years. After that, the Devil must go out to deceive all the nations scattered around the world – referred to as Gog and Magog – and then himself be cast into a lake of fire and brimstone, so that John finally can see the Lamb's wife, a "new Jerusalem" with a street of pure gold, where "there shall be no more death, neither sorrow, nor crying, neither shall there be any more pain: for the former things are passed away" (Revelation 21: 1–4).

The significance of the Apocalypse over many centuries stems from the myriad ways that it has been interpreted, sometimes with astonishing exactitude compared to the often shadowy visions of John. His Apocalypse must have been taken at the time as a prophecy about the near future, for the angel who guided him in his vision ordered, "seal not the sayings of the prophecy of this book: for the time is at hand," and God will "come quickly" to "give every man according as his work shall be" (Revelation 22: 10, 12). With the disappointment of this expectation, Christians concerned with the last days over the centuries have wrought two major channels of interpretation – pacific and militant, each with alternative internal possibilities.

In the more pacific line, the task of Christians is to prepare themselves, or, sometimes, the world, for the Second Coming of Christ and the day of final judgment, for if Revelation is clear on one thing, it is that heaven only has room for the faithful. Yet John, writing in the first century CE, did not bring his visionary yet often worldly metaphorical account to anything like modern historical exactitude – despite intriguing references to the time that has come, to a series of kings and their reigns, to the thousand-year reign of God's angel over Satan, and to Christ's thousand-year reign with "the souls of them that were beheaded for the witness of Jesus, and for the word of God, and which had not worshipped the beast, neither his image, neither had received his mark [666] upon their foreheads" (Revelation 20: 4). Apocalyptically attuned Christians subsequently varied the durations of their anticipations according to the immediacy of salvation quests, historical constraints, theological needs, and mathematical reasoning, and especially, when "prophecy failed."[63] History could be coming to an end very soon, or the revealed and anticipated events might emerge only on the far distant horizons of history, leaving the faithful with the problem of what to do in a Christian life that would end before the end.

Either the immediate or the distant interpretation is open to far more detailed specification. Under a regime of apocalyptic immediacy, believers may undergo intense experiences that disrupt their previous lives. Thus, in the latter second century, Montanus and his two noted converts Priscilla and Maximilla went into ecstatic trance states from which they spoke prophecies; followers separated themselves into a community to await the end, and, when it did not arrive, continued to live together in a sort of post-apocalyptic "heaven on earth."[64] As the example of the Montanists suggests, the apocalypse offers prophets a ready and compelling basis to elaborate freelance narratives. For a religious organization seeking either to establish itself as a church or to maintain its established position, this opening to prophecy poses a problem. The apocalypse either must be contained by a religious organization, or it will offer a cultural conduit for heretical and heterodoxical religious movements, especially in times of tribulation.

The important alternative to pacific readings of the Book of Revelation derives from its militaristic imagery. Already in less militant interpretations there is the possibility that proper actions of believers could hasten the arrival of the day of judgment, a day that, terrible though its process may be, lays the foundation for the final redemption of believers. After the crucifixion of Jesus, some followers came to regard martyrdom as an event that might actually *quicken* the coming of the apocalypse and thereby help establish the Kingdom of God on earth, at the same time offering martyred believers immediate heavenly salvation.[65] Of course, martyrdom might unfold as an act of non-resistance, as it had with Jesus. However, the militaristic and violent imagery of the Book of Revelation builds on apocalyptic scripts previously enacted by the Zealots, of using violence to achieve God's purposes, or, in failure, as at Masada, of accepting collective martyrdom in the form of mass suicide rather than submitting to slavery or worse at the hands of God's worldly foes. For both the Israelites and the early Christians, martyrdom was hardly inevitable. Like Jesus, they were often given the choice of recanting, and thus avoiding death. The rabbinic Jews acquiesced to Roman rule and religious regulation that still left them the right to worship Yahweh. On the other hand, the early Christians sometimes aggressively propagated their faith, and they thus encountered boundary problems with Roman rule. Many Christians in the first three centuries worshiped privately and never faced persecution, but others actively sought it, and over the centuries tens of thousands of believers died as testaments to their faith.[66]

The historical records of this pursuit of martyrdom clearly show that it did not spring forth as the personal choice of individuals acting on their own. To the contrary, the attitudes and behavior that would be necessary to stage one's martyrdom were shaped through practices of social control carried out by religious communities. As the *Martyrs of Lyons* reported concerning a trial of Christians in 177 CE,

> Then ... the proto-witnesses were manifestly ready, and finished their confession with all eagerness. But some appeared *unprepared* and *untrained*, weak as yet, and unable to endure so great a conflict. ... Then all of us feared greatly on account of uncertainty as to their confession; not because we dreaded the sufferings to be endured, but because we looked to the end, and were afraid that some of them might fall away.

In the end, those at Lyons who survived torture came to death in the spectacle of the public arena. Such practices of martyrdom among early Christians raged to the point of group or mass suicide that echoed Masada, and they may have led Augustine to his strong injunction against taking one's own life.[67]

Beyond martyrdom, the Apocalypse can be taken to an even more militant reading. It depicts angels sent forth from heaven to mete out God's wrath on the unrepentant nations. "Unclean spirits like frogs" gather kings and people together at Armageddon. "The Lamb" overcomes those who make war with him. Amidst the smoldering rubble of destruction that ensues, a "mighty angel" affirms, "Thus with violence shall that great city Babylon be thrown down, and shall be found no more at all" (Revelation 18: 21). On a white horse comes one "called faithful and true, and in righteousness he doth judge and make war" (Revelation 19: 11). John sees "the beast, and the kings of the earth, and their armies, gathered to make war against him that sat on the horse, and against his army" (Revelation 19: 19). After the beast and the false prophet got cast into a "lake of fire burning with brimstone," "the remnant were slain with the sword of him that sat upon the horse," leaving the fowl of heaven to sup on the flesh of those who have been slain – "the supper of the great God" (Revelation 19: 16–21). These events all precede the establishment of the New Jerusalem, a city that has the glory of Rome and more, but under the rule of God. There is not a little *ressentiment* here, an anger at persecution that seeks its revenge, and an envy that would fulfill its revenge by emulation of the power and position of the fallen kings: the last shall be first. No longer under the boot-heel of the oppressor, they shall have the rule of their God on earth as it is in heaven. Their opponents and those without faith are destroyed.[68]

This violent cataclysm is all divinely orchestrated. However, how believers participate is open to interpretation. The Christian Church did not directly address this question until the medieval era (see chapter 3), in part because Augustine moved strongly early in the fifth century to counter apocalyptic expectations that the end of time would come any time soon, by the solution of shifting history (and, thus, the millennium) to a spiritual plane that occasionally becomes injected into this world, in a way as Paul had transcendentalized the death of Jesus.[69] Augustine would not warrant intense apocalyptic anticipation, for he lived in a Roman Empire that became increasingly Christianized once the emperor Constantine converted early in the fourth century and founded a new capital at Byzantium (later renamed Constantinople). In Augustine's magisterial book *The City of God*, the spread of Christianity became the symbolic flowering of millennial history, albeit in a world where turmoil called Augustine to contemplate the problem of when "just war" on behalf of the empire might be legitimate: "it is the wrong-doing of the opposing party which compels the wise man to wage just wars," as a matter of defending the peace of Christians – especially the innocent and helpless – and their homelands.[70]

With Augustine, the millennial kingdom has arrived – certainly transcendentally, and, in some interpretations, as an historical epoch. Apocalypse is contained by its delay to a distant future, after the millennium. Into the bargain, history – and, with it, the power of emperors and kings and queens – acquires a Christian *telos* as the fulfillment of God's purpose. In 525 CE, the monk Dionysius Exeguus inscribed this *telos* in the passage of time itself, proposing to order the passing of years from the presumed date of the Virgin Mary's announcement about the upcoming birth of Jesus. However, he seems to have miscalculated the year, now conventionally dated to 4 BCE.[71]

Islam, history, and jihad

In Islam, Jesus was not the divine son of God. He was a major prophet in a series that ran from the Israelite Abraham through Muhammad, the last prophet, to whom Allah revealed the Qur'an. The origins of Islam in the prophecy of Muhammad are closely bound to the historical circumstances of his day, the social context of Bedouin and Arab culture, the economic location of Muhammad's birth city of Mecca on the Arabian Peninsula, and the trajectory of Muhammad's career. Pietistic and egalitarian aspects of Islam are central to the faith. Yet the rapid conquest that spread this faith in the decades after Muhammad's initial visions of Allah marks Islam as a religion with a vivid originary apocalyptic dimension that on more than one occasion has figured strongly in its historical development.

Islam builds upon the ancient Israelite and Christian monotheistic emphases on history. In addition, mystical sectarian developments of Sufism offer an Islamic avenue to the transcendence of ordinary time in an ecstatic here-and-now. However, a central construction of temporality in Islam derives from the doctrine of jihad, sometimes (controversially) translated into English as "holy war." Whether jihad centers on the inner ("greater") struggle of the individual toward perfection or the outer ("lesser") struggle involved in the conduct of warfare is a theological question bound up in the historical circumstances of Muslims facing questions of how and how soon redemption is to come, and how believers are called upon to fulfill the expectations of Allah.[72] The significance of greater jihad (*al-jihad al-akbar*) as a religious ethic is not to be discounted. However, it is the lesser jihad of warfare on behalf of the faith (*al-jihad al-asghar*) that is of broader historical significance, for it builds the apocalyptic further in the direction of religious triumphalism. In the initial Islamic conception, as the last of Allah's prophets, Muhammad was to preside over the end of time.[73]

Muhammad was born around 571 CE in the town of Mecca, which sat astride western Arabian caravan trade routes that connected the Byzantine province of Palestine to the north with the relatively opulent south of the Arabian Peninsula.[74] Mecca was surrounded by harsh desert lands peopled by nomadic pastoral Bedouin clans and occasional agricultural settlements centered on oases – some of them Jewish communities. The town prospered as an entrepôt that serviced the caravan traffic with guides, supplies, and commercial exchange, and as a destination of pilgrimage to its shrine, the Ka'ba. Orphaned by the age of six, Muhammad was taken in and raised by his uncle, Abu Talib. Eventually Muhammad married an older wealthy widow, Khadija. During retreats to a cave near Mecca, he heard a voice announcing, "You are the Messenger of Allah." Visions and voices persisted. Around 610, Muhammad's visions made him understand that he was to transcribe the messages he was receiving from Allah, and those that he recorded over the course of his life came to constitute the Qur'an – "The Recitation."

The early history of Islam as a religion is bound up with the astonishing life of Muhammad, who, in a polytheistic world filled with spirits and gods, advanced the creator god Allah as the one god, proclaimed himself the last of the prophets, and warned of a coming day of judgment. His monotheism strictly limited clan warfare and vengeance struggles, and emphasized family obligations, ritual piety toward Allah, and a broadly egalitarian view concerning the status positions of the faithful.

Muhammad gathered an initial community of followers around him in Mecca. However, they met strong opposition from other townspeople, and in 622 CE, perhaps believing that doom awaited the town so hostile to him and his claims for the authenticity of his visions, Muhammad and a band of his followers undertook what came to be known as the *hegira* (emigration) from Mecca. They travelled some 200 miles north to the oasis town of Yathrib (now Medina), where contending clans welcomed him as a mediator. From that date, the dawn of the Muslim calendar was later reckoned.

In Medina, positioned as the messenger of Allah, allied with no single tribe or clan, or even necessarily with Arabs over Jews or Christians, Muhammad came to serve as the arbiter who would resolve intergroup quarrels. But the landless Meccans who had come to Medina lacked any basis of livelihood, and under these circumstances, Muhammad forged a distinctive alloy, joining the ancient practice of brigandage with blessings of Allah. This fusion produced an expansionary warring theocratic regime that governed the *umma*, or community of the faithful. In this trajectory, Muhammad proved over and over again to be both an effective prophet and a superb strategist. In practice, he connected a novel religious dispensation to the conduct of politics and war in unfolding historical time. The first incident apparently occurred in 624, when Muhammad ordered followers to undertake an attack on a Meccan caravan. To Muhammad went a fifth of the booty – coupled with obligations to Allah to care for orphans and the poor. The rest of the spoils were to be shared out equally among those who carried out the attack.[75] This undertaking differed little in structure from preexisting patterns of caravan raiding. However, Muhammad many times received Allah's endorsement for the religious exercise of violence:

> And fight in the way of God with those
> who fight with you, but agree not: God loves not the aggressors.
> And slay them wherever you come upon them,
> and expel them from where they expelled you;
> persecution is more grievous than slaying.[76]

Thus emerged a pattern of religiously sanctioned spoils warfare. Two months after the initial caravan raid, in the battle of Badr, against forces from Mecca organized to defeat Muhammad, conflict attained apocalyptic overtones, with 3,000 angels said to take his side. As one scholar of Islam, David Cook, has summarized the outlook of proto-Muslims, they "were at peace with God and with fellow human beings who believed in God and the Last Day (Qur'an 48: 16), but at war with those who denied these basic realities."[77] Victory was interpreted as a sign of Allah's support, and Muhammad became emboldened not only to initiate further expeditions for plunder, but also to take hostages for ransom, and women for wives, to exact tribute through threats and force, and to encourage ruthless assassination of apostates and those poets and propagandists who mocked him, his visions, and his message.[78]

Muhammad did not command a standing army. Rather, men – and the occasional woman – decided whether to participate in any given mission. No doubt the increasing numbers of people in those groups that made common cause with Muhammad participated for diverse reasons. Some joined out of religious belief or hope for salvation in the sensual paradise of Eden that Allah depicted through Muhammad, others out of fear of dispossession or political calculation concerning the likelihood of Muhammad's increasing sphere of power, and others for the spoils. Yet the consequences exceed any individual or group motives.

Not quite ten years after the *hegira*, Muhammad and his followers returned to take Mecca in triumph, meeting only token opposition. From then on, Muhammad and those who "surrendered" to Allah (that is, in Arabic, Muslims) built out wider and wider circles of direct rule, alliances, and tributary client regimes that came to dominate the western half of the Arabian Peninsula. Ironically, however, the pacification of vendetta conflict and brigandage that accompanied political success left many tribes bereft of their traditional bases of economic support, and their men emasculated. The Prophet's solution to this dilemma fortuitously redirected Arab armed conflict toward the north, toward Palestine and Syria, for further conquest, spoils, and religious conversion.[79]

Here, with Max Weber, we can trace a genealogy of how holy war became constructed in the monotheistic religions of the West. To begin with, the ancient Israelite idea of a promise that God's chosen people would be elevated "above other nations" provided a legitimating framework. Zealots rebelled against imperial domination. Christianity had its martyrs, and Augustine (354–430 CE) eventually came to affirm a doctrine of forced conversion of recalcitrants. But in Weber's analysis, Islam was the first religion to establish a connection between "religious promises and war against religious infidelity," aiming at "the subjugation of the unbelievers to political authority and economic domination of the faithful." Yet under traditional Islam, Weber pointed out, "if the infidels were members of 'religions with a sacred book' [i.e., Jews and Christians] their extermination was not enjoined," and in many instances they were allowed to continue the practice of their faiths so long as they paid their taxes or tribute and deferred to the political authority of their conquerors.[80]

Muhammad's formula of warring theocratic expansion was apocalyptic in the broad sense that it entailed decisive action meant to hasten the triumph of Allah on earth and the redemption of the faithful in paradise. This expansionary religious logic was to transcend the death of the Prophet in 632 CE, with Abu Bakr's consolidation of rule over the Arabian Peninsula by 634 and the victory over the declining Byzantine and Sasanian empires through the conquest of Syria and central and southern Iraq accomplished by Omar in the 640s CE.[81] In early Islam, then, the world came to be divided into two regions – *Dar al-Islam*, the house of Islam, and *Dar al-Harb*, the house of war, where Muslims were expected to engage in jihad, thereby expanding the *Dar al-Islam*, in principle to the entire world. By the 850s, the Islamic empire was unequaled in size: it stretched from the Indus River in the east to the Atlantic shores of the Maghreb in North Africa, and over the Strait of Gibraltar to the Iberian Peninsula and across the Pyrenees to the city of Toulouse.

In the emergent Muslim community, both internal conflicts among believers and the external process of Islamic conquest generated apocalyptic expectations. Among the believers, the question of succession of leadership following Muhammad's death led to the split between the dominant Sunnis, who followed the leadership of Abu Bakr and established the institution of caliphs (literally, successors) to be chosen by the Muslim community, and the Shi'a movement, which traces hereditary leadership to Muhammad's cousin and son-in-law, Ali ibn Abi Talib. Civil war, sedition, and heresy claims (all comprising the Arabic word *fitna*) created tremendous turmoil among the faithful from the death of Muhammad through the 690s, and this turmoil was often defined in the terms of apocalyptic tribulation.[82]

Over the same time period, the Last Judgment was expected to come soon, seventy – or in some texts a hundred – years after the *hegira* that inaugurated the Muslim era. These intense expectations may have provided impetus to the extraordinary conquests, to bring as much of the world as possible under theocratic rule before the end of time. As David Cook, argues, jihad was to bring on the apocalypse. Quoting early Syrian jihad texts to the effect that "swords are the keys to paradise. … The first drop of blood dripping from the sword brings forgiveness with it for every sin," Cook suggests that the conduct of holy war "was roughly equivalent in its redemptive and salvific qualities for the early Muslim as the doctrine of the cross was for the Christian." He goes so far as to argue that the stamp of Islam as a religion was forged in the army camps, on the way to battle. Yet it is important to recognize that the apocalypse of Muslim conquest did not inherently result in either forced conversions or purges of infidels.[83]

As with Christians anticipating the final battle of Armageddon, Muslims found their apocalyptic expectations disappointed. Muhammad did not usher in the end himself, nor did it come after the prophesied seventy or a hundred years. As with Christianity, doctrines arose that postponed the apocalypse while maintaining the possibility that it might occur at any moment. A redeemer, a *Mahdi*, would come at the end of time. For Twelvers in the Shi'a wing of Islam, apocalyptic expectations became bound up in the "Twelfth Imam." In some accounts, this was Muhammad ibn Hasan, who disappeared in the 870s CE in a process deemed "occultation." As the last, "hidden," imam, he is expected to return again at a time of God's choosing, ushering in jihad and God's final justice and redemption of the world from its tribulations. Though developed independently, as in Judaism and Christianity, this doctrine of future redemption produces both intense expectations and, sometimes, disappointments at the delay in the appearance of the saviour.[84]

In its broad parameters, Islam both reprises the apocalyptic possibilities of Judaism and Christianity and extends the apocalyptic in a significant direction. An apocalyptic sense of history seems inherently important to religions that are monotheistic, for such religions link history and the destiny of believers with the purposes of God, who must somehow triumph in the end. Yet the apocalyptic is open to diverse resolutions. As with its antecedent monotheisms, Islam provides a basis for telescoping the apocalypse in relation to historical time, sometimes bringing its anticipation to a time soon to come, sometimes delaying its arrival until a time so remote as to make no difference in people's immediate lives. Yet the apocalyptic innovation of Islam is profound. With Muhammad, in a way that far exceeds the Zealots' hopes at redemption from oppression at the hands of an evil empire, jihad, as apocalyptic war, became a triumphant manifestation of God's destiny. In this vision, the religion of the faithful offers conquest of territory as the basis for the salvation of the participants in its jihad and the success of earthly jihad as the basis for preparing God's final victory. The strategic time of military action in history is the matrix that will yield eternity.

When Muslim armies of Arabs invaded Persia in the seventh century CE, after one battle, they encountered a Zoroastrian hereditary ruler who asserted a competing apocalyptic narrative. The Zoroastrian, Iran son of Rustam, announced to his council, "we are not powerless to make war, for this is a land of brave men and heroes," but he added, "this is not an event that will end in a day or a year or a thousand years. This is revealed in texts." When the ruler was brought in to see the Arab general Rabi' ibn Ziyad and work out terms of peace, he observed to the general, "It is said that Ahriman [i.e., Anga Mainyu, the spirit of evil] is not visible in the daytime. Behold, Ahriman became visible, there is no doubt about it."[85] The Zoroastrian ruler accepted historical fate, girded by the messianic assurance that the salvation of the good would come at the end of time. When, and whose good, remain to be seen.

The end of the beginning of modernity

There is no date that can stand as "the" beginning of modernity, for the relevant developments are diverse, and diffuse in their origins. This chapter has traced the deep origins of certain temporal structures of social enactment. I have identified the here-and-now as the initial primordial and archaic temporal locus of the social, and traced its elaboration along the synchronic axis in three interrelated forms: (1) a direct and unfolding here-and-now; (2) a here-and-now centered in community that defines the sacred and fosters solidarity through ritual; and (3) a transcendental here-and-now of ecstasy (or, alternatively, awesome contemplation) borne of absolute present consciousness (often socially orchestrated in its access). Evidently, primordial and archaic societies lacked any strong sense of either history or apocalypse. Of course, ancient elites took an interest in history, especially as chronicle, and sometimes as explanatory analysis, in ancient India, in China, and in the emergent Hellenizing world where Thucydides produced his subtle account of the Peloponnesian War. But it is especially in the vein of religion that historical temporality took form as the shared *telos* of a people, and it is in the most intense experiences of historicized time that we find the emergence of an "apocalyptic axis" in its manifold possibilities as an intensely experienced end of history held to give way to a timeless eternity. These forms of temporal enactment were borne of the trials, challenges, hopes, and disappointments of people who deemed themselves to participate in a community of fate, often under conditions of subjugation, occasionally, in triumph. Thus, history and the apocalypse are connected in a continuum, history as the extended unfolding of *telos*, apocalypse as its most intense moments of crisis, when hopes for redemption spawn a variety of courses of action, depending upon how the apocalypse is construed, and what role people as agents are deemed to have in relation to it.

In these terms, the apocalypse must be seen like historical narrative more generally as something other than a literary genre or objective account of events. As philosopher of history Hayden White has shown, narratives bear one or another specifically moral energy.[86] Textual apocalypses, then, are ideational vessels of narratives concerning the meanings of immediate, imagined, or reconstructed social situations. Although they offer important evidence about how the apocalyptic is structured in any given situation, it is to the temporal enactments of the apocalyptic in the vivid present that we must look if we are to avoid an idealism that spiritualizes history or creates a gulf between texts and meaningful action. Thus, in the present study, I seek to "read through" the texts in a way that aims to explore connections between texts, beliefs, and actions.

On the apocalyptic axis, the ancient religions – Zoroastrianism, Israelite religion, Christianity, and Islam – formulated diverse meaningful situational interpretations and responses, from quietistic fatalism and conformity, through hope and faith, to militancy, holy war, and escape to the "other" side – paradise, either a utopian "heaven on earth" in this world or, through martyrdom or collective suicide, the realm beyond life. In any of these possibilities, the apocalypse is not simply an anticipated future event, for life unfolds in relation to that which is unveiled.

This point reinforces a broader one. Social temporality is something other than the backdrop to our lives by which we measure the passing of events. Indeed, "it" is not singular. There are multiple kinds of social temporality. We do not simply live in "society." As philosopher Jean-François Lyotard insisted, we *enact* "the social" in shared streams of actions in the here-and-now that constitute social temporalities.[87] In turn, any given temporal order leverages distinctive capacities of power to organize social life. Just as collective ritual empowers the group and its ritual specialists, so the apocalyptic can empower those who charismatically invoke it. To unearth genealogies of temporality, then, is to develop a phenomenological basis by which to chart how historically emergent temporal structures of the social became layered onto and articulated with earlier ones in ways that have shaped "modern" complexes of power.

There is no "beginning" of modernity, but there is this: by the time that Muhammad's successors had completed their conquests, the "end of the beginning" of modernity had been reached, specifically in the elaborations of history as *telos* and apocalypse as the end of time, which together began to envelop the earlier primordial and archaic possibilities of the here-and-now. Yet a central modern kind of temporality – time not merely as passage but as measured duration, and then commodity – remained nascent at most. And for this modern temporality to become widely established, the time of the apocalypse would have to be contained. It is to these developments that we turn in the following two chapters.

3

Medieval Christendom and Its Others

By the end of the era of Islam's initial expansion in the 850s CE, the basic possibilities of historical and apocalyptic time had become manifest, layered onto the immediate, communal, and transcendent possibilities long established in the primordial here-and-now. A *telos* of historical time could be linked with the destiny of a people, and a dramatic turning point in history could be taken to mark the beginning of a new era. Apocalyptic expectations might posit an imminent moment of divine intervention to rectify the injustices that God's chosen had endured. Those of faith might prepare for the end of time through conversion, or advance the divine cause through war. Or they might retreat from the unfolding debacle in the established social order to a post-apocalyptic heaven, on earth or beyond. Finally, if the apocalypse were pushed back far into the indefinite future, the chiliastic expectations of millennial transformation would recede, leaving the bedrock of life in the here-and-now, orchestrated to varying degrees through tradition and ritual, enveloped within wider developments of historical change.

These temporal possibilities are still all with us today. They continue to play out within a world that we call "modern" (or, sometimes, "postmodern"). Yet no one would mistake today's temporal possibilities for those of a millennium or more in the past. One important reason is that the dynamics of apocalypse have undergone considerable transformation.

To examine the apocalyptic offers a rather unconventional facet through which to view "early modern history." That era used to be dated from the decline of the medieval world, beginning concertedly in the late fifteenth century, to the onset of the industrial revolution toward the end of the eighteenth century. These days, some scholars question whether periodization of an *early* modern historical era makes sense. In their view, many supposed modern advances in "the West" fail to distinguish Europe from other civilizations, for example, China. Furthermore, a self-sustaining modern world that has transcended the "Malthusian trap" (in which population growth cancels innovation) can only be dated from the late eighteenth century, when the industrial revolution triggered by invention of the steam engine resulted in irreversible social transformations.[1] But the end of the "early modern" era is not at issue here. Rather, tracing the history of the apocalypse undermines the periodization from the other end – its supposed beginning point in the late fifteenth century.

From the nineteenth century onward, the intellectual blood sport of debating the emergence of modern economic and state structures in Europe has zeroed in on the relative importance of technological, economic, and cultural or religious developments. Central debates concern the decline of feudalism and the emergence of absolutist states, the rise of cities and towns, the development of proto-industrial processes of production, and the Protestant Reformation. The historical developments that these debates address come into quite a different focus in this and the following chapter, where I rotate the analytic lens to consider the apocalyptic and how it has become transformed. In the present chapter, this refocusing centers on how Christendom became consolidated in Europe. It brings into view the *differential recomposition* of the apocalyptic in relation to sacred versus secular powers. In turn, chapter 4 explores the interplay between apocalyptic recomposition and other modernizing dynamics, including those associated with the rise of objective time and secularization of the apocalyptic. Together, these two chapters initiate an alternative account of modernity in relation to multiple forms of temporality.

Apocalypse, the sacred, and the secular

In the latter twentieth century, it was still possible to entertain the notion that religious institutions and the modern state in the West were "separate." The prevailing thesis was that society had undergone a long-term process of "secularization" whereby religion's influence on public life had declined. Religion was taken to have become "privatized," both in its organizational forms – set apart from the public sphere – and in the religious outlooks of individuals, increasingly argued to be matters of personal choice. Today, even cursory consideration shows this account to be inadequate. In Europe, the German government makes decisions about what organizations are "religious," and therefore qualify for state subsidies. France draws a strong line between religion and public life, but, in doing so, ends up regulating public religious expression by banning children in schools from wearing the headscarf – the *hajib* – or the Jewish *yarmulke* or large Christian-cross necklaces. The United Kingdom offers Christian theological education in its publicly funded universities. And in the U.S., the presumed paragon of the "separation" of church and state, the boundary recently has been blurred by state funding of religiously run social programs. "Secularization" and "separation" as terms are overdrawn, and therefore fail to describe, much less explain. Debates about secularization thus can easily become muddled.[2] As we will see in chapter 4, secularization and the apocalyptic are entangled with one another historically. Because arguments about secularization have been important to the idealization of modernity from the Enlightenment onward, considering anew the transformation of the apocalyptic in relation to modern states constitutes a crucial step in retheorizing "modern" society.

The thesis in this and the following chapter is that in the European milieu, apocalyptic dynamics have shaped how sacred powers have become recomposed in relation to the emergence of comprehensive state power, and that recompositions have shifted the relation of the apocalyptic to both sacred and secular powers. An efficient way to explore this thesis for medieval Christendom is to trace out an apocalyptic genealogy of religious versus secular political power, first, for the Roman Church in the medieval Crusades and subsequent confrontations with "heresy," and, second, during the onset of the Protestant Reformation in the sixteenth century.

The arc of change that I trace is driven by the relations among the Roman Church, heterodoxical religious movements, and emerging absolutist states – states that, within their own boundaries and over time, had to contend less and less with serious countervailing powers, either feudal or religious. In the time of the Reformation, states rearranged the relationship between religion and power, partly by absorbing "sacred" religious powers to define religious deviance – most importantly, apocalyptic "heresy" – and partly by regulating religions that thereby *de facto* became state-sanctioned as "legitimate." (The historically emergent relation of Islamic regimes to jihad and the *Dar al-Islam* is a subject in its own right, which I will only touch upon in relation to Europe.)[3]

The conduct of the Crusades against external (Islamic) hetero-doxies – and internal ones as well – might have yielded an enduring theocratic rule of the Roman Church over Christendom in the West. Instead, medieval kings and queens, although they were "secular" rulers, claimed a divine right to rule and incorporated religious considerations into their exercise of power. The Protestant Reformation, as it played out, institutionalized the relative religious auton-omy of European states in ways that proved irreversible.

Two scholars – René Girard and Max Weber – provide theoreti-cal context for understanding these shifting relationships between Christendom, power, and the apocalypse.

- In *The Scapegoat*, René Girard theorized sacrifice – the ritualized taking of animal and human life – as an act of collective murder directed at a "surrogate victim" who stands in for wider ills, crimes, or malfeasance. Ritual killing – an extreme scapegoating – affirms the purity of the sacred in its positive aspects, separat-ing it from sacred evil, and from the profane. Girard's model of sacrifice initially concerns action within a shared social domain, but his scapegoating thesis has been broadened in its applicabil-ity to individuals or groups that become stand-ins for *external* threats.[4]
- Max Weber observed important continuities, points of contesta-tion, and transitions between religious communities and secular or military powers. As Guenther Roth has noted, Weber "trans-ferred the concept of the congregation or community ["*Gemeinde*"] from the religious to the political sphere and came to define it as the typical charismatic association."[5] This continuity creates tensions. On the one hand, a "hierocratic" religious organization claims ultimate social authority on a sacred basis, and it thus typically seeks to define the limits of non-religious political authority. On the other hand, secular powers pursue autonomy from religious authorities but often depend on religious legiti-mation, as in the asserted divine right of kings. On a different front, so long as God's authority trumps secular authority, polit-ical insurgents may seek to legitimate their struggle against a state by framing it in sacred terms. In turn, to the degree that secular power receives its legitimation from a religious organi-zation claiming a monopoly (in Weberian terms, a territorial

"church"), "the political power can offer exceedingly valuable support to the hierocracy by providing the *brachium saeculare* [secular arm] for the annihilation of heretics."[6]

When a genealogy of the apocalypse is traced in relation to both institutional scapegoating and the question of how community is constituted in religious versus political terms, the stunning and brutal violence of medieval and early modern Europe connects the ancient world directly with the modern world dawning in the late eighteenth century.

The medieval Roman Church, the Crusades, and heresy

Apocalyptic visions occasionally erupted within the popular imagination during the first millennium, despite Augustine's hopes to contain them within a spiritualized church as the vessel of divine history on earth. Probably in the fifth century the Latin poet Commodianus put forward the idea that a "hidden, final, holy people" would emerge to take up arms against the Antichrist, achieving victory and everlasting life. Other prophecies, the medieval Syballine Oracles, treated the first Christian Roman emperor, Constantine, as a warrior-king who, though he died, would somehow become resurrected to defeat the enemies of Christ and rule as the Emperor of the Last Days. The Christian idea of "holy war" is thus indigenous to its traditions, and does not derive from Islamic doctrines of jihad. In time, the medieval church came to conceive of conditions under which violence could be religiously justified, especially if carried out through institutions that are instruments of God's will.[7]

The fate of the Christian Church changed substantially because the Roman Empire did not survive. Its gradual division between East and West made possible the persistence of the Byzantine Empire (and an intact Eastern Church) even after the sack of Rome by Visigoths and Vandals and the collapse of the Roman Empire in the fifth century. In the east, the Byzantine Empire took an almost theocratic form, with the emperor carrying forward certain projects of the church. But in the west, the admixture of surviving Roman institutions and the culture and social organization of the Visigoth and Vandal invaders yielded a "Germanized" church that incorporated elements of pagan folk and magical traditions, and it left intact Germanic traditions of honor that were to become important to the feudal order. Persistent pressures from expansionary Arab invaders further exacerbated already uncertain post-empire conditions.[8] Only occasionally did warrior rulers such as the Frankish kings Clovis (d. 511) and Charlemagne (742–814) consolidate territorial rule. Already before the death of Charlemagne, Frankish and Carolingian rulers had to contend with countervailing feudal powers, and with Muslim armies pressing in on the boundaries of Christendom – on the Iberian Peninsula and even to the north of the Pyrenees.

Under the conditions of political instability that prevailed in the ninth and tenth centuries, eschatological ideas about the apocalypse percolated through occasional popular movements. Whether the end of the first Christian millennium was marked by any concerted apocalyptic anxieties is a topic of scholarly debate.[9] However, no one to my knowledge has argued for any substantial *consequences* of millennialist concerns around the year 1000. Rather, the medieval significance of the apocalyptic – both for the Roman Church and its relation to secular powers, and for the popular classes – became radically recast only when the medieval church moved to establish Christendom as a civilizational culture of world-historical importance. The ideological mold was set in the Cluny monastic order, begun in 910 in Burgundy. However, the apocalyptic consequences did not come until the Crusades, over 175 years later.

Christian monasticism can be traced to Basil the Great, who in the fourth century borrowed from the anchorite traditions of Egyptian hermits to establish an ascetic rule by which monks living communally could sacrifice their personal lives to devote themselves to God. Famously, Benedict developed a *Rule* in the sixth century that would set the standard for an orderly collective life of monks serving God through their labors and their intellectual endeavors. But Benedictine houses operated in relative autonomy, and the Roman Church lacked administrative control over monasteries and convents. By the ninth century, in the Carolingian Empire, aristocratic interests effectively subordinated the orders and their properties to the enhancement of their own estates. Moreover, the church lacked autonomy: like the cloistered domains, its administrative and clerical hierarchies were fully subject to the decentralized play of feudal interests. However, during the tenth century, the Cluniac order promoted a reform that would provide a platform for freeing the church from diffuse secular subordinations. Cluny advanced a model of centralized control and clear differentiation of monasteries and convents from feudally held lands. Administratively, Cluny would be only one monastery, even though, as the movement spread through Burgundy, France, Germany, Italy, and to England, there were many houses, or priories. Opposing the previous quasi-feudal relative autonomy of monastic houses (and the local feudal influences on monasteries that often resulted), Cluny established an administrative absolutism. This monastic centralization foreshadowed an absolutist development within the wider Roman Church promoted by an outsider, the German King Henry III (1017–56), and strongly pushed forward by Pope Gregory VII during the latter part of the eleventh century.

Just as Cluny pursued independence from the temporal world of feudalism, so Gregory sought to eliminate lay investiture (appointment), the practice in which monarchs and lords would select bishops and abbots within their own territories, sometimes by practicing simony – the sale of offices. Gregory's effort to establish the autonomy and temporal power of the church aimed to reaffirm a clear hierarchy – the divinely exercised power of the church above the secular power of divinely ordained kings. "Who can doubt," he asked, "that the priests of Christ are to be considered the fathers and the masters of kings and princes and all of the faithful?"[10] By the thirteenth century, the church would have the trappings of a kingdom of God on earth – a theocratic state in the making, with an extensive bureaucracy that reached across Europe, the capacity to raise money and finance and undertake wars, and, through the organization of the Knights Templar, control of a nascent international banking apparatus unequalled at the time.[11] This drive toward absolutist papal monarchy anticipated secular ambitions of state absolutism that were to come only centuries later.

Organizational reform was one side of the Cluny vision. But Cluny also became a major channel through which the church defined its "Others," both internal and external. The man who served as abbot of Cluny from 1152 to 1156, Peter the Venerable, wrote three treatises on what he regarded as the major threats that Christianity faced.

- one treatise attacked a parish priest who failed to heel to orthodoxy;
- a second put forward the first ever Christian condemnation of Muhammad and Islam; and
- the third depicted Jews as having committed deicide, thus reaffirming the Markean gospel's account of the trial of Jesus.

As social historian Jacques Le Goff described Peter the Venerable's treatises, "They became to some extent the textbooks on Christian orthodoxy." In effect, a broadly apocalyptic struggle in the name of a "political Christ" against those defined as Other by the church became the ideological basis for pursuing internal organizational absolutism, autonomy from feudal and royal interests, and increased political influence in the secular world. This adoption of the Cluniac program by the church created tensions between the two, for Cluny sought to bring people to an other-worldly monastic life, whereas the church sought to gain greater power in the wider world.[12]

Within the cloisters, there was no ostensible need for power other than the authority of the abbot. To be sure, monasteries faced significant challenges of discipline. Already in his *Rule*, Benedict had decreed that the hard-hearted and unruly among the monks "should be punished with whips, even at the first signs of sin." This discipline, following the ideas of Paul and Augustine, amounted to a spiritualization of apocalyptic struggle and its deployment within the cloisters. As Benedict wrote, obedience was necessary for the Christian "fight under the true King, the Lord Jesus Christ."[13]

Outside the cloisters, seeking broader power for the church, Gregory began to consider relocating the fight, by having Christians actually take up arms to advance its purposes. He even entertained the idea of leading a force of 50,000 to Jerusalem. The pope would gain the ultimate trappings of secular power – the capacity to use force.[14]

The church's pursuit of the ideological program framed by Peter the Venerable had diverse reverberations in the medieval period – in the Crusades, in Christian heresies and the Inquisition, and in the persecution of Jews in medieval Europe.[15] Yet what is the relevance of these developments to the apocalyptic? Not all heresies were apocalyptically tinged, or even particularly theological in character: in matters of religious heterodoxy, politics was sometimes the strange bedfellow. Nor can the Crusades be reduced either to purely apocalyptic religious undertakings or to the pursuit of elite interests – religious or secular – in geo-strategic conquest.[16] Nor does responsibility for quasi-apocalyptic medieval anti-Semitism lie wholly in the hands of the church. However, these and other diverse developments during the Crusades and after reworked and relocated elements of the apocalyptic in ways important to the emergence of modernity in what was to become the West.[17]

At the Council of Clermont in 1095, Pope Urban II proposed the first expedition in what became known as the Crusades (so named for taking up the Cross, and wearing it as a symbol on one's chest). *"Deus lo vult!"* the pope told those assembled, "God wills it!" In his origins a Cluniac monk, Urban anticipated much of Peter the Venerable's vision, and he built on Gregory's reforms and pursuit of secular political and military power. Urban saw Christendom beset by Muslim incursions, and he sought to aid the Eastern Church in reconquering eastern inland Asia Minor from Seljuk Turkish warriors (in the eleventh century, the Seljuk Empire had quickly expanded westward from Persia, taking parts of Anatolia). This expedition was to be undertaken by seasoned knights of the secular feudal order, thereby channeling their warring energies outward, in the hopes of building on the Truce of God aimed at controlling feudal in-fighting. In fact, however, the efforts by Urban and others to build support for expeditions to the east played upon and further aroused popular sentiments that were relatively indifferent to the fate of the Eastern Church, but apocalyptically obsessed with wresting Jerusalem from Muslim rule. The Crusaders captured Jerusalem in 1099, a victory over infidels subsequently described in terms borrowed from the Book of Revelation, which had "blood rising to the bridles of their horses." However, this first Crusade went well in part because it came at a time of conflict between rival Muslim regimes – the Seljuk Turks to the north and the Fatimid Caliphate that claimed rule as successors to Muhammad in the Levant and North Africa. The Crusaders' advantage was not to last, for the Islamic doctrine of jihad, which had fallen relatively dormant, became revitalized at the hands of the Muslim religious classes and poets who glorified Muslim warriors as leaders and martyrs. Amidst "highly successful campaigns of jihad propaganda," the Second Crusade, in 1144, was not successful, and in 1187, forces of the Kurdish sultan Saladin retook Jerusalem. By 1291, the Crusaders were driven from Acre and Tyre, their last strongholds in the Levant. The Crusades had all but failed, even if their spirit and institutional logic were to persist for centuries more.[18]

What, then, is the significance of these enormous undertakings? There is no single answer. The Crusades marshaled intense collective political and religious energies in a fusion of war and penitent pilgrimage. But geopolitically they ended up binding Jerusalem away from the Christian world, they weakened the Byzantine Empire (and with the Fourth Crusade against Constantinople, brought the Roman and Eastern Orthodox Churches to a final parting of the ways), and they left Arab rulers continuing to control the southern half of the Iberian Peninsula. When we view these developments through the lens of the apocalyptic, important threads of religio-political dissidence and contestation come into focus: first, in the Crusades themselves; second, in the treatment of Jews as Other; third in the church's delineation of heresies; fourth, in its use of crusades and the Inquisition to control heresies; and, fifth, in the ascetic, mystical, and apocalyptic religious movements that were followed by the Protestant Reformation.

Holy war

Most important, the Crusades set in motion a sea change in the relation of the Roman Church to war, secular powers, and Islam. To be sure, armed conflict had not been a complete stranger to Western Christianity. Augustine had specified the conditions of a just war; occasional messianic poets and preachers had foretold that the coming apocalypse would require battalions of the faithful to fight the Antichrist and prepare the way for Christ's Second Coming; and kings like Clovis and Charlemagne had proclaimed that their military endeavors served divine purposes. But during the ninth and tenth centuries, western areas of Europe were beset by invaders – Vikings from northern Europe, Saracens from North Africa and the Caliphate of Córdoba in what is now Spain, and Magyars from the base in the Hungarian plain that they had conquered from the east. The survival of Christendom was thus threatened on multiple fronts.

Prior to the Crusades the Roman Church had insisted on keeping the carnage of war separated from the direct works of the church, and Christians and Muslims had maintained relatively peaceful relations that permitted trade, the diffusion of important Arab cultural, scientific, and technological innovations to Mediterranean Europe, and Christian pilgrimage to the Holy Lands (if they were willing to pay the hefty levies). With the Crusades, all this changed. In the years just before the First Crusade, Christians increasingly came to view Islam as the earthly embodiment of the Antichrist, and this view gained more adherents with the launching of the mission to the east.[19] When Jerusalem was captured on July 15, 1099, the church's emissaries negotiated with the conquering feudal barons, hoping to establish direct religious governance of the new kingdom. Secular politics foiled this hope. However, even though the church did not achieve anything like theocratic rule over Christendom, the Crusades enhanced its position in the politics of feudal Europe, and its coordination with secular powers thickened.

Theologically, these developments hinged on a shift away from Augustine's careful acknowledgement that some wars might be "just" and toward an active endorsement of holy war as military action undertaken to serve God's purposes. Even in relation to this shift, the eleventh-century involvement of a pope in calling for a military expedition and the role of the church coordinating the recruitment of participants were historically unprecedented. Emblematic of the quantum shift was the transfer of monastic rhetoric into crusading. In effect, "spiritual warfare," originally formulated by Paul in his letter to the Ephesians as a struggle against evil metaphorically equivalent to war, and later invoked by Benedict for the cloister, now became the basis of earthly apocalyptic war.[20]

This shift necessarily yielded religious concerns about the salvation of participants in the Crusades. The organizationally most striking development came when the church sanctioned a fusion of the religious and the military within the Order of Poor Knights of the Temple of Solomon, or Knights Templar, which was formed to protect Jerusalem and the pilgrimage routes to it after their conquest. The man we now know as St. Bernard, abbot of the Cistercian monastery at Clairvaux, helped obtain official religious status for the Order of Solomon. Bernard was not particularly enamored of the knights' religious fervor. "You will find very few men in the vast multitude which throngs to the Holy Land," he suggested, "who have not been unbelieving scoundrels, sacrilegious plunderers, homicides, perjurers, adulterers." Europe, St. Bernard argued, would be better off without such men, most of them badly educated and illiterate, drawn from the lower echelons of the feudal order's warrior class. As Knights Templar, they could serve the church in the unseemly duty of killing infidels. But this plan would require doctrinal revision. Whereas medieval theologians previously had insisted on keeping the carnage of war separated from the direct works of the church, Bernard produced a fusion: "For Christ! hence Christ is attained. ... The soldier of Christ kills safely: he dies the more safely. He serves his own interest in dying, and Christ's interests in killing!" With Bernard's endorsement, killing became a means of self-cleansing. As Pope Innocent II declared in a papal bull in 1139, knights of religious orders who died fighting infidels "consecrated their hands to God in the blood of the unbelievers."[21]

The apocalyptic inversion from early Christianity is profound. Early martyrs saw themselves as a persecuted minority who sought and passively submitted to death as testament to their beliefs. With the Crusades, Christianity combined personal penance with the military pursuit of religious geopolitical interests. Augustine had hoped to defuse intense eschatological expectations about the end of the world by substituting a fusion of eternity with history. But in the Crusades, apocalyptic war against an external Other, the Islamic infidel, came to the center of the church's worldly enterprises. Henceforth, the Christian apocalypse would not only animate the oppressed, the weak, the outsider. There would also be what has been called "an apocalypticism of the powerful, or a triumphalist millennialism."[22]

Religious historian Christopher Tyerman asserts that holy war did not have the doctrinal or operational centrality for the medieval Roman Church that jihad had for Islam in its early centuries.[23] However, we should not underestimate the opportunities that holy war provided for pious pilgrimage, and, in death, martyrdom that assured salvation.[24] Both Islamic military jihad and Christian crusade placed religion in the political position of pursuing violent military action to advance the purposes of God in human history, offering religious benefits to the participants in the bargain. Institutional religion would not passively await the End Days, it would act to ensure the earthly fulfillment of God's will. In the Crusades, the apocalyptic pursuit of strategic military action in unfolding historical time became conjoined with pious sacraments provided by the church to bring the individual participant the eternal salvation of God.

Crusaders against the Jews

The embrace of the apocalyptic within the Church of Rome not only transferred popular eschatological sentiments to the institutional domain. The church's "crusading spirit" also amplified long-standing popular apocalyptic fervor that it proved incapable of containing. Literally tens of thousands of people from diverse social strata – men, women, sometimes children – participated in crusading over two centuries or more, many of them traveling some two thousand miles, countless of them dying on their journeys or in the Holy Land. Despite elite efforts to organize and command the crusaders, the warring ethos and popular millennial sentiments proved a heady mix that could lead to massacres and pillaging far removed from any strategic purposes, much less sacred ones. And from very early in the movement, the scapegoating of the Other to be purged sometimes shifted from Muslims to the more proximate Jews who, over the centuries after the Romans destroyed the Second Temple in Jerusalem in 70 CE, had migrated to form communities in Europe.

In the Holy Land, the poor and undisciplined among the crusaders would pillage and rape, and engage in brutal beheadings of infidels. But long before they arrived there, as the expedition of the First Crusade started out in Europe, crusaders began to go after Jews in Europe. "We have set out to march a long way to fight the enemies of God in the East," one crusader observed, "and behold, before our very eyes are his worst foes, the Jews. They must be dealt with first."[25]

Institutionally, the church did not expect Jews to convert to Christianity until the last days, and following Augustine, it projected that date into the distant future. But in popular sentiment – excited by the Crusades – the Day of Judgment might take place soon. As the historian of the apocalyptic Norman Cohn points out, "the first great massacre of European Jews ... occurred during the First Crusade."[26] In some French towns, Christians reportedly threatened Jews with massacre if they did not convert. Then, along the Rhine River, crusaders in Speyer murdered a dozen Jews in the streets while others fled to their synagogue. At Worms, the synagogue was sacked and all adult Jews who refused to convert were killed. Some Jews who sought refuge in the bishop's castle refused his offer to convert them in order to save them from the mobs, and they committed suicide. Elsewhere too, religious and secular authorities sought to stop the violence, and they rejected efforts to force conversions, but their successes were limited. It is estimated that between four and eight thousand Jews met their death. And this was only the beginning. As crusaders passed through, they sometimes inspired Christian townspeople to take up their own pogroms, and at the onset of the Second Crusade, a renegade monk, Rudolf, led a People's Crusade that began by killing Jews. His movement spread to towns across Germany and France.[27]

Christian anti-Semitism had a deep source in the New Testament synoptic gospels' positioning of the Jews as responsible for the crucifixion of Jesus, and as Norman Cohn commented, "the eschatological tradition had long associated the Jews with Antichrist himself." The historical archives dating from the Christian emperor Constantine on through medieval times are replete with legislation limiting rights of Jews on many fronts, from owning Christian slaves to holding office. But aside from an episode in 554 in Clermont, where Jews were killed or forced into baptism, there seems to be no historical record of Christian-initiated violence against Jews until the Crusades.[28] However, once initiated, the pogroms continued to erupt long after the Crusades – in the *reconquista* of Spain, in the disarray that followed the death of the Holy Roman Emperor Frederick II, in the latter thirteenth-century Rhineland with its self-proclaimed *"Judenbreter"* (Jew-roasters) and *Judenschächter* (Jew slaughterers), and during the period of the Black Death in the fourteenth century.[29] Historians sometimes have pointed to other motives – pillaging, class resentment, and ethnic antagonism, for example – but such explanations are necessarily incomplete in that they account neither for the unrelenting religious rhetoric of the pogroms nor for the frequent willingness to offer conversion to Christianity as a means by which Jews could escape persecution. Conversion of the Jews became a perennial theme of apocalyptic anticipation.

The Crusades and heresies

The possibility that the Crusades themselves spawned heresies can be taken at least three ways. In the first place, the church and secular powers were able to contain neither the Crusades' theology nor their strategic goals. Literally hundreds of thousands of people became caught up in the crusading spirit over the period of its most intense mobilization in the twelfth and thirteenth centuries, including not only the aristocratic and knightly classes but people of all stations of life, down to urban paupers and landless peasants. Popular religious sentiment, partly fanned by those who preached the Crusade and partly inspired by religious ideas gained through travels to the east, took heterodoxical directions that the church would come to treat as heretical, and seek to eliminate.[30]

Second, the Crusades brought to a head the church's general concern with heresy as a problem in its own right. Of course, controversies over doctrine and practice had been central to Christianity from the beginning. Already, late in the second century, the Roman Church argued against gnostic doctrines and contended with followers embracing the revelations of Montanus and his two women companions, Priscilla and Maximilla. Early in the fourth century, Augustine led the Roman Church to challenge schismatics and sectarians such as the Donatists and Circumcillions, who flourished in North Africa.[31] However, during the late first millennium, similar doctrines and movements arose that the church could have deemed heretical, but it did little to try to root out and control unorthodox ideas and practices.[32] Why was this so? The historian of heresy Malcolm Lambert argues that early medieval religious authorities did not go after heretical movements "presumably because they presented no significant challenge to the church."[33] But another answer beyond Lambert's also bears consideration: the Roman Church of the ninth and tenth centuries lacked the organizational coherence of authority that would have been necessary to define, report on, and oppose heresy. It was too permeated with decentralized feudal interests and heterogeneous monastic practices. Only with the rise of the Cluny movement toward monastic and, subsequently, papal organizational absolutism did the church have the institutional aspiration (and, increasingly, the organizational means) to identify heresy as a problem to be acted upon. As Peter the Venerable of Cluny later put the matter, "Whom is it better for you and yours to fight, the pagan who does not know God or the Christian who, confessing him in words, battles against him in deeds?"[34]

Third, the church actually used the crusade template to oppose heresy. Crusades became the basis not only for organizing military campaigns against distant Muslim infidels, but also for firming up the church's predominance over the European peripheries of Christendom – on the Iberian peninsula, in Italy, and in the lands bordering the Baltic Sea. Some expeditions amounted to political crusades to settle scores with secular powers, or colonial crusades to pacify territories, the better to Christianize their inhabitants. But the church's purpose in Pope Innocent III's Albigensian Crusade (1209–29) was to eradicate a Christian "heresy" embraced by nobles and the popular classes alike – the Cathar movement.[35]

Not all heterodoxical medieval religious movements embraced the apocalyptic, and so it is important to distinguish questions about the kinds of beliefs and practices of dissident movements from the question of whether they became caught up in struggles with the church over heresy, and whether such struggles became apocalyptically defined – on either side. Here, a problem arises: much of what is known about shadowy medieval religious movements comes to us through the lens of the church. The church, however, confronted an "underworld" that was, we might say today, loosely organized as a "counterculture," a *bricolage* of popular religious ideas. The church may have rendered greater coherence to various threads of this counterculture than they obtained in dissident practice.[36]

Religious authority, the Cathar heresy, and the Albigensian Crusade

From what evidence persists, there is every reason to think of medieval heresies as countercultural movements. Heterodoxical ideas and loose alliances of kindred spirits – often the poor and dispossessed, but occasionally more settled peoples and even members of the aristocracy – flowed across regions and developed over time. Christian historian Ronald Knox identified two major medieval currents that came to be treated as heretical, their followers therefore subject to execution. Albigensian Catharism and the Waldensians both rejected the doctrine of "office charisma" under which the church claimed the institutional power of even sinful priests to absolve the faithful of their sins. Such movements were roundly persecuted by the church for refusing to accept the doctrine of the Trinity, the authority of the Roman Church, or even the divinity of Jesus.[37] The ideas at issue are not simply doctrinal niceties: they challenge basic theological and organizational rationales for the existence of the Roman Church.[38]

The Albigensian Crusade against the Cathars is one important episode in which the way heresy played out relative to the apocalyptic had broader consequences. Catharist ideas traced to rejection of the Roman Church when the Empire institutionally legitimated it, and they had circulated across Europe for centuries. However, Catharism eventually gained a strong institutional foothold in the economic and cultural crossroads of Languedoc, just to the north of the Pyrenees mountains in what is now southern France. This was a region of cosmopolitan social toleration, in part because of Arab influences, for example, in the diffusion of troubadours' ideas about knightly honor in matters of love and scholars' ideas about mathematics and technology.

Cathars trafficked in the apocalyptic coin of medieval Christian opposition to the church in Rome – that the pope was the Antichrist. However, there are two possible ways of identifying the pope or the Roman Church as Antichrist – either in a generic indication of corruption, or in relation to a specifically apocalyptic interpretation concerning an historical shift.[39] In the latter terms, the Cathars did not hold apocalyptic ideas at the center of their teachings. Rather, they rejected the institutionalized church account of Jesus's life, death, and significance, and substituted a radical dualist theology of pure souls imprisoned in impure earthly bodies, which gave rise to extreme self-denying other-worldly asceticism as a pathway for

liberation of the soul. Despite their clearly Christian ideas and practices (they said the Lord's prayer), historian Ronald Knox could
assert, "the theology they preached was not, in any recognizable
sense, Christian."[40]

By the twelfth century, Catharism was spreading across
Languedoc via an elite of clerics and missionaries, attracting followers from the nobility as well as the popular classes, and effectively
establishing an organized church, complete with a clergy, regional
dioceses, and a lively public life that included debates with Catholic monks in the city of Toulouse. Not only were the Cathars heretical beyond belief, but their degree of establishment on the ground
flaunted the Roman Church's presumption that it possessed an at
least tacit alliance with – and spiritual authority over – the region's
secular feudal nobility. Languedoc represented what was intolerable to the church: a potentially politically autonomous region
of Western Europe that already possessed its own alien but
flourishing institution of a dramatically alternative Christianity.
The church's response was crusade, followed by inquisition.

In the Albigensian Crusade, royal interests overshadowed religious aspects: the French crown sought to counter emergent nationalism in Languedoc by expansion of its own domain centered in
Paris. The crusade was brutal to the extreme in its violence against
both heretics and Languedocian Christians, but it failed to accomplish its religious goals. Thus, the church in 1233 shifted from a
model of military conquest to employing mendicant religious orders
like the Dominicans to attract spiritual seekers to the church through
their own examples of asceticism. Where this failed, the church
would root out individuals' theological deviance through the Inquisition's more fine-grained panoptic surveillance, which brought
torture of people deemed to be Other in order to elicit their confessions so that they could be put to death, the threat to the divine
order eliminated.[41]

For its part in the Albigensian Crusade, the French crown succeeded in initiating the incorporation of Languedoc. This did not
fulfill Pope Innocent III's vision of a "Christian republic," but it did
inaugurate the French formula of what would become a Catholic
nation-state. There are two points to consider about this outcome.
First, as the church would find again and again over the next two
centuries, although monarchs tended to respect the church's spiritual authority, the "spiritual sword" of the church was not sufficiently powerful to counter, or even delimit, the "physical sword"
wielded by secular powers. Warring knights and monarchs would

claim divine legitimacy, but spiritual authority could not dominate them. Second, the Cathars were true believers, doggedly holding to their faith and accepting the consequences. However, they lacked any messianic apocalyptic zeal, and, indeed, seem to have forsworn violence. The *absence* of any strong apocalyptic orientation among the Cathars made the military success of the Albigensian Crusade a foregone conclusion. Whether the *presence* of such an apocalyptic orientation would have yielded a Languedoc proto-nationalist movement is a question that has no answer. But as we will see in chapter 4, the character of the seventeenth-century English Revolution suggests at the least that an apocalyptic orientation would have enhanced the prospects of Languedoc autonomy.[42]

Heresies of asceticism and mysticism

Overall, the Cluniac reforms, Pope Gregory's initiative to reform the church, and the Crusades unleashed both widespread popular religious quests and higher expectations for the institutional church. Some new religious orders – notably the Cistercians, Franciscans, and Dominicans – made room for lay seekers, either by recruiting them for colonization schemes, as the Cistercians did, or by instituting Third Orders in which people could continue to live outside the cloisters, in society-at-large. But the new orders did not completely contain the popular interest, and the church was an unwieldy organization that could not effectively meet its own goals of reform. Under these circumstances, by the middle of the thirteenth century, heterodoxical wandering preachers and popular movements thrived in certain regions of Europe. Many of the "heresies" (and this is largely the lens through which we know of them) centered on either intense quests for self-denying asceticism or the development of mystical possibilities of transcendence. On the axis of asceticism, some people apparently found the church's sacraments insufficient to wash away the sense of personal unworthiness that the church taught was their fate, and they sought expiation of sin through intense self-flagellation. Thus, it is reported, after whipping himself with a scourge that tore off bits of his flesh, one fourteenth-century friar "stood there bleeding and gazed at himself. It was such a wretched sight that he was reminded in many ways of the appearance of the beloved Christ, when he was fearfully beaten. … [H]e knelt down, naked and covered in blood, in the frosty air, and prayed to God to wipe out his sins from before his gentle eyes."[43]

At the other extreme, people called the Beghards and Beguines of Germany gravitated toward a movement of mystical transcendence, sometimes referred to as the Brethren of the Free Spirit. Whether and how far the Free Spirits ever existed as anything other than a diffuse counterculture, and whether they actually embraced the "mystical anarchism" that Norman Cohn has attributed to them remain open questions. However, even by the most conservative assessments, the men and women (and there seem to have been significant numbers of women) attracted to Free Spirit ideas held out the possibility of personal perfection on earth that would allow them direct union with God. Thus, they sidestepped the institutional mediation of the church to experience transcendence directly. From there, it was not difficult to embrace an antinomian belief that conventional mores no longer applied to the adepts who directly experienced grace. Libertine anarchism freed by God's grace from answering to any earthly authority opened out toward a sensual embrace of open sexuality without sin. At least, those were the tendencies that worried the church. "Rejoice with me," one Sister Katherine is said to have told her confessor, "I have become God."[44]

Ascetic and mystic tendencies already existed within the church, but when they began to flourish outside it, they could become treated as heretical. These developments testify to an increasing medieval popular interest in what sociologists call "construction of the self." Yet they were not inherently apocalyptic. Thus, the Free Spirits seem to have pursued mystical transcendence, not an apocalyptic engagement with history.[45] True, apocalyptic expectations might be invoked to promote self-denying asceticism, as a way of preparing for the Second Coming, but for many medieval ascetic and mystical movements, the more pronounced apocalypse came from outside, in the church's use of the Crusade and the Inquisition to stamp out heresies.[46]

Apocalypse as heresy

Apocalyptic sentiments, amplified in both institutional and popular channels of the Crusades, sometimes eclipsed both the church and the Crusades, spreading through religious movements that the church came to deem heretical. In particular, possibilities and consequences of messianic countercultural apocalypticism can be found in movements over some three centuries, animated to varying degrees by the meditations of Joachim of Fiore (c. 1132–1202).

The medieval Roman Church was hardly insulated from serious engagement with the apocalypse, for example, in the ecstatic visions and art of Hildegard of Bingen (1098–1179) concerning the Antichrist born of the church, the failure of his strategies, and his defeat at the end of history. However, more than any other known medieval thinker, Joachim of Fiore advanced a detailed theology. His close readings of the Bible and complex calendrical and numerological calculations about the opening of the seven seals described in the Apocalypse of St. John cast the die for the "date setting" arithmetic of apocalyptic anticipation. Calculating the apocalyptic timeline would surface again and again over the centuries.

In effect, Joachim shifted away from Augustine's transcendentalist and metaphorical displacement of the apocalypse, back to a more worldly theology connected to unfolding human history. Though Joachim's ideas later inspired movements deemed heretical, he lived and worked under the auspices and encouragement of the Roman Church. Having decided to renounce worldly affairs after a pilgrimage to the Holy Land, Joachim became a Cistercian monk and undertook an intense decades-long study of the New Testament Apocalypse, which he advanced in part by composing detailed esoteric diagrams of world history. Joachim was encouraged to submit his findings to the Holy See, and he did so in 1200, but died before any pope evaluated them. Eventually, the church condemned his analysis, and it is not difficult to understand why. Joachim posited three ages of world history ruled in turn by the Father, the Son, and the Holy Spirit – corresponding to the era of the Hebrew Bible, the Roman Church, and an age expected to dawn after a cataclysmic event in the year 1260. "A new leader will rise up from Babylon," Joachim enthused. Forthwith, all Christians would be reunited, the Jews finally converted. A transcendent eternity of universal love and justice on earth would negate any further need for the institution of the church.[47]

Joachim was a deeply committed Christian, admired by Dante and Richard the Lionheart. He remains venerated by Catholics today. However, his ideas were another matter. Whether Joachim meant to predict a social upheaval around the year 1260, others took inspiration.[48] Disenchanted Franciscan "Spirituals" and dissidents began reading Joachim, creating pseudo-Joachite prophecies, and talking about how Francis of Assisi, founder of the Franciscan order, had been the angel of the sixth seal. For the Spirituals, the Holy Roman Emperor was the Antichrist. But many a wandering preacher believed that the "carnal church" at Rome had become the

Antichrist, leaving the faithful to participate in a "spiritual church." Either way, the shift was dramatic. Augustine had wanted to reduce the apocalypse to spiritual metaphor. Joachim de Fiore, and those who followed in his wake, restored it to history.[49]

Popular ideas about the emergence of a messianic king flourished particularly in Germany. Anticipation of Joachim's third age fueled the belief that the Last Emperor might be Frederick II. Frederick died in 1250, a decade before the heralded dawn of the New Age, but this hardly dampened enthusiasm. Instead, a string of fantasies demonstrate the capacity of the apocalyptic for seemingly endless reinvention and reconstruction. It was said that Frederick never really died but simply went into hiding in Sicily, or if he did die, he would be resurrected. And indeed, various incarnations of "Frederick" did appear, met with wild popular acclaim in the midst of warring among German principalities and eschatological movements among the urban poor. One Frederick was burnt at the stake after a suitable trial, a procedure reserved for heretics and witches, not for usurpers to the throne. But the rumored absence of ashes and the recovery of a small bean at the stake yielded the inevitable conclusion: the resurrected Frederick had not died, he had been rescued through divine intervention. He would return.

Mere fire does not douse apocalyptic narratives, it forges them. During the worst episodes of the Black Death in 1348 to 1349, and again and again for centuries, the wavering masses seized on anticipation of Frederick's return. And "he" did return, more than once, right down to the early sixteenth century, when the "Revolutionary of the Upper Rhine" predicted the appearance of the "Emperor from the Black Forest" – an apocalyptic messiah of a German king who would "control the whole world from West to East by force of arms," ruling for a thousand years over a world organized in communal equality. All this could only come to pass after the extermination of sinners, especially lechers, the clergy, usurious moneylenders, unscrupulous merchants, and lawyers. "Soon we will drink blood for wine!," proclaimed the Revolutionary. "All property shall become one single property, then there will indeed be one shepherd and one sheepfold." The Hebrew Bible had gotten it all wrong: in this Christian socialism, the Germans, not the Jews, were God's chosen people. As Norman Cohn noted concerning the Revolutionary, "nobody before him had combined such devotion to the principle of communal or public ownership with such megalomaniac nationalism."[50]

The Revolutionary of the Upper Rhine was a pamphleteer, not a leader. However, apocalyptic fantasies sometimes inspired collective action against the established church and the feudal order. Already in the early 1400s, radical followers of Jan Hus in Bohemia were calling themselves Taborites, their community, Mount Tabor, after the spot where tradition had Jesus making his proclamation that he would come a second time. The Taborites asserted the authority of their own personal scriptural interpretations, and they formed anarchical egalitarian communities. Subjection to relentless persecution only deepened their apocalyptic ideas. They asserted their complete autonomy from the existing political order and their messianic right to kill "the enemies of Christ," a category that included lords, nobles, knights, and merchants. Prague became the new Babylon. In 1421, seventy-five captured Taborites were burnt at the stake as heretics, some of them laughing as they went to death. That same year, a pillaging band of Taborite holy warriors led by a man called Adam (or Moses) was brutally exterminated. But small-scale insurgent holy wars continued to erupt. Amongst diverse movements of peasants and people living marginal lives in the emerging towns, some uprisings, initiated by the *Bundschuh* (literally, the laced-shoe league), combined Christian millenarian visions of egalitarian utopia with plans for class annihilation of the rich and powerful. Echoing Taborite beliefs, they envisioned the last apocalyptic battle as giving way to an earthly egalitarian utopia. These uprisings were duly put down, along with countless non-religious incidents of peasant unrest.[51] However, they anticipated far more significant developments. The apocalyptic was to come into play both in the Reformation itself and in the broader realignment of monarchical European states in relation to religion.

The Reformation and the religious realignment of European states

The eleventh-century reforms set in motion by Pope Gregory consolidated the church as a major medieval political power. The papacy, in the words of Perry Anderson, was "the one medieval monarchy which had achieved complete emancipation from any representative or corporate restraints." Acting autonomously yet drawing other powers to its cause, the church collected taxes to finance the Crusades as pilgrimages of apocalyptic war – mostly against external Muslim Others labeled infidels, sometimes against internal Others such as the peoples of Languedoc, where Catharism had taken such strong hold.[52] However, though the Albigensian Crusade succeeded in the French crown's political goal of expanding its territory, this outcome demonstrated the church's military dependence on increasingly powerful European monarchs who sought to advance their own agendas. In effect, the church ceded some authority to deal with popular apocalyptic radicalism to secular powers. And the Albigensian Crusade's failure to accomplish the church's goal of suppressing the Cathar heresy led it to put in place the institution of the Inquisition as a basis for much more closely targeted policing, torture, trial, and punishment of those found beyond the pale of church doctrine.

Many of the ideas and movements subsequently deemed heretical by the church lacked any substantial apocalyptic basis. However, compared to other heresies, apocalyptic ones proved especially resilient. After all, whereas other contending religious ideas centrally concerned piety, ritual, and access to the transcendent, the apocalypse is specifically historical in its narrative possibilities, and thereby open to manifold adaptations, treating one event or another as the opening of one of the seals, now positing one individual or group as Antichrist, now looking to another as the Second Coming. The church might undertake holy wars in the name of Christ, but a pope just as easily could come to be labeled as the Antichrist himself, the church as an institution of the great Satan. Or the entire medieval order – monarch, church, manorial lords, traders, and merchants – could become the target of apocalyptic resentment and eschatological hopes for redemption.

Through the early 1500s, the church experienced a series of contestations with the secular powers that wielded the physical sword. Pope Innocent III had crowned Frederick II Holy Roman Emperor in 1205, but Frederick pursued autonomous claims of legitimacy and military campaigns that weakened the church. The papacy, relocated to Avignon from 1305 to 1377, emulated much of the secular style and trappings of monarchy, but it suffered diminished authority relative to the French kings, a situation exacerbated more broadly when two, and then three, rival popes made claims to lead the church during the Great Western Schism from 1378 to 1417.[53] Occasionally the church's conflicts with secular rulers took on an apocalyptic aura, each side projecting onto the other the label of Antichrist. However, never in these medieval conflicts did the church lose to any secular ruler its effective and legitimate claim to the spiritual sword. Even during the Western Schism, when who could legitimately claim the papacy was contested, the pope remained the pope. Only the Protestant Reformation produced a radical and irreversible shift in these circumstances. Yet what we call "the" Reformation involved complex developments in diverse societies at intersections of religion and nationalism, as those societies contended with the apocalyptic.

Trajectories of reformation

In its ideological and institutional sources, the Reformation seems to trace to the widespread medieval clerical and popular discontent with the church and to popular movements to gain more direct access to the Bible by making it available for lay reading. The Lollards embraced the translation of the Bible into English by the Oxford theologian John Wycliffe (c. 1320s–1384), and, like Wycliffe, they emphasized the spiritual status of a person as decisive in the efficacy of sacraments such as communion. For Wycliffe and the Lollards (and the followers of Jan Hus and the Taborites in Central Europe, who in part borrowed from Wycliffe), the pope presided over a sacramentally counterfeit and organizationally corrupt church. They readily embraced the culturally available characterization of the pope as the Antichrist.[54]

University of Wittenberg and church theologian Martin Luther (1483–1546) was thus hardly original when he put forward his famous Ninety-Five Theses in Wittenberg on October 31, 1517, challenging the sale of indulgences to raise money for a crusade against the Turks. Luther subsequently developed a series of radical theological positions: notably the priesthood of all believers, which eliminated the church's role as mediator between believer and God, and salvation by faith, without necessary recourse to confession or sacraments other than baptism and the Lord's Supper. Penance would be a largely personal matter, not accomplished through institutionalized ceremony. Theses and theology alike resonated with deep currents of medieval opposition to a church already seen as corrupt and worldly. Luther, like his predecessors, and like others in the Reformation that ensued, identified the pope as Antichrist, but he used especially florid rhetoric in dismissing "flatterers of the pope" and "enemies of Christ."[55]

Historically, it would be tempting to read the Reformation back onto Luther, rather than seeing Luther as a person of his times. He began as a monk dissatisfied with his church. But Luther developed his theology in engagement with history, including the historical relationship of Europe to Islam. As in the Crusades, at the onset of the Reformation, Islam figured strongly in apocalyptic visions that swirled around Europe. In the political chaos of the thirteenth century after the breakup of the Seljuk Empire under Mongol pressure, the Ottoman Empire had emerged from small beginnings to rapid expansion that would make it, by the sixteenth century, the largest empire in the world. The Ottomans prospered on the basis of a formula reminiscent of early Islamic history – an expansionist jihad ideology against Christian and "pagan" infidels pursued by a patrimonial state that appropriated war booty to fund its administration. In conquered territories, the Ottomans tended to follow older Islamic strictures of toleration toward "peoples of the book," so long as those conquered recognized the legitimacy of Islamic rule and paid their tribute (considerations sometimes less onerous to peasants than the feudalism that the Ottomans displaced). Under this formula, the empire conquered parts of Europe – Bulgaria and Serbia in the late fourteenth century, and Constantinople and most of the rest of the Balkans, including Greece, by the latter fifteenth century. By the time of Martin Luther, Ottoman forces were threatening Hungary. Not until the Austrian military initiatives at the end of the seventeenth century would Europe find the Ottoman threat substantially reduced.[56]

For Luther, the possibility of Turks overrunning Europe became a sign of the last days: "the spirit or soul of Antichrist is the pope, his flesh or body the Turk," his *Table Talk* records. Like some crusaders, Luther found the possibilities of converting or eliminating the Jews appealing as a way of preparing for the Final Judgment. The pope, as well as the kings of France and Spain, shared Luther's concern about the Turks, but they also sought to confront the internal threat – Christian heresy. They considered launching a "general crusade," as the French and Spanish kings put it, aimed both at infidels and at "extirpation of the errors of the Lutheran sect."[57]

Overall, these plans did not succeed. Coupled with the mid-fifteenth-century Gutenberg printing revolution based on movable type, Luther and others' translation of texts from Latin to vernacular languages enhanced the mass diffusion of religious ideas, enabling people to read and interpret the Bible to one another, thus making it easier for them to forge direct relationships with God, unmediated by institutional professionals. Religious meanings about the significance of life, individuals' ultimate or "sacred" identities, and the relation of this world to history, the apocalypse, and eternity became increasingly open to innovative formulations. The ideas of Luther and other theologians, most notably the French-born John Calvin (1509–64), spread rapidly around in Europe (between 1517 and 1520, more than 300,000 copies of Luther's various writings were sold).[58]

Even in less radical strands of the Reformation, Protestants killed opponents – including other Protestants – and died at the hands of their opponents as well. The Swiss Reformation theologian Huldrych Zwingli (1484–1531) was killed along with two dozen other pastors when he led soldiers defending Zurich against an attack by Swiss cantons allied with the Roman Church. One cannot walk around the Scottish town of St. Andrews without encountering places where one or another Protestant believer was killed – martyred, in their view. And tens of thousands of French people died in their Wars of Religion. The Protestant Reformation was not simply a religious movement: it mobilized family members, towns, districts, regions, and claimants to state power across Europe to struggles that were widely regarded by protagonists on both sides as apocalyptic wars against Babylon and the Antichrist.

Religion has been called a sixteenth-century word for nationalism.[59] This pithy formulation deserves elaboration: in the sixteenth century, state nationalisms became defined by way of struggles over religious identity – Protestant or Catholic. In some countries, the Reformation would prove irreversible. Yet for all the violence associated with the Reformation, nowhere did insurgent revolutionaries directly overthrow a state allied with the Roman Church. Thus, sociologist Robert Wuthnow has rightly asked, how and why did the Reformation succeed? Few of the ideas that animated it were novel. How was it that newly organized religious sects could survive, and some of them become state-established churches, when previously the Roman Church had been able, if not to eliminate what it deemed heresy, at least to prevent its institutional establishment? Printing and literacy contributed to the diffusion of Protestant ideas, but these factors alone do not explain outcomes, for Reformation success was geographically uneven relative to the spread of its ideas. To address this complex puzzle, Wuthnow engages in careful comparative analysis of states, regions, and towns where the Reformation either became established or did not succeed during the formative period from 1519 to 1559. Overall, he argues, the Reformation had tremendous appeal, especially in emergent commercial towns, for it "offered vernacular worship, access to the sacraments and Scripture, and a greater sense of participation in religious services," and thus a stronger integration of religion into the collective life of the towns. However, "For the Reformation to be successful, some form of institutional leverage was needed to effect change despite resistance of these [powerful rural] elites."[60]

That leverage came in certain German, Swiss, and Dutch regions where the increasing independence of commercial towns gave their councils the capacity to resist state, elite, and religious pressures. The councils might do so for three reasons. First, wide popular support for the Reformation demanded it. Second, many secular urban officials and leading burgher-citizens themselves took positions of leadership in the Reformation movement. Third, Reformation ideas were not all of a piece. Radical ideas might inspire broad popular insurgency that could threaten not only the established church and landed elites, but, potentially, commercial towns as well. Faced with demands from Holy Roman Emperor Charles V (who followed the lead of Pope Leo X) that the new heresy be suppressed, town magistrates often resisted. As Wuthnow puts it: "their greatest fear was not reprisal if they did not comply but the danger of popular insurrection if they did." Either by actively promoting the Reformation or by following a middle path of "passive support or tolerance," town magistrates might gain some direct control over the movement, for example, nominating church pastors.[61]

The apocalyptic lever

The alternative that loomed was apocalyptic war against the established social order. In the Reformation movement initiated by Thomas Müntzer (c. 1488–1525) that became connected to the Peasants' War, the possibilities became vividly apparent – to town leaders, to electors of the Holy Roman Empire, and to the princes interested in state building. Müntzer was born in German Thuringia to a family of middling means. He became a priest and, fascinated by the apocalyptic mysticism of Joachim of Fiore, followed Luther in breaking with the Roman Church, but then broke with Luther in 1520 while conducting a ministry in Zwickau. There, Müntzer came under the influence of a messianic weaver named Niklas Storch, who was also conversant with earlier medieval heresies. He took up Storch's ideas, most notably that the unrighteous should be exterminated. The result was a dramatic quest for apocalyptic war to produce an earthly kingdom of the millennium. Expelled by

Zwickau's town council for his divisive and inflammatory preaching, Müntzer relocated to Prague, where he tried unsuccessfully to form a new church open only to true believers deemed by the strength of their commitment to be the Elect chosen by God. By 1523 he resurfaced in Thuringia, this time in the small town of Allstedt. There he initiated the first liturgy ever conducted in German, translated Latin hymns, successfully preached his radical message to peasants and workers in the copper mines, and founded a secret quasi-military sect, the League of the Elect. When one of the two princes of Saxony visited Allstedt, Müntzer preached him a fiery apocalyptic sermon based on the Book of Daniel, imploring the princes to do their duty to "drive Christ's enemies out from amongst the Elect, for you are the instruments for that purpose." The representatives of the conventional church and the ungodly among rulers should perish, Müntzer asserted, "for the ungodly have no right to live, save what the Elect choose to allow them." When the princes failed to heed his call, Müntzer became further radicalized. Increasingly he saw the millennium as requiring the founding of an egalitarian apostolic community of goods in *this* world, a development that could only be achieved by action to topple the existing social order. Not just the Roman Church was the Antichrist. Luther himself became Revelation's Whore of Babylon, for he would not take decisive worldly action on behalf of God.[62]

The Peasants' War that erupted in 1525 in the south and west of Germany probably connected back to earlier uprisings of the *Bundschuh*. Initially, it lacked Müntzer's millenarian program, though small bands rampaged through Thuringia sacking monasteries and convents.[63] However, an elective affinity developed between the movement and Müntzer, for he offered ideology, leadership, and messianic fervor. In April 1525, in his church (by then at Mühlhausen), under a flag bearing a rainbow on a white field, Müntzer announced plans to march, and he and followers did indeed raid some monasteries and convents. His subsequent letter of April 26 to Allstedt followers spelled out plans for a chiliastic war. "Begin to fight the battle for the Lord," he exhorted followers: "Even if there were only three of you, you would be able to fight one hundred thousand if you seek honor in God and in his name. Therefore, strike, strike, strike! This is the moment." When peasants organized a force of some 8,000, Müntzer led a band of 300 supporters to join them. Together they confronted the princes' smaller but much better equipped army – complete with around 2,000 cavalry. Confident of victory, the princes offered terms. However, as an early history of the event records, Müntzer assured the peasant forces that God had revealed to him their impending victory. Müntzer himself, Norman Cohn recounts, "would catch the enemy cannon-balls in the sleeves of his cloak." A rainbow suddenly appeared, which seemed to confirm to followers that the divine moment had arrived, and they sang "Come, Holy Spirit" as the princes' troops began to fire their cannon, initiating a slaughter of some 5,000. Later, Müntzer, who had fled the scene, was apprehended in a nearby cellar and tortured into a confession about the goal of the League of the Elect – to kill the ungodly in order to establish a millennial kingdom on earth. After confessing, on May 27, 1525, he was beheaded.[64]

With this outcome, Müntzer sealed his legacy as a prophetic failure. Nevertheless, it is important to recognize that he initiated a war against not only the Roman Church and the feudal order but also a nascent Protestant church. This was a new version of the apocalyptic holy war – of Christian insurgents initiating a struggle against ruling Christian powers. Moreover, though Müntzer's prophecy failed, it did not fail to inspire others. The radical Reformation script of apocalyptic holy war would be enacted again.

Just as the Peasants' War was unfolding in 1525, the Anabaptist movement arose in Germany and Switzerland. Anabaptists are known for the doctrine of second, or adult, baptism. However, that simple ritual had a deep meaning. It signified entry into a sect of those reborn to the community of brothers and sisters living apart from the world of sin. Anabaptists sought to establish the millennial kingdom on earth, not through piety, which they regarded as inauthentic to Christianity, but by acting out their vision of how the early apostolic community of Christians lived. They intrinsically viewed external authority of any kind – certainly state authority – with great suspicion, thus sowing the seed for the most apocalyptic of narratives. From the outside, their radical separation from "the world" left Anabaptists to be branded as dangerous, and subject to intense persecution wherever they went. Their treatment in turn fulfilled their righteous sense of persecution.[65]

Almost seamlessly, the end of the Peasants' War at Mühlhausen was followed by the establishment of a short-lived Anabaptist theocratic tyranny at Münster, in the west of Germany. In February 1534, Anabaptists took over the town council, their fellowship augmented by nuns who had escaped their convents along with an influx of Anabaptists from elsewhere in Germany and the Low Countries. The Anabaptists expelled from Münster any Lutherans and Catholics who refused rebaptism, precipitating a military siege by the authorities, who could not countenance a theocratic Anabaptist city that was confiscating property of the banished whilst establishing a collectivized regime of work and a community of (mostly expropriated) goods. Later, with the inauguration of a "king," came a deeply patriarchal polygamy and executions of non-believers and those deemed sinners. Finally, after eighteen months of ever-hardening rule, the Bishop's besieging forces stormed the city, overpowered resistance of the two or three hundred Anabaptists who remained, and despite offering safe conduct to survivors, massacred nearly all of them. The leaders were captured and tortured until death with glowing hot irons, their remains hung in iron cages from the tower of St Lambert's Church, where their bones remained until finally they were removed – after World War II. In the wake of Münster, Anabaptism persisted and spread as a sect, but in a climate of extreme suspicion and periodic persecution, and only because the movement rejected the sword and backed away from its more apocalyptic visions.[66]

Religion, reformation, and nationalism

To magistrates and princes, Luther looked attractive by comparison to Müntzer and the Anabaptists. From early on, he had placed limits on his apocalyptic anxieties, holding to a theology of pious waiting. He embraced the role of moderate reformer who would oppose all radical tendencies: the iconoclasts seeking to destroy religious symbols and statues of the Roman Church; the peasant movements undertaking the destruction of monasteries, convents, and churches; Thomas Müntzer; and the Anabaptists. Luther would forswear violence, at least of a particular kind: "I do not wish the Gospel *defended by force and bloodshed*. The world was conquered by the Word, the church is maintained by the Word, by the Word also the church will be revived, and Antichrist, who gained his own without violence, will fall without violence." But the Peasants' War was different. On that matter, Luther stood "against the murderous and plundering peasant hordes," who he said "must be knocked to pieces, strangled and stabbed, covertly and overtly, by everyone who can, just as one must kill a *mad dog*!" This vehement stance, and Luther's rejection of Müntzer as "Satan stalking, the Spirit of Allstedt," gained him the backing of the nobility and paved the way for the establishment of the Lutheran Church in some German principalities as a state church. Here, the Reformation succeeded by allying with elements of the established political order in containing the more radical formulations of apocalypse.[67]

Elsewhere, the Reformation played out in different ways. John Calvin was notably silent on the Book of Revelation. Even though he seems to have believed the Reformation to be the last great turning point of history before the world's end, his theology was not centrally ordered by dramatic ideas about the unfolding of God's wrath in the last days. Rather, he sought to create a New Jerusalem in the kingdom on Earth based on God's keen justice.[68] So the Reformation certainly was not a purely apocalyptic religious movement. Nevertheless, from the beginnings of the Reformation until past the middle of the seventeenth century, Europe encountered millennial ideas and movements of the most diverse kinds, and even non-apocalyptic developments often were shaped in relation to apocalyptic possibilities.[69]

Overall, the issue that Wuthnow identified, of institutional leverage supporting – or not supporting – religious change, was decisive. In Denmark, and Sweden and Norway, monarchs benefited from increased trade that gained them some degree of autonomy from the nobility, itself traditionally allied with the Roman Church. Church lands were secularized, monasteries dissolved, and Lutheranism established as the state church.

As for England, the initial success of the Reformation had everything to do with a conjuncture of the throne's increased power due to international commerce coupled with the interest of King Henry VIII in divorcing Catherine of Aragon for her failure to produce a male heir. In the absence of an heir for King Henry, Charles V of Spain stood to gain the patrimony of the English crown through Catherine, his aunt. Because the pope was allied with Charles, he would not grant a divorce. Stymied, Henry secretly married Anne Boleyn and subsequently gained the consent of Parliament to have himself declared the "supreme head" of what would become the Church of England.

The Reformation fared less well in some countries. In eastern European regions it initially gained some ground, for example, with the conversion of Duke Albert of East Prussia and through Polish openness to multiple confessions. But ultimately the Counterreformation prevailed. In France, despite some popular and aristocratic support, especially in the south and southwest, where religious dissidence dated back to the Cathar heresy, the state lacked effective autonomy from the landed nobility, and it vacillated in whether to tolerate Protestant worship, finally decisively outlawing it in

1685. Spain, with its empire based on state-dominated patrimonial capitalism and close ties to the church, and with its strong Inquisition and closely interdependent state and nobility, was overall the least hospitable climate for the Reformation in Europe.[70]

Yet to focus solely on the causes of Reformation success or failure in relation to different European societies and their state formations would be to consider only half of the state/religion nexus. Societies as diverse as Germany, France, Spain, and England experienced *differential recompositions* of sacred versus secular power, including power to define the heretical and contain the apocalyptic. Initial Reformation outcomes were significant for how apocalyptic ideas and movements might subsequently take hold or be delimited.[71]

Spain was marked by the greatest continuity with its medieval past, but even there, the Reformation challenge had its consequences: precisely because the Spanish state so successfully suppressed the movement, it could advance modern power without integrating its relatively homogeneous population into a solidary national community. The French state, if anything, became even more strongly associated with the Roman Church, but in a way that royal propagandists used to portray the French kingdom as a sort of holy land, the country of God's chosen people. France prevailed over a more robust Protestant movement than Spain confronted, and by prevailing, it mobilized popular French sentiment against the Reformation in ways that helped further define France as a strong Catholic national-religious community.[72]

The Holy Roman Empire achieved a more hybrid solution, perhaps at the expense of delaying German national integration. The 1555 Peace of Augsburg clarified the rights of German princes to determine what religion would be established within their principalities, creating a parcelized welter of religious establishments, and leaving open the possibility that, within a given principality, religious dissidents (notably Anabaptists) might be prosecuted for heresy – a condition that would persist until the end of the Thirty Years' War and the Peace of Westphalia in 1648 (and even then, the conditions of public worship in non-established faiths could be limited by law).

By contrast, English King Henry VIII's peculiar royal motivations for supporting the Reformation produced a unified monarchical fusion of state and church – a caesaropapism in which royals administered the established religion. Thus, the Church of England bore a striking resemblance to the Roman Church, differing most substantially in who controlled it, but demonstrating a similar willingness to engage in action, as Wuthnow has put it, "to *control* the spread of Protestant ideas, especially among the lower strata, lest heresy lead to popular uprisings." However, the crown's control of a relatively delimited royal reformation created an instability in the succession of Protestant and Catholic English monarchs, and it eventually left an opening for radical Protestants – labeled "Puritans" by the crown – to identify the crown itself as the new Antichrist.[73]

Overall, as Anthony Marx has argued, sixteenth-century conflicts over Reformation Protestantism produced conditions in which monarchs sought to delimit religious zeal, and sometimes mobilize it to their own purposes. However, in the bargain, national identity came to be defined in religious terms in relation to excluded Others – not only infidels outside, but also persons within who aligned with unorthodox religious tendencies. In both Catholic and Reformation states, Christina Larnar has suggested, religious doctrines became political ideologies. Conflicts between European societies – the Dutch Revolt against Spain (c. 1555–1609), for example – increasingly played out across religious cleavages that tended to align with economic interests in relation to the emergent capitalist world-economy. Internal societal conflicts also became important: the French Wars of Religion (1562–98), the Dutch "Religious Quarrels" of the early seventeenth century centered on what Philip Gorski calls Calvinist "Hebraic nationalism," and the Puritan-led English Civil War (1642–51) all helped define the boundaries of national identity and the legal basis and limits of civic participation by religious dissenters. Given these developments, Gorski argues, modern theories of secular nationalism need to be displaced by an understanding that religious varieties of nationalism emerged in Europe, beginning more than two centuries before the French Revolution of 1789.[74]

Conclusion

From the Crusades to the Reformation, European engagement with the apocalyptic helped to shape dramatic recompositions of the relation between church and state, in both Protestant and Catholic societies. The broad contours of this shift can marked by way of the two scholarly arguments cited at the beginning of this chapter – René Girard's account of scapegoating as ritual killing and Max Weber's analysis of ways the political community mirrors and connects to the religious community.

Both in the medieval period of Crusades and heresy and in the Reformation, in both established and dissident religion, apocalyptic meanings typically became fixed in relation to the definition of an Other that constituted a threat to the sacred. In the extreme case of holy war, as Girard's argument would suggest, violence against the Other constituted not merely a strategic politico-military initiative, but a sacred act of scapegoating meant to purify the social order from internal or external threats. Yet the agent that would carry out sacred operations shifted. Shadowing Max Weber's filature between religious and political community, Anthony Marx has renewed the historical argument that the key early modern basis on which European nationalism became built – whether Protestant or Catholic – was a religiously inscribed definition of the nation and its excluded Others. The secular communities that could marshal people to one or another national political cause were, in their origins, religious communities.

The nationalization of religion that the Reformation initiated created a radically changed climate of the apocalyptic. Wuthnow describes the situation well. Noting the overall compatibility of Reformation ideas and state interests, he observes, "What made them especially so was their tendency to *desacralize* existing religious authority, thereby giving the states an opportunity to exercise greater control over religious affairs."[75]

Either way (though in different ways), with the political success of the Reformation or the success of a state in forestalling it, the state increasingly appropriated important aspects of the religious community's authority for policing the boundaries that define legitimate religious organization and personal identity in relation to the sacred. Witchcraft is a telling example. As one historian of religion has remarked, "it was clearly a heresy persecuted with no less enthusiasm by the Protestants than by the Catholics."[76] Similarly, just as Protestants would find themselves subject to persecution in Catholic countries, so Puritans, Anabaptists, and other radical reforming sectarians met with persecution under Protestant rule. For states along the entire continuum, from those aligned with the Catholic Church to those where Protestantism came to hold sway, the state, based as it was in a *de facto* religious community, came to inherit the previously purely religious function of regulating, policing, and containing religion, thus in effect defining the boundaries of heresy. As the medieval Roman Church had learned, so states would also find that many of the most challenging boundary problems – both internal and external – became mapped in relation to the apocalyptic.

The Reformation that began in the sixteenth century, along with other dramatic social changes of the era, confronted states with quite different apocalyptic challenges and opportunities than those elites faced in medieval times. Earlier, during the medieval era, the character of the apocalyptic had shifted, as a channel of action both among religious dissidents and on the part of the powerful. But the basic medieval temporalities of social action had remained largely arrayed among various possibilities of the here-and-now and the apocalyptic.[77] As we will see, the forms of society that developed in objective diachronic time – haltingly in the late medieval period and more strongly in post-Reformation Europe – altered the context of the apocalyptic, with repercussions that would connect directly to modernizing processes and projects.

4

Apocalypse Re-formed

John Calvin, the greatest of the sixteenth-century Protestant reform-ers after Luther, saw the papacy as Antichrist, but in his volumi-nous writings he never chose to comment on the New Testament's Apocalypse of St. John.[1] Instead, Calvin took the Reformation in the direction of disenchantment, opposing the Roman Church's mysti-cism and directing people to this-worldly concerns.[2] Later, Whig-gish histories harnessed Calvin's theological modernism by treating the emergence of modern society as the *telos* of a gradual yet sweep-ing transformation that displaces superstition and dogma with Reason, belief with science, *bricolage* with technology, tradition with progress. However, holistic Whiggish histories have come into hard times, for it is now widely recognized that modern societies are not all of a piece. French sociologist Bruno Latour has made the case in a particularly cogent way in his book *We Have Never Been Modern*, by arguing that the assertion of modernity as a unity masks *hybridic* situations in which "modern" elements become composed in relation to "non-modern" elements.[3]

The previous two chapters have laid the groundwork for identi-fying hybrid societal structures by exploring multiple kinds of temporality – varieties of the here-and-now, history, and the apoc-alyptic. Yet Calvin's theology does not align with any of these temporalities. Like other of modernity's cultural, technological, material, and organizational features, it is centered in objective "diachronic" time – time that can be measured by the hour, minute, and second, time that can be saved, spent (not wasted!), and planned out to organize the future. Objective time knows no beginning, and no end. It is the contrapositive of tradition's "eternal return," and the antithesis of apocalypse. Even so, modernity has not heralded the end of the apocalyptic. Hybridity prevails. Calvin tended to downplay the apocalypse, as have elites in his wake, but modernity needs to be considered in relation to it.

The Reformation amounts to something like a hinge holding two screens together: its apocalyptic aspects connect the world of medieval Europe with modernity, but the hinge rotates relationships of the apocalyptic with religion and the state – whether Protestant or Catholic in its established confession. This chapter explores hybridic modernity on the latter side of the hinge, from the close of the fifteenth century – the time that historians generally date the onset of the "early modern era" – to the end of the eighteenth century, by which point important modernizing developments were well under way. As my general thesis of hybridity suggests, the major modernizing developments during this period of some three centuries are not all of a piece, and they connect unevenly to apocalyptic and other times. To explore this thesis, the present chapter deconstructs hybridic modernity by way of five sketches, each concerning a distinctive development of, or away from, the apocalyptic.

- Objective time (i.e., of the clock and calendar) reconstructs social identities, rechanneling apocalyptic mentalities into rationalized routines of time-bound everyday life.
- Religious, and sometimes apocalyptic, philosophies of history become relocated within a secular construction of historical time.
- Emergence of the capitalist world-economy in the late fifteenth century is undergirded by ideologies of the apocalyptic, and sometimes the apocalyptic becomes relocated through collective religious migration.
- State initiatives regulate religion, and contain and quiet the apocalyptic.
- Apocalyptic violence becomes replicated within the domain of secular politics.

Modernizing tendencies, it turns out, are complex and incomplete. This hybridic character of modernity becomes especially evident when we focus on understanding how it is constituted in relation to multiple temporalities.

Modernizing temporality, identities, and everyday life

The spread of objectively measured time, of calendar and clock, has been by far the most important temporal transformation since antiquity. But objective time remained relatively undeveloped in the West until well into the second millennium. Early medieval chronicles of history lack any strong sense of linear flow, for the simple reason that modern conventions of temporality had not yet been firmed up.

Diachronic time is radically different from any temporality that came before. It gears rationally ordered action into the social and material world – in the assembly line, to take an obvious instance, but also in state and other bureaucratic production of social arrangements, and on myriad other fronts. To the degree that objective temporality comes to predominate, it redistributes social life and power away from both apocalyptic and synchronic time. To invoke Max Weber, the "rationalization" and "routinization" of social action – coordinated in relation to the increasing dominance of the objective time of the clock and calendar – place people within different temporal frames than those concerned with the end of the world, while the "disenchantment" of the world that comes with the rise of diachronic time breaks up the mystery and magic entailed in the previously dominant synchronic rituals connecting the here-and-now, the community, and the transcendent. Thus, the rise of diachronic time fundamentally alters the matrix of temporal possibilities.[4]

Augustine's fifth-century formula of divine history would persist through the medieval era and beyond, but he famously puzzled over time: "I know well enough what it is, provided that nobody asks me; but if I am asked what it is, and try to explain, I am baffled."[5] Even by Augustine's day, the objective measurement of diachronic time had a long history, keyed to the measurement of earthly solar and lunar cycles, candles marked to measure time's passage, sundials, water clocks, and even astrolabes. Yet the coordinated social *use* of objective time did not become widely diffused until well into the second millennium of the common era. True, in the sixth century, Benedict's monastic *Rule* laid out the religious cloister's schedule of prayer, work, and other activities of daily life. But in early medieval society more widely, the passage of duration was not necessarily conceived in rationally equilibrated units: in some times and places, the number of hours of daylight always equaled the number of hours of night, with the consequence that hours' lengths differed depending on the season.

Mechanical water clocks (invented in China and possibly independently elsewhere, probably before 1000 CE) had the potential to change all this with their tick-tock escapements that regularized temporal passage. However, diffusion of temporal innovations did not come quickly. In Islamic civilization as it flowered up to the thirteenth century, reckoning of months and years was tied to a lunar calendar that does not synchronize with yearly orbits of the earth around the sun. Arabs seem to have developed the earliest ideas of objective time as a "thing" divisible into very small units (ultimately down to the indivisible "time-atom"), and they invented measured duration in musical notation. Yet the famous thirteenth-century Arab water-driven mechanical "elephant clock" remained an elite novelty.[6]

Elements of clock technology, along with other Arab scientific, technological, and intellectual innovations, diffused to Europe during the medieval period, in part through Andalusian Iberia. In Europe, the measurement of diachronic time gradually became increasingly important to the organization of social life. Church bells had long rung out the hours of prayer, but not necessarily with any precision. Ringing the bells told the time, but time did not always determine the ringing of the bells. However, by the fourteenth century, in towns dominated by merchants interested in regularizing business activities, time began to be measured with ever greater exactitude. Clocks with equal day and night hours began to appear in town hall towers across Europe. As social historian Jacques Le Goff comments, "Time was no longer associated with cataclysms or festivals but rather with daily life, a sort of chronological net in which urban life was caught." Yet the capacity to *measure* diachronic time does not assure its *use* in the organization and coordination of social life. This point is underscored by one negative medieval view of the usurer who lent money to be repaid at some future point in time. Such a person amounted to a thief of time, Thomas of Chobham (c. 1158–c. 1236) argued, which "belongs only to God." Equally problematic was the *internalization* of diachronic time-consciousness. Two situations, almost 500 years apart, show that objective time was the time of merchants and employers. Already in the fourteenth century, the city of Amiens in France issued an ordinance regulating workers' hours of labor in the cloth trade.[7] However, even by the early nineteenth century,

E. P. Thompson has shown, English capitalists could not count on their workers to care more about objective time than they did about the pleasures of the here-and-now.[8] And in agrarian and rural communities, where the vast majority of people still lived in the nineteenth century, time remained centrally ordered by the seasons and weather, not by units of measured time.

Technical developments and economic interests enhanced and promoted the emergence and diffusion of diachronic time. However, this was a complex historical development that cannot be reduced to economic determination, much less technological innovation. Religion was particularly important as a channel of temporal regulation. St. Benedict's (imprecise) monastic regulation of diachronic time by the ringing of bells long preceded the clock and the factory. And, as both Weber and the French historian Georges Duby pointed out, cloistered monasteries and convents in the West attained a degree of regulation of work that was unheard of in the wider manorial economies. Feudal lords could exact rent from peasants in the form of a share of crops or labor, but they had next to no way to control the efficiency of peasant work. By contrast, some monastic orders, the Cistercians, for example, combined rationally ordered scheduling of time with an ideal of other-worldly work asceticism – self-sacrifice in devotion to God, socially regulated by monks monitoring their peers.[9]

Outside the monasteries and convents, things were different. As early as the sixth century, the church invented a new way to distribute religious meanings by using a rational system of notating music on paper, yielding a yearly calendar of uniform liturgy that could be replicated across its domains.[10] But the church rationalized its liturgy in order to produce a mass cultural experience. Salvation in medieval Christianity remained strongly centered on the ancient synchronic axis: it overlaid onto everyday life in the here-and-now a complex web of religious symbolism. A calendar of rituals, public piety, devotion to the saints, and confession, perhaps pilgrimage, offered the keys to eternal transcendence in life after death.[11] Alternatively, the Crusades, by combining pilgrimage with holy war, provided an avenue in which apocalyptic death promised immediate post-apocalyptic salvation. But neither the medieval liturgical calendar nor holy war connected pursuit of salvation with diachronically scheduled or regulated conduct in "this" world. Peasants might hope for redemption in the next world, and members of the knightly and aristocratic orders might hope for forgiveness that would assure their places in God's heaven. But ever since God had sent Adam and Eve out from the Garden of Eden, humankind had lived in a fallen world.

The theological innovations of most dissident medieval religious movements also fell elsewhere than along the line of diachronic time. The radically antinomian Free Spirits pursued ecstatic transcendence in the here-and-now. Apocalyptic movements variously projected hopes for salvation from the desperation of life onto an imminent Second Coming, or they sought, through war, to bring on the millennial kingdom. But such movements did not break out beyond the synchronic and apocalyptic axes.

However, a religious embrace of rationalized time did begin to take hold in some religious groups during the medieval period. The fleeting time of an uncertain life had long been a Christian theme emphasizing the need to prepare for death by assuring one's salvation. "Nothing is more precious than time," St. Bernard was widely quoted as saying.[12] In the cloistered monasteries and convents, the importance of other-worldly work asceticism became concentrated among lay brothers and sisters who increasingly did the non-intellectual labor of the cloisters, working in its kitchens, shops, and fields. Around the same time, the lay heterodoxical Waldensian and Cathar movements began to develop ideals of discipline internalized by believers and oriented to craft vocations in "this" world. These movements failed to spread their ideals of work discipline – both because of their organizational limitations and, by the mid-thirteenth century, due to the success of the Inquisition against them.[13] Nevertheless, by the early fourteenth century there is evidence of a broader religious ethic emerging. An Italian preacher, Domenico Calva of Pisa, used the vocabulary of merchants to suggest the need to "save and take account of time," and he railed against sinful "waste of time." And sloth, a term earlier used to describe monastic boredom, was becoming more generally understood as idleness or waste of time.[14]

Any radical shift in the religious valuation of time, however, required effective organization that could challenge the institutional conservatism of the Roman Church, committed as it was to synchronic liturgy, ritual, and magic. This organizational challenge came only with the Reformation. And even in the Reformation, Martin Luther emphasized salvation by faith and the priesthood of all believers, and thus did not move the synchronic formula of medieval salvation very far in the diachronic direction of worldly asceticism. He regarded the Reformation as the beginning of the last days, and his followers mostly took up his retooled piety as "faithful patience" while awaiting the Final Judgment. Only in the early seventeenth century, with the disasters of the Thirty Years' War, did the apocalyptic expectations of Luther's followers wane.[15] Luther did preach that believers should place sacred importance on their worldly vocations, but as Max Weber famously argued, this emphasis on a personal calling did not translate into a pervasive self-regulation of work, only an embrace of one's duties in this world. In short, Luther largely reorganized the theological and institutional bases of the synchronic formulae of medieval piety toward more direct communion with the divine, but he did not open up any substantial diachronic theology.[16]

It was Calvin whose theology gave rise to the workaday yet religious self-discipline that became centrally ordered by internalized diachronic time.[17] In Max Weber's account, Calvin relentlessly opposed the magical liturgy of the medieval church. He formulated a theology of "predestination" that emphasized the complete inability of individuals to change their prospects of salvation: those who were to be saved already had been chosen by God. To believers who became obsessed by anxieties about salvation that this dour and uncompromising doctrine precipitated, Calvinist preachers urged constant activity as an antidote and protection against the Devil, who would find work for idle hands. In effect, the other-worldly asceticism of organized self-sacrifice within the cloisters resurfaced in the wider world. Protestant "monks" internalized rational and efficient use of time in everyday life (hence, "inner-worldly asceticism"). For Calvinists, Weber remarked, "Waste of time is thus the first and in principle the deadliest of sins." Time became the subject of preachers' admonitions: "use every moment of it as a precious thing, and spend it wholly in the way of duty," Richard Baxter advised.[18] To the degree that this ethic took hold, independent of any technological or economic determination, religious meaning reconstructed personal identity and everyday life in protomodern ways.

Certainly Calvinism did not spell the end of either magical liturgy or the synchronic channel of salvation more generally. The new disenchanted and diachronic ethic of inner-worldly asceticism hardly became pervasive. Agricultural work continued to involve its daily rounds, and as my general account of hybrid modernity anticipates, belief in magic and devils persisted, as did the synchronic here-and-now as the site of both life's enjoyments and the rituals that can offer a taste of sacred transcendence.[19] Catholic and Lutheran theologies promoted piety over works, and from the early seventeenth century onward, reactions against the woeful Calvinist doctrine of predestination led to a series of Protestant sectarian theological innovations. Among the Baptists and later the Methodists, the Arminian doctrine opposed to Calvinist predestination took hold: salvation is in principle open to all, and individuals may take steps to improve their prospects. Yet Protestant sects continued to emphasize that hard work was a sign of God's grace conferred, and they thus sustained inner-worldly asceticism as an ethic even without anxieties about predestination.[20]

The spread of clocks and pocket watches, which increasingly affected the temporal organization of life, even of people who did not own them, helped encourage the internalized objective time-consciousness that Protestantism promoted. Whether Calvinist asceticism and a new "spirit of capitalism" were accompanied by an "industrious revolution" in the seventeenth and eighteenth centuries remains a question of debate. What historians have documented is that well before the industrial revolution, objective diachronic time was becoming an ever more widespread feature of European life, far earlier than in other parts of the world. Yet diachronic time opened up multiple constructions.[21] After the industrial revolution began to take hold in the late eighteenth century, differently rational English and German constructions of labor time arose in the nineteenth century.[22] By the twentieth century, institutional mechanisms of socialization and social control wrested inner-worldly asceticism from its religious foundations and translated it into a more generalized "work ethic," while modern industrial production based on organization of the assembly line created a material basis of labor discipline. In turn, with the use of Taylorist ideologies to organize production as efficiently as possible, and with long-range planning – for example, through use of PERT (Planning Evaluation Review Technique) charting – future time in effect could be colonized through anticipatory organization. By the latter twentieth century, with the "post-industrial" emergence of knowledge production as a central driving basis of economies, linear time had broken down into interactive episodes among people that organize economic activity.[23] Today, objective time is the central temporal axis for the organization of social life, yet it is subject to myriad elaborations, in part in relation to other forms of temporality. Ironically, the partitioning of time that diachronic scheduling facilitates yields social and private occasions within a here-and-now that is relatively autonomous.

Beyond the technological and economic consequences of diachronic rationalization and routinization of action, their implications for popular engagement with the apocalyptic are important. Already, the Calvinist "disciplinary revolution," Philip Gorski argues, had substantial consequences. Calvinist states (the Netherlands, England, Brandenberg-Prussia), more than others, adopted new models of labor regulation, poor-relief, and administration that increased their rational efficiency and effectiveness, and routinized their operations. On a different front, Gorski suggests, insofar as the disciplinary revolution took hold "from below," increased religious inner-worldly ascetic discipline among the popular classes eased problems of social control.[24] This development parallels a wider one: to the degree that Calvinist and other Protestant movements stripped religion of magical intercessions toward God, and to the degree that disciplined social action marked by internalization of diachronic time-consciousness became predominant, the world was, as Weber suggested, disenchanted and demystified. Popular life became more routinized, and thus rechanneled away from apocalyptic passions. Disciplined selves geared into this-worldly affairs. Despite all these changes, however, objective temporality has not become pervasive. Rather, the time of the clock remains in play with other times, importantly, through transformations of historical consciousness.

History and the apocalyptic

We may define historically oriented action as action that builds upon other action to produce change (rather than only to maintain the status quo, reaffirm the past, or sustain domination). When historical action is defined in this way, history itself may be recognized to be a gradually emergent social innovation. As I argued in chapter 2, in the ancient civilizations order was valued, and change represented a threat to order. When they engaged in historical actions, notably conquest, the ancients, even the Greeks, tended to fold them back into the eternity of social archetypes through processes of mythicization. This cycling back of history into myth began to break apart when Zoroastrian dualists and Jewish, Christian, and Muslim monotheists separated the beginning of history from its end, placing the unfolding earthly struggles of God's people in the middle, in historical times.

Islamic territorial expansion, the Christian Crusades, and medieval European heretical movements all reinforced the connection of the apocalyptic with history, but none of these developments substantially transformed historical consciousness. Joachim's medieval apocalyptic theology of the three stages, by contrast, not only reopened the door to historical considerations of the end times, but also offered a crack through which a new temporal opening later would be chiseled, toward secularized but somehow still sacred engagements with history.[25]

Beginning in Joachim's times and more concertedly with the Reformation and the "scientific revolution" of the sixteenth and seventeenth centuries, the construction, locus, and, in some quarters, credibility of assertions about the divine *telos* shifted. Historian Anthony Kemp goes so far as to argue that Reformation ideology required a new historical consciousness that broke with the older model of history. Subsequently, the eighteenth-century Enlightenment yielded new philosophical models of history, and the study of history became transformed as well. Thinkers proposed models of historical process in cycles, spirals, and stages. In turn, Kant and later Hegel puzzled over the relationship between history as divine purpose and history as the unfolding of Reason. Animated by the emergent ideology of progress, Hegel and Marx proposed alternatively spiritual and materialists accounts of history as dialectical movement toward perfection. In all this, some way of giving value to history – from God's will to progress to liberation of the masses – provided the basis for constituting history as a universal and holistically meaningful moral unity. Even the "scientific" history initiated by the nineteenth-century German historian Leopold von Ranke, though it meant to tell "what actually happened" (*wie es eigentlich gewesen*), would simultaneously unveil divine purpose. "Every action of the past gives evidence of God, every moment preaches his name," Ranke wrote. In turn, with the rise of neo-kantian relativism in the latter nineteenth century and the elaboration of historical and social-scientific methods and postmodern critiques of metanarrative during the twentieth century, the transcendent "meaning *of* history" substantially gave way to multiple and contested meanings *about* history.[26]

From today's vantage point, historical consciousness cannot be reduced to theological and scholarly ideas. We recognize that people engage in action with one or another embodied sense of historicity. Thus, in early medieval Christian Europe, Augustine's formulation of a dialectic between history and transcendent *telos* continued to accord well with widespread pessimism about this world and anxious hope about the next. As historian Carl Becker put the matter, "Life on earth was but a means to this desired end [of pardon for sin and error], a temporary probation for the testing of God's children."[27] Just as among the ancients, in the sixteenth-century history written by Gregory of Tours, Anthony Kemp observes, historical consciousness remained "without plot or narrative, without development or *telos*."[28]

By the late medieval period and more strongly with the onset of the Reformation, history became engaged in relation to other temporal possibilities, most notably, transformation of the here-and-now in relation to the emergent framework of objective time. These changes were reflected in increased interest in annals, chronicles, and historical periodization.[29] In turn, some strands of Reformation thought, notably Calvinism, inverted Augustine's anti-apocalyptic dialectic of history and eternity by constituting the community of the elect in theocratic terms, as stewards of God's earth who could fulfill God's purposes by this-worldly endeavors. Divine history was brought to earth. Here, Calvin, with his general aversion to apocalyptic thinking, twisted apocalyptic urgency into something new – an almost Augustinian indifference to exactly *when* the apocalypse might come, welded to an always immediate yet enduring struggle against the forces of evil. This ongoing battle to defeat the Devil on earth ultimately would yield a gradualistic pursuit of God's plan in *this* world. Time became something not to be wasted in sloth, and collective historical action became a basis to transform society into the millennial kingdom.[30]

Religion of course was not the only vehicle through which people began to act with historical consciousness, that is, to "make history." Colonization, trade, advances in technology, the scientific revolution, the Enlightenment – these sixteenth- and seventeenth-century European agendas – of states and entrepreneurs, scientists and social philosophers – yielded new kinds of initiatives that possessed a transformative dynamism. Historians do not fully agree upon the causes and interrelationships of these diverse new initiatives, but their hybrid character is not difficult to recognize. The Reformation had its continuities with medieval religious dissent. Magic, mysticism, and ritual piety persisted, and Protestants were not all as ascetic as some of their exemplary prophets.[31] So too, science did not suddenly and dramatically become dissociated from alchemy and craft knowledge to burst forth as full-bore positivism. And although the Enlightenment was centered on reason, for all the deist, agnostic, and atheist refusals of revealed religious doctrines, its flag nevertheless attracted many Christians who saw no conflict between reason and religion.[32] In short, Bruno Latour's thesis that "we have never been modern" certainly applies from the sixteenth to the eighteenth centuries, when social institutions from religion to science and the state seem like alloys themselves, filled with impurities, forged by alchemists. An important case in point concerns European colonization in relation to the apocalyptic.

Apocalypse, exploration, colonization, migration

To suggest that apocalyptic orientations somehow "caused" the emergence of competing European state-centered colonial empires would be reductionist in the extreme. Nevertheless, their interplay had consequences both for colonization and for the conditions under which apocalyptic developments would unfold. Already before the Reformation, European societies – especially Spain and Portugal – engaged in exploration and colonization. After the Reformation, other European states pursued similar projects. These endeavors initiated the formation of a capitalist world-economy centered in Europe. In different ways, colonization both before and after the Reformation bore markings of the apocalyptic.

Before the Reformation

A famous philosopher once argued that "the historical destiny of Christian peoples is no possible subject of a specifically Christian interpretation of political history."[33] However, world history would be very different if Christians had not invoked connections between history and apocalypse. Certainly, Christian holy war has characteristically involved an apocalyptic struggle *in* history. The Roman Church organized the Crusades in order to counter both external Muslim and internal heretical threats to its dominance over a Christian civilization. It thus employed a broadly "colonial" logic, one that consolidated *internal* and *external* territory where Christians reigned.[34] In turn, early European state projects of colonization have direct origins in the Crusades.

The Crusader states in the Holy Land were not deliberately established as colonial projects centered on economic exploitation, and they did not bring much in the way of wealth or tribute back to the papacy or European monarchs. Nevertheless, from 1099 until

1291, invading foreigners held on to their identities as Europeans while ruling four Crusader colonies that amounted to trading entrepôts. The Christian rulers did not force conversion any more than Muslims had. However, they maintained European hegemony in their territories – colonies that the French referred to as *Outremer*, that is, lands across the sea.[35] Materially, Europeans settlers in *Outremer* adopted both slavery and the cultivation of sugar – two practices that later would become central to the spread of Portuguese and Spanish colonies along the Atlantic islands off Africa, and in the Americas.[36] Thus, although the Crusades were not based in a colonialist economic ideology, they spawned material practices and forms of social organization that undergirded subsequent European colonial expansion.[37]

The argument that the Crusades – and especially the Iberian *reconquista* – provided the original template for colonization by Europeans was first made early in the nineteenth century by Leopold von Ranke. As another historian put the matter more recently, "The European Christians who sailed to the coasts of the Americas, Asia, and Africa in the fifteenth and sixteenth centuries came from a society that was already a colonizing society."[38] The early Portuguese explorer Henry the Navigator (1394–1460) headed the Order of Christ, the successor to the disbanded crusading Knights Templar, and he brought a crusading and imperialistic spirit to his campaigns along the coast of West Africa. The church sanctioned Henry's endeavors with official papal bulls, proclamations that authorized him to enslave peoples he encountered on his voyages "to convert and combat the infidel." The islands of the eastern Atlantic thus were colonized on the basis of crusading grants authorized as a way to advance the *dialatio*, the expansion of Christendom.[39]

The same basic pattern carried forward to the Latin Americas. "Veterans of the *reconquista* and crusades in North Africa became the conquistadors of the New World," one historian has observed.[40] Christopher Columbus claimed that his explorations to reach the Indies would advance the coming of the last days by building the world mission of Christianity.[41] In America, as in the Crusades, spoils, booty, and conquest for Christendom went together. But because the papal bulls empowered monarchies to act on behalf of the church, as in the Crusader colonies, religion was a subordinate partner. In the spread of the Portuguese and Spanish empires to the Americas, conquest was first and foremost a military achievement to colonize lands thereby deemed part of a monarchy's patrimony, and allocated to loyalists who would undertake development of production, whether of sugar or silver, for the emerging capitalist world market.[42] For its part, the church engaged in varying practices of encouraged or forced conversion, and it organized indigenous populations and slaves through highly successful networks of missions established by the Jesuits, Franciscans, and other religious orders.[43]

For the church, the Portuguese and Spanish colonizations of the Americas advanced a triumphal march toward realization of world Christendom. But for Portugal and Spain, the central concern was empire. Yet what justifies the pursuit of empire? The great economic theorist and historian Joseph Schumpeter defined imperialism as "the objectless disposition on the part of a state to unlimited forcible expansion." For Schumpeter, imperialistic states use force to increase their domains without being able to calculate the economic costs and benefits in advance. Therefore, imperialism has to justify its program to the masses in terms of an "objectless disposition" – one that exceeds economic rationality – and Schumpeter thought it could do so only by appealing to "dark powers of the subconscious" – by mobilizing "the need to hate," or "inchoate idealism," or some similar non-rational motivation.[44] A good deal of evidence suggests that the template of the apocalyptic crusade furnished an ideological appeal along such lines at the very origins of Western imperialist conquests beyond Europe.

Colonies and migration in the wake of the Reformation

With the Reformation, the relation of the apocalyptic to migration and colonization shifted radically. Protestant theological debates raised the question of whether the Americas might be the site of the New Jerusalem. Prince Henry, son of King James I of England, sought to counter Catholic Portugal and Spain by establishing "true" Christianity in the colonies. In 1629, Reverend John White proposed to create a "bulwark" by colonizing New England "against the kingdom of Antichrist which the Jesuits labor to rear up in all quarters of the world." Over the years, English elite and state-centered tendencies to identify colonization with the cause of Protestant Christian world hegemony would resurface on numerous other fronts – in Oliver Cromwell's colonizing agenda toward Ireland during the Puritan Commonwealth; in concerns about whether the Antichrist might arise in England's Protestant economic competitor, the Netherlands; and in debates about treatment of native Americans in relation to apocalyptic theologies. On the latter front, in North America, seventeenth-century Puritan minister Cotton Mather would speculate, "we may guess that probably the devil decoyed these miserable savages hither in hopes that the gospel of the Lord Jesus Christ would never come here to destroy or disturb his absolute empire over them."[45]

Yet the apocalyptic discourses of state-sponsored and elite Protestant projects of colonization pale in comparison to waves of religious migration that *relocated* the apocalyptic. When Europeans experienced religious persecution at the hands of either Catholic regimes toward Protestants or Protestant regimes toward Catholics and radical Reformation movements, collective migration was one important response. Such migration promoted colonization at the edges of the world-economy, and in the bargain, provided a safety valve that relieved sending societies of their strongest dissenting religious elements. Of course, most European colonization of new territories in North America and elsewhere was undertaken by trading companies, adventurers, transported criminals (some of them for crimes of insurrection connected to dissenting religion), vagabonds, and people of few religious convictions who sought land. But people also migrated in streams connected to larger religious communities, and sometimes traveled as a group. The consequences were diverse.

When Catholics left a Protestant for a Catholic European country, or Protestants fled to a state open to Protestantism, their migrations enhanced networks of religious association across European national boundaries, stimulating the circulation of religious ideas. In addition, migration frequently increased the diversity of confessional traditions and organizations within societies, provoking issues of religious tolerance.

For religious migration outside Europe, the structures of colonization after the Reformation were quite different from before. Portuguese and Spanish colonization had brought a church that claimed to monopolize access to salvation within colonized territories, but made salvation available to all who participated in the church's rituals. By contrast, those who fled persecution during the Reformation sometimes sought to establish a sect of God's chosen people. Few religious migrants would try to establish a theocracy ruled by the elect, as did the Pilgrims coming to Massachusetts in 1620 or the Mormons arriving in Utah in 1847. But religious migrants would at least hope for the collective freedom to practice their religion, sometimes to the exclusion of other religious practices within their colony. Thus, religious migrations could put a cultural stamp of meaning or purpose onto colonization of territories that often came to include other people who were less religiously inclined. Sometimes that stamp centered on one or another apocalyptic endeavor – of flight from "the Beast," or building what the Pilgrims envisioned – a "City on a Hill."[46]

States containing the apocalyptic

What, then, of the European countries from which religious dissenters migrated? After the Reformation, the state became the central node in relation to which modern alignments with the apocalyptic were to be established. Developments were highly complex, both within and across states, for the Reformation did not succeed everywhere, and dramatically different versions took hold where it did – Germany, the Scandinavian states, the Netherlands, and England. Yet all European states shared with both the nobility and the emerging bourgeoisie an interest in controlling and policing the most apocalyptic or otherwise radical versions of the Reformation, ones like the early Anabaptist movement. Thus, tracing modernizing projects of "containment" offers an efficient basis on which to identify the realignment of the apocalyptic in relation to modernizing states.

With the Reformation, Catholic, Protestant, and mixed states all increasingly took up the containment of religion by regulating and sometimes administering it, and they did so in ways that eventually undermined the most intense apocalyptic doctrines. In the long term, two centuries after the beginning of the Reformation, the book of prophecy was largely closed: both within establishment national religious confessions and in heterodoxical religious movements, the range of permissible revisions to religious doctrine became circumscribed in ways that discouraged radical new messiahs from stepping forward. Both where the Reformation took hold and where it did not, states shifted away from the medieval formula that reserved matters of theological controversy to the church and left kingdoms to act as the *brachium saeculare*, the secular arm for church enforcement against heretics. Now, unevenly and incompletely, states themselves took up the delineation and enforcement of boundaries of religious toleration and deviance, and they would deal harsh repression to groups and movements that fell beyond the pale. Thus, by the early eighteenth century, after two centuries of Reformation episodes when the apocalyptic might operate at the center of history, strongly apocalyptic religious movements became marginalized. Where they did arise, they unfolded largely in tension with states rather than, as in medieval times, in tension with the church.[47]

We can get a good sense of the range of state containments of the apocalyptic by considering two quite different countries – Catholic France, where strong opposition to the Reformation was mounted, and England, where Protestantism ultimately prevailed. Both English and French developments are rooted in the development of the Reformed church in Switzerland and Geneva, where thousands of refugees came during the sixteenth century to flee persecution. In Switzerland, after theologian Huldrych Zwingli's death, Lutheran apocalypticism found its way into the doctrines of his successor, Heinrich Bullinger (who predicted the end of the world to come in 1666, a millennium + the sign of the Beast). For his part, Calvin pursued a decidedly less messianic theology. Lacking any strongly apocalyptic orientation, he shifted zealous and uncompromising collective religious action toward the affairs of this world. In Geneva, these ideas blossomed into the brief establishment of a Reformation theocracy that required religious confession for citizenship.

French Huguenots, dominated by secular aristocrats, and proto-Puritan English and Scots *émigrés*, most of them ministers, absorbed the ideas circulating in Switzerland and Geneva according to their status positions in their own countries. Moreover, the English and Scots may have had greater exposure to Bullinger along with Calvin, whereas the latter proved the predominant influence among the French.[48] In turn, when the *émigrés* returned to the two countries, Reformation theologies had differential consequences as they played out in relation to social forces in England versus France.

England

Any account of events in England during the two centuries beginning with the Reformation is likely to imply a coherence to history that even historians most given to metanarrative have not been able to identify.[49] An amazing and diverse array of millenarian and other tendencies both shaped and emerged out of the cauldron called the English Revolution, itself linked to developments in Scotland, France, the Netherlands, and the Catholic Church. The interplay of the apocalyptic, religion, and politics among diverse and shifting alliances is of a complexity unrivalled in its day, and it anticipates the great conundrum of the twenty-first century's global jihad and counterposed "war on terror." Among the myriad aspects, I focus here on how apocalyptic ideas and movements became reconfigured in relation to state power.

Because the monarchy initiated the English Reformation at first on the basis of Henry VIII's marital aspirations, its officials abjured any apocalyptic underpinnings. Yet the vicissitudes of English monarchy from the time of Henry VIII's rule until 1649, when King Charles I was tried and executed, were both driven by and in turn produced shifting constructions of religious legitimacy. The regency that governed during the brief reign of Henry VIII's son, boy king Edward VI, pursued the first serious institution of Protestantism. When Edward died in 1553 at the age of 15, his Catholic half-sister Mary – daughter of Catherine of Aragon and Henry VIII – married the Catholic King Phillip II of Spain, thereby fueling flames of English opposition. During her five-year reign, Queen Mary endeavored to reestablish English Catholicism by reversing policies that Edward's regency had advanced – the reformed liturgy and the permission for clergy to marry. When "Bloody" Mary's regime condemned some 275 Protestant leaders and believers to be burned at the stake, Protestants came to view them as saints – especially after the publication of John Foxe's 1563 *Acts and Monuments of the English Martyrs.*[50]

The Marian exile – in which proto-Puritan English Protestants like Foxe sought refuge in Switzerland and Geneva – ended when Mary died in 1558, leaving her Protestant half-sister Elizabeth to take the throne. Queen Elizabeth reinstated Protestantism in a relatively conservative Anglican church that would again be governed by the state. In addition, concerned by rival – and Catholic – claims to succeed to the English throne, she had her cousin, Mary, Queen of Scots, confined.

Initially, Catholic belief, if not worship, was permitted. However, by 1570 Pope Pius V had issued a bull declaring Elizabeth a heretic, thereby challenging both England's Protestant church and the very legitimacy of Elizabeth's rule. "Effectively," according to one analysis, "the Bull made sedition a religious duty for all English Catholics, and gave crusader status to any Catholic prince who made war on Elizabeth, deserving Catholics' loyalty and support."[51] Parliament responded by outlawing the bull, and over the course of Elizabeth's reign, Catholicism in England increasingly became an isolated sect followed mostly by fractions of the wealthier classes.

Elizabeth adopted an increasingly harsh anti-Catholic stance, and she thereby hoped to placate radicalized Marian exiles who had returned to England. Though prosecutions of Papists were pursued under the rubric of treason rather than heresy, this distinction made no significant difference for the more than 100 Catholic priests who ended up executed. Elizabeth further solidified English Protestantism in 1585 by going to war with Spain and declaring all ordained Catholic priests guilty of treason. After the 1587 trial and execution of Mary Queen of Scots for plotting to overthrow Elizabeth, and in the wake of the English victory over the Spanish Armada in 1588, Elizabeth consolidated the establishment of Protestantism by using secret police to identify Catholic priests and exiling or placing under virtual house arrest Catholics who refused to recognize the authority of the Church of England.[52]

For all this, Elizabeth's Protestantism was of a politic sort that maintained respect for tradition and authority. Strong followers of Calvin attacked lingering organizational forms and liturgical practices as the "dregs of popery."[53] However, mainstream Puritan clerics tried to contain the spreading radical popular movement and seal off routes to separatism and millenarian and antinomian heresies by deploying a "covenant theology" that, borrowing from capitalist models of contract, would bind individuals to God through the church.[54] In the wake of the Spanish Armada's defeat, by 1593, Protestant radicals found themselves subject to similar penalties to those applied to Catholic recusants. In the latter sixteenth and early seventeenth centuries, struggling against what they regarded as an incomplete Reformation, radical ministers and theologians used secret meetings, propaganda pamphlets, and university bases at Cambridge and Oxford to attract followers. Many of those who joined were gentlemen. In the 1620s and '30s, some, men like John Milton and Oliver Cromwell, in effect became "the first Puritan lay intellectuals."[55]

With Elizabeth's death in 1603 and for the next half-century, debates about how to purify the Anglican church (or scrap it altogether in favor of independent sects of gathered saints) would make Puritanism an ever more visible religio-political movement of opposition to the English state that governed its church, and the movement increasingly counted members of Parliament among its numbers. Reform historically had meant the correction of existing social institutions. But as the Puritan movement developed into a counterculture with huge numbers of participants of diverse religious and political tendencies, many Puritans came to believe that

reform required something far more comprehensive – the construction of an entirely new edifice of state committed to creating a
Calvinist millennial kingdom. Already in the sixteenth century,
proto-Puritans had emphasized the importance of social discipline,
leading to the establishment of workhouses such as London's Bride-
well Hospital, meant to encourage moral and spiritual discipline
though methodical work activity.[56] By the 1620s and '30s, the movement was becoming increasingly political at the very time when
people across economic classes sought to stem what they regarded
as social disorder spreading under conditions of falling wages and
rural cottager encroachments onto commons lands and forests.[57]

The Puritan movement preached virtues of sobriety and discipline that proved widely attractive in these conditions of crisis. But
its focus on discipline spilled beyond sermonizing. It spawned
highly committed groups of individuals who derived their claims
of legitimacy from a degree of religious conviction that yielded
zealously engaged political action without previous historical parallel. In effect, Michael Walzer has famously argued, the Puritans
invented modern political opposition politics as a social form, and
like other sixteenth- and early seventeenth-century groups such as
the Huguenots, the Catholic League, and the signers of the Scottish
Covenant, they carried into that politics a belief in their right to
wage war. In turn, to war they brought a new Calvinist-inspired
discipline of troops – not mercenaries but religiously inspired citizens. "Those who fought for God," Walzer observes, "would have
to *know the reasons*; only then could army regulations and religious
fervor come together in a new discipline." When the Puritans' New
Model Army conducted war, it would transcend merely secular
purposes. Protestant sermons invoked the Crusades. Cambridge
scholar Joseph Mede, whose 1627 work *Clavis Apocalyptica* was
translated to English in 1643, followed millennial ideas of the
German scholar Johann Heinrich Alsted (1588–1638), but gave them
a decidedly English twist. He proposed that victory in a crusade
against the Beast would give way to the millennial kingdom – on
earth.[58]

Virtually from the onset of the Reformation onward, apocalyptic
theologizing and popular anxieties shadowed English religious
thinking. Sometimes deep scholarly readings of the Book of Revelation proposed complex mathematical and astrological methods to
recalculate the exact date of Armageddon. Scots mathematician
John Napier's 1593 *Plaine Discovery of the Whole Revelation of St. John*
employed logarithms, which he had invented, to pursue his real

passion, determining the Day of Judgment, finally calculated to fall between 1688 and 1700; Francis Potter, who became a Fellow of the Royal Society, used the Book of Revelation's 666 to prove that the pope was the Antichrist; and in 1642 John Archer assured his readers that the papal Antichrist would be defeated in 1666.[59]

By the 1630s, English writers had published the major learned apocalyptic treatises of their generation, and the center of apocalyptic gravity shifted to preaching and Parliament. Every party to the political disputes over religion and state had its apocalyptic theology. Despite some diplomatic doubts, the Anglican church held to identifying the Catholic Church and its popes as Antichrist. Strong Calvinists sought to purify the Church of England and England itself by instituting a theocracy along the lines of Calvin's Geneva. And for the most radical Puritans, the Church of England became "the Beast," all the more so when William Laud, chosen as archbishop by King Charles I in 1533, ratcheted up persecution of Puritans.[60] In these apocalyptically charged circumstances, in 1637, King Charles sought to bring Scottish worship under the wing of the Anglican church. But the Scots revolted, forcing him to call English Parliament into session in 1640, even though by then the Puritans dominated the House of Commons. After Charles had settled with the Scots in 1641, he tried to arrest leaders of the Puritan faction of Parliament. However, in the ensuing military struggles, the Puritans' highly disciplined New Model Army defeated the forces of Charles, brought him to trial, and had him convicted of treason. He was beheaded in 1649. Subsequently, Cromwell led the New Model Army in retaking Catholic Ireland, which was by then in alliance with Charles's son, Charles II.

The legally orchestrated but unprecedented regicide of Charles did not dampen apocalyptic politics: it shifted them in a post-apocalyptic direction. In a climate of high hopes, utopian visions brought into question all the eternal verities of the established order. Far beyond Calvinism, a much broader range of radical countercultural religio-political proposals for building the millennial kingdom came on offer. Already the Reformation had begun to revolutionize marriage, shifting from a property relation to a partnership in principle based on individual decisions about mutual affection and commitment. But people in the movement known as the Ranters took jaundiced views toward preachers railing about sin, especially coded for sex. Ranters mocked Puritan self-righteousness, and, if accounts are to be believed, they embraced free love and gathered in taverns to revel in blasphemy. Another group, the Family of Love, claimed that heaven and hell are to be found in this world, and they lived holding all things in common. In April 1649 the True Levelers, or Diggers, occupied some commons land on St. George's Hill at Cobham in Surrey for a fortnight, proposing the organization of Christian society into communal groups that would grow their own food. And one Digger, Gerrard Winstanley, raised an objection that resonated more widely, against any legal or governmental organization of religious affairs.[61]

Many English people with less utopian visions nevertheless argued for "no king but Jesus." The most militant program emerged among the Fifth Monarchy Men. This movement, especially popular in the towns and the army, foresaw the coming of the rule of Christ as the fifth monarch after the four monarchs described in the Bible's Book of Daniel 2: 36–44 (on the premise that the fourth monarch had been the Roman emperor, whose rule had been extended by the popes). Compared to the Ranters and the Diggers, the Fifth Monarchists developed wider support for their programs, which included the substitution of biblical for English law. But in 1653 they lost out to the man who had begun to lead the New Model Army, Oliver Cromwell. Much inspired by deep meditations on God's divine purpose, Cromwell became Lord Protector of the Commonwealth. Afterwards, a Fifth Monarchist preached at St. Anne, Blackfriars, "Let us go home and pray, and say, 'Lord, wilt Thou have Oliver Cromwell or Jesus Christ to reign over us?' "[62] By 1556 the most radical of the Fifth Monarchists were forming quasi-military terrorist cells of from five to twenty-five men and plotting to overthrow Cromwell's Protectorate. Anticipating revolutionary anarchists in the nineteenth and twentieth centuries, the insurgents apparently believed that their heroic chiliasm would somehow precipitate a revolutionary transformation, in their case, the defeat of the newest whore of Babylon. It was chaotic circumstances like these that Thomas Hobbes had anticipated in his *Leviathan*, published in 1651, where he proposed rule by an all-powerful secular sovereign who, in the long stretch of time between Christ's first and second coming, would govern a religious kingdom without brooking religious dissent.[63]

The Puritans under Cromwell had their apocalyptic visions, but unlike the Fifth Monarchists, they did not anticipate any miraculous intervention. Rather, they would have to build the millennial kingdom themselves, harnessing the discipline and fervor of the New Model Army to a pragmatic politics concerned with the challenges of ruling a country both traumatized and animated by its historic moment.[64] For Cromwell and Parliament, just as for Anglicans, circumstances required the strict regulation of public outbreaks of millenarian or ecstatic religiosity, whether pacifist or militant. Yet Cromwell also instituted Puritan-inspired reforms. He arranged for Independents, Presbyterians, and Baptists to minister parish churches, established a policy of tolerating private worship by non-Puritan people of diverse confessions, and initiated a policy, partly driven by his Puritan convictions, of welcoming Jews to return to England, more than three centuries after they had been banished.[65]

Following Cromwell's sudden illness and death in 1658, the Restoration of the monarchy in 1660 ended any Reformation effort to legislate exactly who might constitute the elect rulers of Christian society. Cromwell's body was exhumed, hung in chains, and his decapitated head placed on a pole outside Westminster Hall, where it seems to have remained until at least 1685. Severe punishment thus was meted out to an already deceased perpetrator of regicide.

Nevertheless, Charles I's son, King Charles II, initially sought religious peace. His Declaration of Breda in April 1660 affirmed that "no man shall be disquieted or called in question for differences of opinion in matters of religion which do not disturb the peace of the kingdom."[66] Yet the popular movements unleashed during the Puritan Revolution clearly unsettled both aristocracy and bourgeoisie, and Parliament, dominated by Anglicans, reacted by reestablishing the Church of England and outlawing dissenting religious meetings of more than five people. Under these conditions, strong dissenters found migration to the continent or the Americas attractive. For others who stayed in England, historian Christopher Hill has argued, the ensuing persecution "drove all but the most dedicated believers back to the state church. So the sects became restricted to a self-selected elite: the elect."[67]

On the opposite front, Charles's tolerance toward Catholics provoked the suspicions of antipapists, and this suspicion seemed to them validated when he converted to Catholicism on his deathbed. His brother, King James II, had long affirmed his own Catholic faith, and he naively tilted toward Catholicism and a French alliance from the beginning of his rule until he was deposed in the Glorious Revolution of 1688. This was a revolution "from above" that Parliament encouraged by inviting William of Orange – married to Mary, Protestant daughter of James – to invade. Their rule consolidated a distinctive and relatively enduring pattern – anti-Catholic Protestant nationalism. The Catholic mass was outlawed, priests were to

[margin note: of French / Rights of Man]

be subject to "perpetual imprisonment," and the person who reported Catholic offenses was to receive the tidy sum of £100.[68] On the other hand, in the 1689 Act of Toleration, Puritan dissenters, Quakers, and other sects, already well established on the ground, gained state legitimation of their freedom to pursue their own religious visions so long as they were willing to forgo any effort to create a single kingdom of saints.

The Puritan Revolution and its aftermath in the Restoration produced widespread disenchantment with religious enthusiasm and increasing apathy toward religion more generally.[69] The sum total of diverse tendencies yielded a collective outcome: the state brought the general population back from the apocalyptic precipice, and contained apocalyptic and other dissenting sentiments within identifiable groups. By the eighteenth century, according to Christopher Hill, dissenters might pursue expanded rights, "But always the knowledge that an overthrow of the Whig régime would be far worse for them than its maintenance prevented them going very far."[70] More broadly, in the account of Francis Fukuyama, with the rise of political liberalism in Europe, "religion was defanged by being made tolerant."[71] As pacification became a reality, Lawrence Stone recounts, "the Church of England became a part of the spoils system of the government, and both the dissenters and the Catholics went their own way relatively unmolested."[72]

Already by the end of the sixteenth century, Protestant clerics had appealed to English elites by proposing that preaching a sober and disciplined Calvinism would inoculate England from the sort of Anabaptist millennium that had unfolded in Münster.[73] By the beginning of the eighteenth century, the waves of apocalyptic excitement that peaked with the English Revolution had long waned. But the three-cornered struggle between Anglicans, Catholics, and Puritans and dissenters left a considerable residue in the formation of England as a state. Now it was ordered on the basis of legally instituted control of Catholicism, and steeped in hard lessons about the benefits of striking a balance between religious toleration of diverse Protestant (and Jewish) believers, and, on the other hand, the risks to social order that a revolutionary fusion of apocalyptic beliefs with political agendas could pose. The apocalypse would be contained, but not simply on the basis of preaching as social control. By the eighteenth century, in a Hobbesian solution, the state unambiguously ended up as both the guarantor of religious freedom and the enforcer of the boundaries of toleration necessary to maintain the established political order. In the bargain, emergence of a wider regulatory state, Christopher Hill has argued, enhanced predictable conditions for capitalist development, paving the way for England to become the country where the industrial revolution first took hold.[74]

France

The fate of the Reformation in France, and its implications for state regulation of religious dissent, might seem more straightforward than in England.[75] The Huguenots returned from Geneva to spread Calvinism in France among both common people and political elites, and the specific character of elite support stamped the character of French Protestantism. The Huguenot movement did not take the modernizing direction of independent political factions that marked English Puritanism. Instead, it became caught up in the struggle of nobles to reform feudalism in order to counter the absolutist tendencies of the French throne. Militarily, the nobles anticipated the discipline of the New Model Army, but their practices remained infused with medieval notions of personal honor, and their political goals did not produce the zeal that the English Puritans would muster. Early on, the Huguenot movement established congregations under the patronage of feudal lords whom Calvinist leaders might both chastise for their conduct and seek out for their protection. Thus, the Huguenot movement was beset by contradictions that proved difficult to resolve. In particular, the nobility would not work to depose the monarchy and create a Protestant political order, for, as one nobleman frankly put it, "if there were no longer a king, each village would free itself from its gentleman."[76]

As in England, the prospects of Protestantism intertwined with royal politics. The contestations of the Catholic Guise family versus the Protestant Bourbons in the wake of the death of King Henri II in 1559 initiated France's Wars of Religion, which continued over three decades. Catherine de' Medici, ruling in the name of her two sons, Francis II and Charles IX, initially believed that religion was a smokescreen being invoked to obscure secular political rivalries, and she sought to appease the factions. But in this belief, she was mistaken. Efforts to compromise satisfied neither the zealous Catholic League, which sought to eliminate Protestantism completely, nor the Huguenots, who believed that efforts to resolve the crisis – such as the 1563 Edict of Amboise – were tilted against them. Terrible conflicts ensued. The bloodiest single event, the St.

Bartholomew's Day Massacre in 1572 – began as a narrowly framed political plot to assassinate prominent Protestants. But it quickly grew into a mob massacre of anyone identified as Protestant, initially in Paris, and then more widely. Somewhere between six and twelve thousand Protestants were killed. Through 1581, one estimate puts the total death toll in the Wars of Religion, Catholics and Protestants combined, at 750,000. Even by more conservative estimates, the carnage was historically without parallel in Europe.[77]

By 1585, Henri III moved away from any hopes of accommodation, decreeing that "there will be no practice of the new Reformed Protestant Religion but only that of the Catholic religion."[78] After his death in 1589, a Protestant heir, Henri of Navarre, succeeded to the throne, but only by converting to Catholicism (famously saying, in jest or not, "Paris is worth a mass"). Henri sought to end the recurrent wars and place France on a more even keel, and, against the pope and the Catholic League's wishes, in 1598 he put forward the Edict of Nantes, which permitted the free exercise of religion by Protestants. He also secretly subsidized Protestant minister salaries and paid for military garrisons to defend Huguenot forts. Henri found some success in encouraging stability, but in 1610 a Catholic opponent of the Edict of Nantes assassinated him. By 1616, elements of the nobility were using Huguenot strongholds to challenge royal absolutist interests and develop religiously bounded "states within a state." In turn, the crown pushed to assert royal power over religion. However, it did not just move against the Protestant Huguenots. Eventually, it found a new target in the Catholic Jansenist movement that originated in the 1640s, oriented toward doctrines of divine grace, predestination, and salvation through the church alone. For the monarchy, any heterodoxical movement, even a Catholic one, would have to be contained.

In 1682, the French government got a representative assembly of Catholic Church clergy and hierarchy to agree to the Gallican Declaration, which asserted significant autonomy of the French Church from the pope and lent legitimacy to the French crown's *de facto* power to regulate the church, in part by appointing bishops. In 1685, with the Protestants already strongly suppressed, Louis XIV would revoke the Edict of Nantes. It had been a necessary framework for creating a stable French society, he asserted, rather than a principled basis on which to organize society. "Members of the so-called Reform religion, while awaiting God's pleasure to enlighten them," could continue to live in France without interference, but public or private Protestant worship was forbidden, ministers were ordered to convert or emigrate, and private Huguenot schools were prohibited. There would be *une foi, une loi, un roi* – one faith, one law, one king.[79] In England, nationalism was being built on suppression of Catholics and regulation of Protestant dissidents. In France, a distinctively religious form of absolutism would both define the boundaries of Catholicism and require the exclusion of Protestants.[80] The French would no longer be Catholics; Catholicism would become French.

Reprise: containment and progress

Contestations in France between the monarchy and Protestant competitors based in the nobility bore medieval trappings of honor and chivalry in war rather than the apocalyptic zeal that animated developments in England and Scotland, where insurgent Protestants saw themselves fulfilling a messianic mandate. In essence, the French Wars of Religion ended up enhancing the power of the monarchy, as the Albigensian Crusade had in the early thirteenth century. These differences between France and England reinforce the argument that apocalyptic movements pose special threats when they identify the state with Antichrist, their battles with Armageddon. Overall, it is not implausible to think that the absence or presence of an apocalyptic manifest and its particular implementation contributed to the difference in Reformation outcomes in France and England.

Nevertheless, the consequences for the containment of religion were similar in the two countries: they differed only in what religions were to be contained – Catholicism and dissenting Protestantism in England versus Protestantism and dissenting Jansenist Catholicism in France. Containment of religion by the state was a *general* outcome of the interaction of the Reformation with political struggles, rather than a *specific* outcome only occurring when a strongly apocalyptic movement threatened a state.

With the Reformation, Christian historian Ronald Knox argued, religious enthusiasm became all but a dead letter. In his telling, Martin Luther's alliance with the German princes not only marginalized the Anabaptists, "it cemented from the first that alliance between church and state which so long governed the outlook of official Protestantism; and it deepened in official Protestantism a contempt for those enthusiastic movements towards which, if it had consulted its own genius, it should have been sympathetic."[81] Reformation efforts failed to create a single national church ordered by the elect according to strict theologies. Instead, to invoke the classic distinction between church and sect,[82] establishments of national Protestantism came to approximate churches, that is, religious organizations offering salvation to all, not just the elect. These outcomes aligned with broader developments of social power, but they did not spell the end of the apocalyptic in Europe.

The multiple sources of social power had increased significantly by the sixteenth century. Revolutions in navigation and gunpowder weaponry not only initiated centuries of European colonial expansion, but enhanced what the Reformation also promoted: possibilities of centralized power over bounded state territories.[83] Non-state apocalyptic movements in an increasingly modernizing world thus found themselves overwhelmed by the diverse kinds of power increasingly exercised by secular states – not only brute military force, but also the power to channel populations into workaday life at considerable remove from the episodic eruption of apocalyptic charisma. The Puritans, however, exhibited an alternative tendency, in which the apocalypse became threaded into worldly, historical pursuits, nevertheless animated by religious commitment and enthusiasm for the fulfillment of God's purposes on earth. Here, chiliastic apocalyptic eruption gave way to a form of apocalyptic fervor tempered by Calvinist discipline that yielded sustained and strategic action. The apocalypse became harnessed in relation to historical time and the emerging rationalized and routinized diachronic social order.

This hybridic mixing suggests that the apocalyptic was subjected to disenchantment and desacralization, and redirected toward an ideology of progress in the bargain. Although progress as an ideal is often traced to the Enlightenment (with the Enlightenment inadequately interpreted as an intrinsically secular development), the origins of progress arguably derive in part from Calvin's theology. Previously, mainstream Christian teleology had been marked since Augustine as history eternally open to believers' personal experience of an eschatological present when transcendental, divine reality could become manifest. For his part, Calvin focused this eschatological present onto the diachronic time of goal-oriented action.[84] In seventeenth- and early-eighteenth-century England and America, this conception supported the idea that building the millennial kingdom on earth contributes to progress as a Christian mission. Only a pale shadow of the apocalypse remained, in something of a "postmillennial" theology that Christ's eventual return would depend on preparing the soil.[85]

In this light, it is not so easy to disentangle the Enlightenment from religion. In our day, social theorist Jürgen Habermas has argued that a key institution of the Enlightenment – the public sphere as a secular arena where politics might be freely debated – emerged toward the end of the seventeenth century. Thus, Habermas noted, pubs and coffeehouses of the 1670s were "considered seedbeds of political unrest."[86] However, practices of public communication in England have their origins well before the Enlightenment, partly in religious discussions of politics.[87] Already during the Puritan Revolution, Christopher Hill tells us, "the lower orders could meet, discuss, and organize themselves, free from the control either of a parson safely educated at Oxford or Cambridge or of the squire, and free too from the paternal supervision of heads of families."[88] Baptists were gathering to worship at inns, smoking their pipes during services. In 1641, one could hear the complaint "religion is now become the common discourse and table-talk in every tavern and ale-house."[89] In the Civil War, Puritans debated whether the violence of their actions ought to be justified as holy war or under more secular auspices of natural rights. Enlightenment concerns in England thus arose initially in religious discourse: "The state, or civil society, came to understand itself as, at bottom, a religious entity."[90]

Similar connections can be traced in England between science and mainstream Puritan "Latitudinarians" who accepted the Church of England during the Restoration and sought to curb religious enthusiasm, but wanted to prepare for the millennial kingdom. To do so, they worked to harmonize religion and science through an ideology that naturalized society. They thus made God's divine plan open to study by new-style mechanical philosophers such as Robert Boyle and the apocalyptically minded Isaac Newton, who themselves contributed to the legitimation of Christianity as a "natural religion."[91]

During the eighteenth century, secular aspects of the Enlightenment would continue to gain primacy, notably in the emerging view that history no longer should be read as the flowering of God's will. Yet there are religious bearings to be found in Enlightenment thinkers. Hints suggest, for example, that in France, Voltaire viewed himself as something of a secular saint, putting forward Enlightenment ideas as a sort of non-fanatical faith. In the nineteenth century, French social theorist August Comte would proclaim positivism as a philosophical faith in progress through the application of science.[92] Providence would be displaced by increasingly secular understandings of free will, cause and effect, and history.

However, the Enlightenment and positivism did not shear either knowledge or ideology of their religious bearings. Rather, they moved Augustine's Heavenly City onto earthly foundations. The future in this world became the promised land, to be built not through divine intervention, but by people acting progressively, in concert with one another in the unfolding of historical time, from generation to generation.[93] Progressive people of faith kept to much the same vision, but through religious engagement. On both religious and secular fronts, progress defined in relation to abstract goals increasingly oriented the here-and-now toward action on projects to be realized in unfolding diachronic time, through planned efforts.[94] Yet the apocalyptic did not simply wither away.

Secular rechanneling of the apocalyptic

Calvin consolidated a postmillennialist theology that ended up lending support to the modern ideology of progressive action in historical time. With him, the apocalyptic sword began to be hammered into the ploughshare of modernity. The Peace of Westphalia in 1648 brought an end both to the Thirty Years' War centered in the Holy Roman Empire and to the Eighty Years' War between the Habsburg Empire and the Dutch Republic – both of which centrally involved issues of religious confession. After the Glorious Revolution of 1688, England entered a new era in which religion was to figure far less strongly in either civil or interstate war.

However, what would prove a more ominous development came into play. In any number of instances, instead of being beaten into ploughshares, the sacred sword of the apocalypse would be moved from the religious to the secular realm. A distinctly "modern apocalyptic" would center on state power and its contestation. A central moment of this development can be marked by a comment of historian Dale Van Kley about the French Revolution. Its "dechristianization," he observed, "bore an uncanny resemblance to the Calvinist iconoclasm of the French Reformation more than two centuries earlier."[95] How to account for this similarity between religious and secular radicalism? Let us take stock.

Before the Reformation, knightly principles of honor and vengeance had permeated medieval European warfare. Absolutist monarchs could supplement the fighting ethos of feudal codes only by offering those who would serve their cause tangible material incentives (shares in spoils or payment as mercenaries). Alternatively, they simply pressed their subjects into service. Insofar as people were willing to die for a cause on a basis other than honor or material incentive, their motives tended to have strongly religious origins in the ancient forms of martyrdom that had become channeled into military action for a sacred cause in Islamic jihad and the Christian Crusades. In at least one case, a religiously based nationalism emerged. As one historian observes, "The crusade and the providential destiny of France and its ruling dynasty merged in the later Middle Ages into a form of apocalyptic royal or national messianism."[96]

In the Reformation, the vehicle of nationalism carried the apocalyptic ideology of a sacred cause into the terrain of secular warfare. As we have seen, the New Model Army in England held to an apocalyptic narrative about the Puritan cause within a military organization that embraced proto-modern forms of discipline and pursued objectives in the secular world. The Puritans thus brought religious zeal to the pursuit and exercise of political power in a way consonant with their broader Calvinist theology. In effect, the personal Calvinist war of repression against the self was replicated in a struggle against social disorder.

The dual reconstruction of self and the social, it turns out, is a cultural template that later would be employed in other totalistic modern social movements. Parallels can be found, for example, in the Jacobin ideology of the French Revolution and in Lenin railing against "disorder" and "slovenliness" during the Bolshevik Revolution. For the Puritans and subsequent disciplined revolutionaries, Michael Walzer therefore proposed a program of comparative analysis, arguing, "Their great achievement is what is known in the sociology of revolution as the *terror*, the effort to create a holy commonwealth and to force men to be Godly."[97] Even in sixteenth-century England, however, this was not only a Puritan project. As philosopher Jacques Derrida has commented, at a number of junctures in *Leviathan*, Hobbes invoked terror as a principal basis of the commonwealth (he wrote, for example, "there must be some coercive power, to compel men equally to the performance of their covenants, by the terror of some punishment, greater than the benefit they expect by the breach of their covenant"). In its modern origins, terror as a social technology of intimidation supports the broad capacity of the state to regulate the conduct of people within its jurisdiction.[98]

The Holy Commonwealth of the Puritans did not persist, but two centuries later a strong version of the "terror" emerged again – in the French Revolution. For France, the history of historical interpretations might seem stacked against any thesis that religiously apocalyptic zeal found its way into the secular realm of politics. After all, French royals successfully prevailed against the Reformation, and they did so by delimiting a specifically French Catholicism that was anything but apocalyptic. By 1789, state and church were so tightly linked that the French Revolution overthrew not only the monarchy but religion as well. Was not the French Revolution the child and the triumph of the Enlightenment? Addressing this question will help crystallize our understanding of a possible lineage by which the apocalyptic relationship to modernity emerged. To pursue this puzzle, we need to ask: how the French Revolution developed in relation to religion, whether the revolution had an apocalyptic dimension, and if so, what its character was. By this route, it will be possible to consider whether terror in the French Revolution descended through a genealogical relationship from earlier religious messianism (and if so, from what sources), or was instead a functionally equivalent apocalyptic reinvention within a secular domain.

Sociologist S. N. Eisenstadt recently characterized modern secular revolutionary movements in a way that goes beyond suggesting their functional equivalence with medieval and Reformation revolutionary religious movements. Such modern movements, Eisenstadt argues, were "fundamentalist" in the sense that the Jacobins of the French Revolution were fundamentalists – in their highly disciplined yet zealously radical efforts to remake society according to a total and encompassing utopian vision. During the Reign of Terror that lasted from September 1793 to July 1794, with ultimate conviction concerning the rectitude of their vision, the Jacobins freely used the guillotine to achieve and maintain the power that they would need to implement their program. This violent fundamentalism is distinctly modern, yet its unrelenting reason stands in opposition to the values of the Enlightenment that are conventionally associated with modernity. How could this be so? In Eisenstadt's account, Jacobin participants in the French Revolution acted within utopian and millenarian temporal frameworks that already had arisen in the proto-fundamentalist radical Reformation and the Puritan Revolution in England. The difference was that in France chiliastic millenarianism took on a secular but nonetheless sacred character. The Puritans had undertaken apocalyptic violence to defeat Antichrist and fulfill God's divine plan by building an orderly kingdom of God on earth. The Jacobins under Maximilien Robespierre also treated violence as a sacred vehicle, but they sought to build a "republic of virtue" as a secular yet quasi-religious utopia. As Robespierre held, "the sphere of popular government … in revolution … is at one and the same time virtue and terror; virtue, without which terror is quite deadly; and terror, without which virtue is powerless. Terror is nothing more than rapid, severe, and inflexible justice; it is therefore something that emanates from virtue." Eisenstadt's juxtaposition of the French Revolution with earlier apocalyptic European religious movements suggests more than functional equivalence. It strongly implies a diffusion of the apocalyptic from religious to secular auspices. Yet Eisenstadt does not spell out whether or how such a diffusion occurred, perhaps because historians of France themselves have only incompletely addressed the question.[99]

Certainly, apocalyptic ideas persisted during the eighteenth century in the shade of the Enlightenment in France. Indeed, the onset of the French Revolution in 1789 marked "the messianic expectation of regeneration," as an early twentieth-century historian put it. In this climate, considerable excitement surrounded prophetresses Suzette Labrous and Catherine Théot, who came forward to proclaim the momentous events to be part of the divine millennial plan. Christian critics later declared the revolution something like the bastard child of a union between the godless Enlightenment and Antichrist.[100] Diverse contemporary and *ex post facto* interpretations thus show that apocalyptic meanings were still readily available for appropriation in the late eighteenth century and after. But they do not account for the apocalyptic character of the revolution.

Since medieval times, the filaments of apocalyptic cultural diffusion in Europe had often spread underground like mycelia of mushrooms. The Jacobins thus might seem to be enacting apocalyptic narratives that simply popped up under propitious conditions. However, the relationship is at once more specific and more complex than this metaphor would suggest. Conventional histories of the Revolution give pride of place to the Enlightenment *philosophes*, not to religion. But these readings may derive from metanarratives of secular scholars less than interested in giving religious developments their due. More recently, revisionist historians have argued that events on the ground linking religion and politics did a great deal to unravel the French monarchy in the eighteenth century.[101]

The genesis of revolutionary conditions in France has much to do with the history of the Huguenots and Jansenists. Already in the sixteenth century, Huguenots drew on Christian just-war theory to assert a proto-revolutionary doctrine – "the right to resist authority when they deemed it to be tyrannical or illegitimate."[102] Louis XIV's 1685 revocation of the Edict of Nantes ended religious toleration. However, in agreement with Voltaire, we may suspect that the king's action breathed new life into a Huguenot movement that otherwise would have continued its non-apocalyptic trajectory of decline into insignificance. With the king's decree, apocalyptic visionaries among the Huguenots saw dark days ahead. In 1687, one scholar, Pierre Jurieu, aligned Revelation 11: 13 with an earthquake that he predicted would occur in France a century after the Edict, in 1785, plus or minus nine or ten years.[103] Forced to choose between their faith and conversion, and fearing persecution, at least 200,000 Huguenots, perhaps hundreds of thousands more, departed for Switzerland, the Netherlands, Germany, England, and North America. In its day, this was the largest, most dramatic episode of religious migration ever. However, perhaps 800,000 Huguenots remained in France. Many converted to Catholicism, at least publicly. But child prophets emerged, and Huguenots, often armed, continued to worship in secret, increasingly regarding themselves in prophetically apocalyptic terms. In 1700, there was a bloody Huguenot revolt in southern France by the Camisards (so named either after the everyday shirt worn by the rebels or after the word *camisade*, "night attack"). Prophets played a not insignificant role, sometimes giving the signal to begin battle, and deciding whether prisoners were to live or die. The insurrection lasted for four years, and unrest lingered for years afterwards. With so many Huguenots following these events from exile, they attracted international attention. As the turmoil died down, Huguenots remaining in France hardened into a community of memory, leaving French authorities concerned not to overplay their hand in religious persecution.[104]

During the eighteenth century, the Catholic Jansenist movement confronted the French throne with a similar challenge. At the urging of Louis XIV, in 1713 the pope issued a bull, *Unigenitus*, declaring Jansenist ideas "seditious, impious, blasphemous."[105] With their beliefs declared heretical, some Jansenists began moving in messianic directions. Miracles were witnessed. In the 1730s, believers began experiencing ecstatic spiritual convulsions and speaking in tongues. Faith-healing appeared. A Jansenist abbé with one leg fourteen inches shorter than the other was found hopping on a tomb in the cemetery of Saint-Médard, claiming that his shorter leg was growing longer. The Abbé Etémare offered an apocalyptic assessment: the War of the Beast had begun in 1730, and it was to end in 1733, seventeen centuries after the death of Christ. By the 1740s, the waves of public Jansenist eruptions subsided, and private Jansenist meetings shifted toward often highly ascetic "treatment" of convulsions. But by then, the once esoteric clerical theology had spawned a popular underground movement involving perhaps hundreds of thousands of people.[106]

Huguenots who worshiped in secret had for a half-century faced the wrenching choice of whether to go to a priest to receive extreme unction, the final sacrament before death, or, publicly failing to do so, risk exposing their families to repression as heretics. Now, any Jansenist would find it difficult to receive extreme unction without a *billet de confession* by a priest documented to have endorsed the papal bull rejecting the Jansenist heresy.[107] But on this matter, the monarchy became embroiled in conflict with the *parlement* of Paris, one of those sovereign French courts whose magistrates could resist royal edicts and negotiate with the king concerning them. The *parlement* had opposed the *Unigenitus* bull since 1714. Finally, in 1757, it succeeded in gaining the right of magistrates to forbid priests from refusing to offer the church's sacraments. Later, in the 1760s, Jansenists and *parlements* in Paris and elsewhere worked in concert to force the monarchy to eliminate the Jesuit order from France. In these episodes, the French monarchy lost secular political battles concerning religion, and in effect ceded authority to regulate religion to the *parlements*. In the bargain, it lost considerable symbolic prestige and religious authority. As historian Keith Baker depicts the controversy over religious sacraments, it was the first in a series of events in the 1750s and '60s in which "French politics broke out of the absolutist mold."[108]

Subsequently, the French Revolution aligned strange bed partners of politics. On the one hand, Enlightenment leaders came to embrace absolutism, but they transferred it from the monarch to the will of the people – or at least to the leaders who claimed to represent the people. Absolutism persisted, but under new auspices. On the other hand, the lower ranks of the Catholic clergy increasingly came to resent the wealth and spiritual corruption they witnessed among the bishops, whose numbers were dominated by the nobility. Many of them therefore allied with the more spiritually pure Jansenists, in opposition to the monarchy. But ultimately, the lower clergy found themselves betrayed by the revolution of 1789, for it resulted in a policy of dechristianizing French society. First the National Assembly appropriated church property while affirming that it "would provide in a fitting manner for the expenses of public worship, the maintenance of the ministers and the relief of the poor." Then, early in 1790, it dissolved the religious orders and congregations, and released the clergy from their vows. Committed Catholics belatedly returned to the defense of the monarchy, but this move simply more strongly aligned Catholicism and king under what revolutionaries regarded as a reactionary ideology that they were working ruthlessly to destroy.[109]

Yet the Jacobins did not exactly eliminate religion. Dechristianization in the French Revolution may be read, ironically, as a new kind of religion, what is sometimes called a "political religion" that would replace conventional religion with a totalitarian or quasi-totalitarian religion of the state. The abolition of the old Gregorian calendar in favor of a new, rationally ordered revolutionary calendar, during its brief existence, eliminated the Bible's Sabbath and buried the cycles of yearly rituals and saints' days under a new regime of time. Robespierre wanted his fellow Jacobins to respect the Catholic religion, insisting that "The man who wishes to prevent the saying of Mass is a greater fanatic than he who says it."[110] But in this he was seeking to temper a messianic iconoclasm among Jacobins and the sans-culottes in the street that mirrored the guillotining of the king as a decisive break with the past. The very language of religion – catechism, martyr, missionary – became the language of the revolution. Now, finally, might come what the poet Marie-Joseph Chénier would call that final "single universal religion" in which "the human family burns its incense only at the altar of the *Patrie*, common mother and divinity." In November 1793, the Cathedral of Notre Dame in Paris became the Temple of Reason, where the goddess *Liberté*, later Reason (represented *in vivo* by opera singer Mademoiselle Maillard), was honored in public ceremonies. More profoundly, the Jacobin clubs developed a style of meeting that somehow amalgamated reason with a sort of reworked Christian asceticism, and the movement developed a totalistic moral binary of good versus evil, light versus darkness, that ultimately would consume its own membership in successive waves of denouncements and bring the most diverse "enemies" of the Revolution to the guillotine. Here, the Enlightenment arrived at a theological precision of reason that would serve chiliastic justice. For Alexis de Tocqueville, these developments heralded "a new kind of religion, an incomplete religion, it is true, without God, without ritual, and without life after death, but one which nevertheless, like Islam, flooded the earth with its soldiers, apostles, and martyrs."[111]

For all that is known about the French Revolution, the sources and development of the Jacobin culture and program remain something of a mystery. After reviewing diverse developments preceding the revolution that have been invoked to explain its character, one historian despairs, "links of cause to effect slacken ceaselessly as we rehearse them the better." He concludes, "the lasting message of the revolution's history is dauntingly ambiguous."[112]

However, an apocalyptic analysis yields some clues. Recall that Michael Walzer found the English Puritans to be reacting against what they experienced as disorder, and hoping to establish a new, well-ordered holy commonwealth. A parallel emerges when we trace, as Keith Baker has, usages of the word "revolution" by the French. Through the end of the seventeenth century, conventional French meanings tended either toward the astronomical idea of revolution as a full cycle of turning, or to a plural usage – revolutions – to describe political and social events that had produced disorder. But Huguenot exiles in England began to capitalize the word in the singular to refer to "*la Revolution d'Angleterre*," and they distanced its meaning from disorder. Absolutist authors often repluralized and decapitalized revolutions to describe the twists and turns of English history, but the abbé Mably wrote a history published just before the French Revolution that portrayed French absolutism as lacking in political order. Mably's work opened up the possibility of understanding a revolution as an opportunity to "establish a new order of things." Yet establishing the new order required action. Thus, historical time was brought down to an urgency within the immediate here-and-now. As the revolutionary journal *Révolutions de Paris* affirmed at the time, "in a revolution *each day* has its storms and its dangers."[113] History here was not an inexorable unfolding of God's will, nor progress stretched out in time, but transformation based on collective action in the strategic time of immediately unfolding actions intended to create a new, as it were, post-apocalyptic world. The Jacobin order was, as any number of historians have noted, a moral order. Robespierre's republic of virtue drew its energy in part through the sharp contrast he drew with the immoral and corrupt aristocrats that it displaced.[114] Here can be found a substantial parallel with Puritan revolutionary displacement of disorder by order and discipline, immorality by morality, irrationality by the new rational religion – in France, a secular and political one.

Did a religious cultural template become transferred into the initially secular movement of the Revolution? A possible answer comes from the work of François Furet, who put forward a new interpretive account nearly two centuries after the revolution.[115] Dismissive of Marxist interpretations, Furet goes back to Tocqueville, whom he reads as treating the revolution less as a radical break than as the fruition of changes toward an administrative state based on egalitarian principles that was already well underway within the monarchy. In turn, limitations in Tocqueville's explanation of the genesis of the Revolution push Furet to consider earlier developments, namely, the antecedent sources of the Jacobin ideology and program. On this question, he argues, the early twentieth-century historian and sociologist Augustin Cochin supplements Tocqueville. For Cochin, the cultural seedbed of Jacobinism is to be found in the "philosophical societies" (*sociétés de pensée*) of pre-revolutionary France. Cochin's description of literary societies, Masonic lodges, and patriotic and cultural clubs suggests that religious revolution – with its search for realization of ultimate meanings through the diffusion of a new religious dogma – is the antecedent social form of the philosophical societies that began to spread across France by the 1750s. These secularized social groups brought a decidedly Catholic and French theological effort to arrive at dogma into the realm of direct democracy. There, as in religion, debates about political truth, once resolved, provided a sharp philosophical razor by which to distinguish truth from error, right from wrong, dogma from heresy. As Furet describes it, "The philosophical society, being the locus of the general will, was thereby the enunciator of truth."[116] When, by political sleight of hand, the Jacobin clubs claimed their voice as that of the general will, deviation became a violation both of truth and of the egalitarian democratic process by which truth had been established. Politics embraced a religious logic – specifically that of French Catholicism. What within religion would amount to heresy became treason.

One should pursue the regresses of historical explanation so long as they bear fruit. Furet's reading of Cochin shows the pre-revolutionary French philosophical societies to be "status groups" in which participants, though coming from different social stations, can associate with one another on the basis of a shared sense of cultural values and honor that encourages an egalitarian ethic. Insofar as such a group seeks consensus on a narrow set of ideas, in these terms, it amounts to a sect of true believers, rather than a church open to all comers.[117]

If Cochin is right about the origins of Jacobinism as a social form, its totalizing apocalyptic struggle traces back to particular organizations during the Enlightenment that were largely secular in their self-understandings, but (for example, in the Masonic lodges) could incorporate religious trappings and play out the status-group dynamics of true belief previously most important to sectarian religious movements. When Jacobins adopted sectarian group principles as the basis for violent action against opponents, political religion took on a theology of cleansing violence.

Is there a substantive affinity with English Puritanism to be found in Jacobinism? Or is the logic of the Terror to be found in French Catholicism, and behind it, the Inquisition against heresy? Are the direct cultural sources of the Jacobin reign of terror located in the philosophical societies? If so, to what degree did such societies engage the religious tensions of the mid-eighteenth century in relation to the quasi-legislative court *parlements* and the Jansenists, and how? These questions call for further research on the philosophical societies, their origins, and their agendas in the 1750s, the very time when – outside the societies and prior to the interventions of the *philosophes* – public controversies over refusal of sacraments to Jansenists were beginning to weaken the French monarchy.[118] Even in advance of further research, a broad interpretation can be proposed.

The French Revolution, in effect, telescoped a century and a half of English Reformation and ensuing Puritan and Glorious Revolutions into a much shorter set of developments. The Reformation never having succeeded in France, the Revolution ended up being directed against the crown and the Catholic Church – the connection between the two retightening as the revolution unfolded. A secular yet apocalyptically tinged political struggle overturned both. Victory was meant to establish a post-apocalyptic regime that would retool religious symbolism to create a secular religion of the French nation-state, with citizens to worship at Temples of Reason. France would have its reformation, but it would take place in the shadow of the Enlightenment, and in a secular form. France would have its revolution, but it would draw on the anti-apocalyptic logic of Catholic dogma and the Inquisition rather than the Puritan Revolution's apocalyptic war against disorder. France would seek its new state, but it would aim to establish a religiously secular utopia rather than the Puritans' utopian religious state. The French Revolution would be driven by the most extreme violence, carried out within an even more rationalized matrix of organization than that of the New Model Army. In the French Revolution, the ending of one historical era and the initiation of a new world, achieved symbolically through the "sacred" violence of Reason's sharp guillotine, brought the apocalypse unequivocally into the world of modernizing political contestation, to establish a political religion of universal rights that would reaffirm the principle of dogmatic monotheism on a secular basis. In something of a secular Catholicism, the new heresy would be religion itself, other than the secular religion of virtue. The state would act to contain both religion and its possibilities of public expression – a practice that survives in France today, for example, in regulations prohibiting the wearing of religious dress and symbols in schools.

Conclusion

By the end of the eighteenth century, the apocalyptic had become a hydra, regenerating with each effort to contain it, encompassing multiple polysemic narrative resources that overdetermined the bases for specifying disparate visionary projects constructed under circumstances of crisis. Profoundly altered, the possibilities of constructing the apocalyptic crossed the bridge into secular modernity. How else to understand one incident?: Marc-Guillaume-Alexis Vadier, a Jacobin atheist, stood in opposition to the more mystical and deist Robespierre, and he tried to discredit Robespierre with a letter (probably invented) supposed to have been found under the mattress of the messianic Catherine Théot. The letter proclaimed that Robespierre's mission of establishing a "new cult" had been "predicted in Ezekiel."[119] Thus, Vadier associated Robespierre with an apocalyptic prophetess as a way to try to discredit him. Even an atheist could deploy apocalyptic rhetoric as a political tool. But this was only a footnote compared to what would happen later. On diverse fronts during the nineteenth and twentieth centuries, alternative possibilities of the apocalyptic arose again and again in a modernizing world increasingly ordered by objective time, no longer dominated by the contestations of religion with emerging states.

5

Modernity and the Apocalyptic

The French Revolution was a signal event in the emergence of modern society. It ended the royal absolutism of the *ancien régime*, affirmed Enlightenment values of *liberté, égalité, fraternité*, ushered in the First Republic, and further consolidated the modern French administrative state. Yet the Reign of Terror was an unrelentingly violent utopian pursuit of the new sacred civic order. A founding moment of political modernity was apocalyptic in its logic. To come to terms with this circumstance and the broader developments it anticipates is to explore the idea I put forward in chapter 1, that tracing a genealogy of the apocalyptic can yield a new understanding of modernity.

Modern social theorists once held that archaic forms would be shed along the route of modernity's progress – through the advance of science, the spread of democracy, and the creation of an egalitarian, universalistic, and rationally ordered society.[1] How could the apocalyptic fit into this picture? Some observers maintain that seemingly archaic social phenomena in contemporary society – the ones of central interest here, apocalyptic movements, as well as ethnicity, nationalism, and fundamentalism – are quintessentially modern.[2] However, at least for apocalyptic movements, such a thesis contradicts what we have seen in the previous three chapters. The apocalyptic has origins in the most ancient civilizations and societies, and apocalyptic phenomena have sporadically come into play over millennia. To say that contemporary apocalyptic movements embrace modern social practices and technologies is not to say that the apocalyptic is modern. If we really can come to terms with this contradiction, it will open a way to go beyond the obvious point that the social world is complex, and modernization uneven, to deepen our understanding of modernity, the apocalyptic, and their relations with one another.

To pursue this path, let us consider the problem of "sacred violence," that is, violence not simply employed to achieve some strategic goal, but used ritually to affirm a symbolic meaning that separates the sacred from the profane. "The *terror*," Michael Walzer suggested, is a particularly modern kind of violence deployed to establish a sacred social order. However, violence to achieve social purification has been used by both rulers and insurgents, long prior to any full-blown modern "terror." The key modernizing development, in Walzer's view, is the use of sacred violence to try to establish a "godly" utopian order. The seventeenth-century Puritan Revolution for which Walzer characterized "the terror" came before modernity as a self-conscious project had developed. Violence on both sides could be gratuitously brutal in its ritual symbolism, but only one side used violence to further a utopian agenda. After King Charles I was beheaded on January 30, 1649, soldiers dipped handkerchiefs and swords in his blood, cut off locks of his hair, and prised up pieces of the scaffolding to sell.[3] Twelve years later to the day, with the Restoration, the body of Puritan revolutionary leader Oliver Cromwell was disinterred two years after his death, posthumously beheaded, and his head was put on a pole – outside Westminster Hall.[4] Impaling a head on a pike also was an important symbolic feature in the French Revolution. The French thus sealed sacred violence within the program of modernity at one of its founding utopian moments, in the revolution. Yet the head on a pike was hardly revolutionary. To some, the revolution thus no longer seems as "modern" as it once did.[5] But there is an alternative interpretation. Perhaps sacred violence became articulated with modernity.

The apocalyptic does not always play out in a violent way, and not all symbolic violence is apocalyptic. Nevertheless, as I will argue in the present chapter, in the modern era, considerable numbers of violent episodes have been apocalyptic ones – anarchist acts of terror, secular revolutionary movements, anticolonial struggles, wars, and various conflicts between an apocalyptic sect and an established order. To understand these developments in relation to modernity, I begin this chapter by sketching an alternative to conventional holistic or dialectical theories of modernity. My alternative account depicts modernity as a complex marked by multiple and hybrid temporalities. This account offers a new way of under-standing modernity's disjointed elements and their relationships to one another.

The new account identifies multiple lifeworldly frames of moder-nity – for example, bureaucratic organization, war, and moments of community life – in relation to ideal-typical temporal structures of social action. However, I do not seek to reduce modern life and its social dynamics to ideal types. Rather, the point is to use these types as benchmarks to chart more complex hybrid and amalgam-ated temporal structurations. There are two broad temporal devel-opments – the consolidation of administration of social life in diachronic time, and the imperialist quest that nation-states have pursued in strategic time. These two trajectories, I submit, need to be understood *in relation to each other*. They constitute an emergent hybrid "Empire of Modernity" in which the two forms of temporal-ity central to established orders of modernity – diachronic admin-istration and the strategic exercise of legitimate violence – are becoming increasingly articulated with one another, gradually relocating beyond any given nation-state, in a more diffuse and systemic complex.

As we will see, the apocalyptic is not isolated from these develop-ments: apocalyptic logics of action surface in relation to history and bureaucracy, community, and everyday life. After sketching a tem-poral phenomenology of modernity, I trace shifts in predominant apocalyptic structurations along two major twentieth-century axes – secular and sacred – that develop in relatively autonomous streams during the nineteenth and twentieth centuries. As I will show by way of conclusion, toward the end of the twentieth century, the secular and sacred apocalyptic become intertwined again, as they had been in medieval times.

Theorizing modern times

Most people survive each day without taking on the baggage of intellectual debates about the modern (much less the postmodern). In fact, the modern condition assures that the person on the street doesn't need to understand the modern anymore than she or he needs to understand the inner workings of a cell phone or a com-puter. Modern society is based on divisions of labor, divisions of knowledge, and the interfacing of individuals with complex orga-nizations, objects, and practices through the systematization of user routines. Even if modernity might seem like a high abstraction, its features permeate our everyday lives, and, indeed, saturate our ways of being in the world. We enact modernity (and postmodernity) every day, usually without being self-conscious about doing so.

Exploring social temporality provides a way of understanding the differentiated complexities of modern life. To begin, it is useful to review and extend my temporal analysis. In previous chapters I have charted a history of times by reference to the types of social temporality identified in figure 2.1: (1) the here-and-now; (2) collective synchronic time; (3) ecstatic transcendence; (4) diachronic time; (5) historically oriented strategic time; and (6) post-apocalyptic temporality centered on the "timeless" social eternity of a "heaven on earth" (also potentially accessed through tradition as an "eternal return" to a golden age in the past). This account has shown that variants of new temporalities – history, the apocalyptic, and objective time – emerged over the centuries, becoming layered onto earlier temporalities centered in the synchronic flow of the immediately experienced moment.

At its origins, "primordial" social life took place in the unfolding here-and-now, with collective synchronic enactments of ritual orchestrated as either an "eternal return" to a mythic tradition or direct experience of the sacred in ecstatic transcendence. Initially ritualized, strategic time increasingly became detached from traditions but without substantial diachronic coordination: war established, maintained, enlarged, or redrew social boundaries, whether defined by community, clan, tribe, or people. With the rise of ancient civilizations, strategic and historical war increasingly enveloped synchronically ordered communities within wider social hierarchies and lines of tribute, legitimated either by "divine" ideological claims of authority within an "eternal" order, as in sacred kingship, or, more rarely, by legal-rational diachronic law in democracy, republic, or empire. Under these conditions, apocalyptic time emerged in two conflicting affirmations: (1) by subordinate groups in their quest for liberation from domination they deemed illegitimate; and (2) by superordinate powers affirming the rectitude of their vision of triumph – in both cases, in the name of a monotheistic God.

In medieval Europe, apocalyptic possibilities became further differentiated – especially in the Crusades, popular apocalyptic movements, and efforts by the Roman Church to suppress heresies. Yet these developments only rarely overwhelmed the enduring synchronic times of the here-and-now and its communal ritual orchestration – increasingly accomplished through the church's mass-distributed calendar of liturgy. The historically new temporal development came in urban centers, where increasingly precise diachronic time took ever broader root among merchants and entrepreneurs. Fuller development of objective time came later, in the early modern age of discovery, the spread of a nascent European-centered capitalist world-economy, and the increasingly revolutionizing developments of science. In relationship to these developments, a diachronic logic of rationalization and routinization shaped central aspects of modernizing social organization – in the reorganization of the economy and work, in Protestant worldly-ascetic and individualizing selfhood, and in the increasingly legal-rational administrative organization of the state.

Transformations of the apocalyptic were equally dramatic. Both before and after the onset of the Reformation, ideologies of European colonization depicted the triumphal spread of Christendom, sometimes to establish the new kingdom of heaven on earth. In the Reformation, the apocalyptic became remapped onto religio-national contestations over state power. In turn, both Catholic and Protestant states increasingly contained religious apocalypticism through regulation of religion, even as apocalyptic orientations spread into secular political struggles, there becoming fused with diachronic discipline. Finally, an ideology of progress recast the increasing predominance of objective time such that history and diachronic time became articulated with one another, specifically in increasingly effective efforts to plan and construct the future.

Modern social and systemic differentiation (e.g., between home life, work, school, leisure activities, and so on) functionally requires an objective and abstract "world time" as a coordinating basis.[6] Yet the spread of objective temporalizations produces an irony: the vivid present is less and less frequently experienced as the here-and-now, and when it is, we experience it as a counterpoint to life more generally. Mostly, we move across the webs of time, quickly crossing from one frame of reference to another, making meanings by reference to the past and the anticipated future. This fast pace of urban life was already apparent at the beginning of the twentieth century. People had become used to shifting their attention from one person or thing to another, literally, in seconds.[7] Yet today, this pace is hardly ubiquitous. People live out different rhythms during the week and on the weekend. Those who use vacations to "get away from it all" in some rustic setting will sometimes recall that they had no need to wear a watch, and even "lost track of what day it was." Thus, despite the seeming triumph of objective time, the character of modern temporality is hardly fixed or static.

With the emergence of a post-industrial society layered onto industrial society beginning in the 1960s, work for many people shifted from routinized actions in commodified units of labor time into a "game between persons."[8] Coupled with this change, increased speeds of communication and transportation have led to a compression of objective time and space.[9] The consequence of these shifts is time that has become "liquid": events of the past slip away, soon to be forgotten; new events and things arrive ever more quickly (but never quickly enough). People come to exist in the blur of a vivid present ever more jam-packed with activities that displace the here-and-now, or construct it from the outside. At the vortex of postmodern time, people no longer take interest in eternity because the present offers what fulfillment can be had.[10] The times of modern life, predicated on history and the clock, are malleable and emergent.

People gear into personal social networks and rounds of activity with distinctive temporal styles and rhythms of action. But the unfolding here-and-now is hardly a blank canvas. Rather, each of us participates in multiple arenas marked by distinctive institutionalizations and conventionalizations of time. Some arenas – the assembly-line and sports events such as basketball, for example – are nested within the more encompassing objective framework of the calendar and the clock, and they are internally structured by objective temporalities as well. Other events – an evangelical religious service, a baseball or cricket game – are scheduled on the calendar but have internal temporal structures more loosely connected to objective social time. In short, the strong modernist emphasis on objective time fosters its opposite – heterogeneous individual and collective engagement in "private time."[11] In the limiting case, people occasionally seek to transcend everyday and institutional social temporalities in spiritual practices such as Zen meditation, disciplining themselves to shed cognitive assumptions and social conventions by which experience is normally organized, to make way for some ineffable "pure" experience of the ecstatic and the infinite.[12]

In the history of times, complex, hybrid, and nested temporal structures have emerged, embodying new forms of social action, relationships, and organization. This phenomenological history of times offers a basis on which to move beyond previous approaches and retheorize modernity. Social theory has long been concerned to explain the shift from "traditional" to "modern" society – from mechanical to organic solidarity, from *Gemeinschaft*, or community, to *Gesellschaft*, or society. But theories of modernity tend to objectify the time of history, resulting in evolutionary, stage, and teleological theories that treat "history" and "society" as holistic and reified "things," and thus fail to come to terms with the multiple and often contradictory realities of modern life. Resolving this paradox has proven difficult because modern social theories typically specify total systems of concepts in relation to one another, supposedly mirroring modern society as a holistic "object" of analysis.

The challenge for any alternative approach is to theorize the non-coherence of "modernity." One line of analysis congruent with my phenomenological account of multiple temporalities has been pursued by historical sociologist Peter Wagner. He describes modernity not as a "thing" or "stage" of history, but as marked by the increasing deployment of "modernizing projects," realized only incompletely across space, that are unstable in their persistence over historical time.[13] Wagner's approach identifies modernizing projects as social activities. It thus avoids reification of "modernity" either as a time period or as an "analytically real" theoretical construct.

We have already encountered several historically central kinds of modernizing projects, but not yet described them as such.

- Diverse early modern projects promoted *rationalization and routinization of material/ideal infrastructures*, for example, in agricultural practice (e.g., in the draining and consolidation of fields), road networks, market towns, and economic calculation and accounting.
- A second early modern stream of modernizing projects has been concerned with the *mass distribution of meanings and the reconstruction of the self*, first using communal ritual to solidify "traditional" identities on a mass scale (e.g., via the medieval Catholic mass), and, second, as Weber famously argued, in Protestant formulations that encouraged a work ethic appropriate to proto-industrial and industrial capitalism.
- In a third stream, to invoke Michel Foucault's thesis of *governmentality*, modernizing projects have enhanced "policing" of society through techniques of "disciplining," in which the state "was able to govern people as individuals significantly useful for the world," in order to facilitate the functioning of emergent

modern economic apparatuses of production and labor, social organization, markets, and social institutions of private life.[14]

- Fourth, what might be called *postmodernizing simulacra* reorganize lifeworlds through *absorption* of action in the here-and-now into an administratively and/or computer-constructed reality – a Disneyland either physical or mental.[15]

On the whole, these modernizing projects are diachronically organized to penetrate and reorder the temporally synchronic arenas of the everyday lifeworld and its institutions of community and power. Thus, "modernity" may be construed as a temporal complex characterized by the increasing predominance of activities ordered within institutionally organized and rationalized diachronic time.[16]

Whereas in earlier times, peoples' identities within collectivities tended to be relatively fixed, and ascribed by birth and status hierarchies, modernizing projects tend to promote the individual freedom of action necessary to gear into diachronic organization of activity – notably in work, but in personal life as well. New temporal regimes, in the terms of Michel Foucault, facilitate the diffusion of practices of governmentality whereby power is exercised through the orchestration of life in the here-and-now.[17] However, the old social forms that predominated under more synchronic arrangements – for example, patriarchal familialism and particularistic networks of personal association – do not simply disappear. Instead, diachronic patterns of organization sometimes layer onto or accommodate forms of the *anciens régimes*. New hybrid social arrangements emerge as a consequence, for example, particularistic patrimonial networks that organize bourgeois enterprise and state politics.[18] Under these complex conditions, as theorists of modernization rightly thought, "primordial" identity in relation to a single community based on ritual affirmations of ascribed status becomes problematic. However, quite the opposite of what theorists of secularization expected, the diffusion of modernizing diachrony does not spell the end of the collective synchronic or the waning of religion. Rather, there is an accelerating spread of new sacred communities of identity – sometimes mutually exclusive, sometimes overlapping with earlier institutionalized communities that persist. Religion, ethnicity, nation, football team, reality TV show – each creates synchronic rituals that produce identity. The result is a modern welter of communities – of varying solidarity. By way of synchronic community rituals, identities proliferate, not only across individuals, but also within us.[19]

The central axis of modernity, however, is diachronic. Diverse modernizing projects and associated practices of governmentality arise both in increasingly rationally organized economic production of goods and services, and in state bureaucratic organizations controlled through legal-rational mechanisms of democratic or authoritarian power. There are implications for other temporal forms of action. Market and political competition and conflict in strategic time are increasingly orchestrated through diachronic planning of strategies, for example, through market research and computer game simulations. A long-term political shift from personal rule to legal-rational government establishes conditions in which outsiders can seek improvements in their legal statuses, and pursue inclusion within the civil sphere (itself a modern reconstruction of synchronic community based on binary moral codes concerning the sacred). In turn, tensions emerge between diachronic legal-rational egalitarianism versus the identity politics of synchronic communitarianism.[20] Yet legal-rational administration also increasingly sets the conditions of synchronic life and community, for example, by regulating religions and voluntary associations, instituting a variety of professional knowledge practices that "police" the everyday world, and appropriating synchronic ritual to the orchestration of diachronic institutions. Conversely, synchronic communities import diachronic principles into the organization of their activities and operations. Overall, in the aggregate of these diverse developments, modernizing projects establish a diachronically organized world centered in individualism, formal bureaucratic organization, economic and political competition and conflict, and practices of governmentality. As Wagner puts it, modernizing projects implement, facilitate, and delimit liberty and discipline.[21]

Diachronically centered modernizing projects incompletely and unevenly articulate with other temporalities. Yet the overall tendency is for developments to converge, combine, and reinforce one another in what Jürgen Habermas has evocatively described as the emergence of an overarching *system* that transcends and "colonizes" the lifeworld, subsuming, ordering, and organizing activities within it.[22] Habermas's theory of systemic colonization, which considers issues similar to those addressed by Foucauldian analyses of governmentality, can be elaborated and contextualized in several ways. First, as we saw in chapter 2, prior to the rise of the diachronic, collective rituals that affirm the solidarity of a community already subjected the unfolding lifeworldly here-and-now to "colonization." Thus, colonization is a broader possibility than one that operates only through modernizing systems. Second, diachronically organized activity that orchestrates the "system" itself takes place *within* lifeworlds, e.g., of the office. The "system" is a socially produced cultural structure – of codes, procedures, laws, conventions, practices, computer programs, web pages, and so on – that potentially colonizes *all* lifeworlds, including, reflexively, the ones that produce it. Third, colonization is not of "the" lifeworld as a single domain. As we have seen, the modern lifeworldly arenas that people move across are heterogeneous and differentiated in their temporal enactments. There are, then, diverse kinds of colonization. Fourth, recalling Wagner's point about modernizing *projects*, the system's colonizations are necessarily uneven, incomplete, and subject to the agency of individuals and groups who may seek to contest, resist, or reverse subordination to the system. Finally, much modern social action is centered in economic and political competition and conflict, sometimes to the point of violence and war. These struggles – often fought for control of systemically colonized regions of activity – are centered in strategic temporality, not the diachronic system.

The scholars I have invoked here – Wagner, Foucault (whose work in key respects builds out from Weber),[23] and Habermas – differ in their characterizations of modernity, but they share a basic insight. Each recognizes that pervasive forms of social control move far beyond formal "authority." The differences between the two most prominent recent theories – those of Habermas and Foucault – have to do with social-control mechanisms and emancipation. For Habermas, control transpires through colonization of the lifeworld, whereas Foucault's imagery is of discipline, governmentality, and diffuse regulation of persons in their embodied conduct. As for emancipation, Habermas locates its prospects in the ethos of non-coerced communication within a political community, whereas Foucault finds some potential in the dispersed actions of subjects who enact resistance as transformation, albeit with results that may transform without liberating.

Even this brief sketch lends support to the thesis that modernity is neither an historical epoch nor a coherent totality. In turn, further considering social temporalities under modern circumstances provides a basis to push toward a fuller theorization. As we saw in chapter 4, modernity is borne up in both historical and diachronic time. The historically emergent ideal of progress in relation to future achievement of goals is central to modernizing projects, and progress is mapped in relation to historically contingent sequences.

Equally, modernizing depends on calculation and rationalization, and these are keyed to diachronic temporality. However, contemporary society is not exhausted by the increasing predominance of objective time described so far. What of politics and social movements, domination, war, colonialism and imperialism, revolution, terrorism? In these domains, competition and conflict are oriented toward events that build upon one another in what I have called strategic time. Let us focus on the widest domain – of world-historical conflict. The hierarchical international political economy is structured not only by institutionalized patterns organized through state and economic regimes of formal association, but also by the strategic exercise of power via imperialism.[24] The modern rise of diachronic time has facilitated economic calculation, routinized production, and the administration of rule-based organization and law. But it is imperialism that underwrites and expands the domains of calculable diachronic time. Central to imperialism is the use of force in strategic conflict that unfolds in the time of history.

Phenomenologically, differences between theories of imperialism and theories of modernity are manifested in their alternative constructions of social temporality. Theories of political power and imperialism invoke conflict in strategic time, whereas neither the system/lifeworld theory of Habermas nor the governmentality/ resistance account of Foucault does so. The theoretical divide between diachronic and strategic time thus marks the disjuncture between theories of modernity and those of imperialism. Empirical social research replicates this divide in the dichotomy between (diachronic temporality) sociologies of organizations and institutions, on the one hand, and, on the other, (strategic temporality) sociologies of social movements, rebellions, revolutions, and wars. To be sure, strategic conflict may take advantage of modern organizational and technical possibilities, and, indeed, this very hybridity of modern conflict is important to strategic options and tactical capacities. However, contemporary conflict in contentious politics, revolution, and rebellion is structured "outside" diachronically routinized modernity.

Thus, on the one hand, modernity is rightly theorized as centrally configured within the diachronic time of the calendar, industrial assembly-line production, time-and-motion studies, PERT (program evaluation review technique) charting, returns on interest over time, and other calculable and commodified forms of diachronic time. On the other hand, imperialism underwrites diachronic time, and, once established, it may operate on the basis of legal-rational administration, but whereas diachronic temporality predominates in organizing modernity, conflict in the strategic time of history is central to the uneven fates of various imperial projects. These contradictory conditions of "integrated disparity" mark an emergent geopolitical hybrid of diachronic order established and sustained through intermittent strategic exercise of force, a hybrid so central that it should be named as such – the "Empire of Modernity."

In its origins this hybrid geopolitical order was based in alternative nineteenth- and twentieth-century imperialist projects pursued by independent nation-states enmeshed in competition with one another in a globalizing world economy. But in the twenty-first century, the fusion of diachronic governmentality with the strategic exercise of violence has increasingly transcended the boundaries of nation-states, resulting in a transnational hybrid.

The Empire of Modernity is no longer simply an imperialistic order dominated by a single state or a "world system" of competing core states in a world economy, but neither is it some sort of centered and coherent world political order. Rather, this emergent world geopolitical complex is at present centered in the West and militarily in the U.S. Historical sociologist George Steinmetz thus is no doubt correct to identify the contemporary U.S. as "the controlling center of a global empire." However, the theorization of empire that Steinmetz has offered acknowledges the importance for the contemporary U.S. of "'just-in-time' political coalitions and alliances," "the privatization of military services," as well as the proliferation of "non-military control mechanisms."[25] Many of these mechanisms increasingly are organized through multilateral, international, or non-governmental organizations, some of them strategically distanced from the hegemony of a militarily dominant nation-state. The upshot, in my view, is that fluid lines of transition are emerging between empire centered in a single nation-state – today, the U.S. – and a more generalized and diffuse Empire of Modernity as a network of governing projects and strategic military initiatives undertaken by an unevenly coordinated web of sovereign states, international governmental agencies, and non-governmental organizations (NGOs).

The Empire of Modernity, thus described, has obvious similarities to the philosophical and historical theorization by Michael Hardt and Antonio Negri in their book *Empire*.[26] One key difference is that Hardt and Negri position Empire *after* modernity, whereas I am struck by sufficient continuities to warrant designating something new, the Empire of Modernity, that is in significant respects an (incomplete) hybridic fusion of two different temporal modes through which *modern* power has become extended in its domains over the nineteenth and twentieth centuries – first, in domination through systematization and governmentality, and, second, in the strategic exercise of power. How, and how far, the Empire of Modernity will displace conventional empire centered in a single nation-state is an historically open question.

What, then, of the apocalyptic? Seemingly, even a temporally specified theorization of the Empire of Modernity has little place for the trauma of the last days that announce the new era. Yet as we have seen, the central developments that altered structural possibilities of apocalypse through the beginning of the nineteenth century had to do with: (1) ever stronger articulations of the apocalyptic with objective, diachronic time; and (2) the bending of the apocalyptic toward ever stronger understandings of history as both *telos* and reflexive project of purposeful engagement.

One of the major modernizing projects has been to "tame" apocalyptic and eschatological expectations – to "close the book" on religious prophecy on the basis of procedures of rationalization and routinization that would, as Max Weber put it, "demystify" social life. In the aftermath of the European sixteenth- and seventeenth-century wars of religion, by the late eighteenth century, religious apocalypticism had largely been contained. To the degree that diachronic routinization of life took hold – in the organization of work and inner-worldly asceticism that became associated with the diachronic organization of work – historically new kinds of people came to live in ways increasingly remote from apocalyptic anxieties. However, religious pacification hardly spelled the end of the apocalyptic. There are two complexly intertwined reasons. On the one hand, like other modernizing projects, efforts to pacify religious apocalypticism were uneven over time and space, and various incarnations of the sacred apocalyptic continued to be nurtured over the nineteenth and twentieth centuries. On the other hand, the sacred violence of the warring apocalypse became grafted onto secular politics and social movements. In the remainder of this chapter, I first trace emergences of relatively secularized apocalyptic movements, and then turn to persistent modern threads of more concertedly sacred apocalypticism.

Lineages of the secular apocalyptic

In the English Puritan Revolution and the French Revolution, apocalyptic war had gone far beyond the chiliastic episode. Apocalyptic struggle, pursued with "religious" fervor, acquired a new, diachronic discipline, and with it, a stronger engagement with both history and visions of progress. But these developments were only the beginning. As S. N. Eisenstadt has argued, religiously infused cosmologies and legitimizations of sacred violence that preceded modernity subsequently became inserted into modern political violence more broadly, in totalistic, jacobin-styled movements. These secular yet sacred movements share with some religious fundamentalist movements both the goal of implementing a reconstruction of society based on a coherent and powerful ideological program as well as the "sacred" ideological justification of violence toward that end. This world is to be remade, either as a heaven on earth or its secular utopian equivalent.[27] More generally, states and state contenders increasingly relocated the apocalyptic within worldly secular politics, where its containment has proven horribly uneven. A new region of the apocalyptic opened up – in modernity.

In the 1920s, a political doctrine with an apocalyptic logic began to circulate. The German political theorist Carl Schmitt witnessed the weakness of the German state during the Weimar era, and he resuscitated Hobbes's concern with the need for a sovereign with absolute power. "Sovereign is he who decides upon the exception," Schmitt wrote, holding that in a time of severe crisis, the sovereign might rightfully take steps outside constitutionally legal boundaries. This concept of sovereignty, coupled with Schmitt's claim that only a politically engaged participant has the capacity to distinguish friends from the enemy that is "existentially something different and alien," yields the theoretical rationale for conceiving of war as something that eclipses any mediation by "neutral" third parties.[28]

Schmitt gravitated toward support of the Nazi Party in the early 1930s, and it would be comforting simply to dismiss him as a fascist. Unfortunately, this move does not work. Schmitt was only giving philosophical voice to realities of war already manifested on the ground. Beginning with World War I (and anticipated by the Civil War in the U.S.), as Hannah Arendt later observed, "the distinction between soldiers and civilians was no longer respected." Possibilities of social organization under diachronic regimes – mass mobilization, modern military organization, mass killing – brought the scale of modern secular political apparatuses and technologies of violence up to what Arendt called "total war." In all this, secular political conflict mirrors and amplifies the theology of holy war:

- The Nazi regime, inspired by an ideology of the millennial Reich, carried out mass, bureaucratically organized genocide, exterminating over six million Jews and others, perhaps millions more.
- The United States dropped atomic bombs on Nagasaki and Hiroshima in August 1945, resulting in a death toll of over 200,000.
- The Cold War, frequently portrayed by Western protagonists as a struggle against godless communism, became shadowed by the potential for nuclear holocaust as the final Armageddon.

Doctrines of nuclear deterrence put in place in the wake of World War II, Arendt argued, "changed the role of the military from that of a protector into that of a belated and essentially futile avenger."[29] The theory, the industrialization of capacity, the collapse of normative boundaries, and the level of destruction can only be deemed apocalyptic.

Modern times and the apocalyptic in their strongest manifestations are antithetical to one another, and, thus, potentially in collision. Yet the temporal orientations became articulated in distinctive hybrids. The apocalyptic became modern, an element of integrated disparity in what was to become the Empire of Modernity. Revolution and terror, war, colonialism and empire – seemingly secular phenomena – are all potentially infused with apocalyptic dimensions.

As with the French Revolution, in later developments, seemingly secular conflicts unfolded on the basis of apocalyptic logics. Under the sign of modernity, the apocalyptic was no longer necessarily religious, or, to reverse the valence, secular conflicts could take on a sacred apocalyptic character. Indeed, the apocalyptic has spread so widely, both geographically and in the forms of its manifestations, that here I only sketch developments connected to two broad world-historical shifts. First, I consider genealogies of violence in the sometimes intertwined movements of Marxism and revolutionary anarchism that emerged in the nineteenth century and became directed toward the Soviet and Chinese revolutions of the twentieth century. I then turn to apocalyptic dimensions of twentieth-century struggles against colonialism and imperialism.

Revolutionary communism and anarchism in Russia and China

"The Communist Manifesto," published by Karl Marx and Friedrich Engels in 1848, posited the central axis of history to be class struggle in the unfolding strategic time of "this" world. However, their depiction of that struggle took a decidedly apocalyptic form. At the outset, Marx and Engels's theory of dialectical historical materialism gained a spiritual substrate by taking as its point of departure Hegel's philosophy of universal history. Hegel in effect had secularized Christianity (or spiritualized the secular). Thus, at his hands, the quest for salvation turned into a world-historical dialectical process moving via the synthesis of opposites toward the complete realization of "absolute Mind" (*Geist*). Marx and Engels inverted Hegel's philosophy, looking not to the idealist triumph of Reason, but instead to change that would come through the worldly dialectic of historical contradictions in how societies are organized. But the material dialectic would not continue until the end of time. "The history of all hitherto existing society is the history of class struggles," Marx and Engels wrote in the Manifesto. Therefore, if class conflict could be eliminated, history as we know it would come to an end. By transcending the contractions of communal but subordinated feudalism versus free but individualistic capitalism, Marx and Engels anticipated, the world-historical communist revolution would inaugurate a final historical epoch of free communalism.[30] After a decisive struggle would come the end of history. After the end of history would come the earthly utopia. Although Marx employed the secular rhetoric of "scientific socialism," Reinhold Niebuhr once suggested, he wrote as an "apocalyptic dogmatist." Engels acknowledged as much, but reversed the valence. Not that the revolutionary communist movement was religious apocalypse made secular, but that medieval and Reformation movements had actually involved material conflicts of class interest "carried on under religious shibboleths."[31] The communist movement could shear the historical process of its spiritualized fantasies and put apocalyptic action onto a scientific basis.

"The Communist Manifesto" famously dismissed the "castles in the air" of secular nineteenth-century worldly utopias such as the communal society established in New Harmony, Indiana, by Robert Owen, the "phalanxes" inspired by Charles Fourier, and Étienne Cabet's Icaria. Engels eventually acknowledged that utopian communal societies demonstrated what he and Marx believed to be the practicality of socialism, and he recognized that people living communally were already confronting real problems of as yet "future" societies. But egalitarian utopias in the wilderness based on enlightened principles of Reason would never overturn capital- ism. The communist revolution could only be accomplished through class struggle in this world. With the revolution, the proletariat would control the means of production in the interests of the entire society. After the end of class conflict, Engels wrote, political power and government would be transmuted into "the administration of things." As for people's lives, alienation would disappear. Marx offered the vision of a communist society that "makes it possible for me to do one thing today and another tomorrow, to hunt in the morning, fish in the afternoon, rear cattle in the evening, criticize after dinner, just as I have a mind, without ever becoming hunter, fisherman, shepherd or critic."[32]

Social theorist Georges Sorel would assert early in the twentieth century that the central revolutionary challenge was to bring about the "catastrophe" entailed in "the passage from capitalism to Social- ism." A guiding myth would be required, in order to inspire people to break with an established order through acts of violence.[33] Marx's depiction of the post-revolutionary utopia was decidedly vague. Anticipating Sorel, he offered a vision of a promised land that never went far beyond general imagery concerning how eliminating the alienating influences of capitalism on labor and the self would assure self-fulfillment. The vision was sufficient to legitimate revo- lutionary violence but also sufficiently mythic as to avoid getting bogged down in endless debates about how to structure post-rev- olutionary society. The communist program entailed by this stance short-circuited the revolutionary voluntarism of nineteenth-century utopian experiments, and it overwhelmed the historical significance of anarchists like the Christian Leo Tolstoy, the quasi-religious the- orist of cooperation and mutual aid, Petr Kropotkin, and Mikhail Bakunin, who warned about the dangers of a centralized dictator- ship of the proletariat.[34] Nineteenth-century Marxism thus avoided what in the twentieth century would become the crucial question – how might society actually be organized after the revolution?[35]

Instead, the communist movement focused on achieving power through intensive efforts in strategic time on "this" side of the apocalypse. Like earlier religious thinkers anticipating dramatic upheaval and change, radical intellectuals debated whether and how action might help achieve utopia. In these debates, apocalyp- tic visions of transformation became articulated with modern pos- sibilities of political mobilization and alternative strategies of revolutionary violence. On one side, some radicals toward the end of the nineteenth century believed that catastrophic conflict would not be necessary. Britain's Fabian Socialists and the German Eduard Bernstein hoped for gradualistic progress through democratic politics, in what Bernstein called "evolutionary socialism."

At the other extreme, insurgents unleashed violence against established regimes and elites – in the revolutions of 1848, and in more directly working-class conflicts such as the Paris Commune in 1871, the secret underground Russian group Narodnaya Volya ("People's Will") that took direct inspiration from Robespierre's Reign of Terror, and the increasingly violent industrial conflicts of workers, strike-breakers, and police in the U.S. "Now or never," proclaimed Narodnaya Volya, and they kept targeting Tsar Alexander II with bombs until they finally succeeded in assassinating him in St. Petersburg on March 1, 1881. The United States experienced similar violence. During an 1886 Chicago rally at Haymarket Square protesting police killings of strikers against the McCormick Harvesting Machine Company, an unknown person – possibly a militant anarchist or an *agent provocateur* – tossed a bomb into a line of policemen who were attempting to disperse the crowd. And in 1892, 22-year-old Russian immigrant Alexander Berkman sought to assassinate the industrialist Henry Clay Frick in retaliation for his deployment of hundreds of strike-breakers at the Homestead, Pennsylvania, steel plant.[36]

Decisive "propaganda of the deed" in the immediate historical present, according to anarchist advocates, amounted to heroic action that could demonstrate the repressive nature of a regime, inspire the masses by example, and precipitate a broader revolutionary movement. The logic is captured in Joseph Conrad's gripping 1907 novel, *The Secret Agent*: like those who hatched the fictional plot to bomb the Greenwich Observatory (striking at modern time itself), the anarchists meant to interrupt unfolding time and intervene in history by violent acts both symbolic and strategic. Indeed, symbolism would contribute to strategy.

By the latter nineteenth century, the character of revolutionary violence had thus shifted dramatically. The French Reign of Terror took hold *after* the initial revolutionary seizure of power, and it operated as a ritualized violence meant to intimidate opposition and purge the new sacred order of contamination. It thus amounted to a powerful symbolic omen of a shift in political fortunes, and a warning to those who might challenge the new order. The Russian and American anarchists claimed inspiration from the French terror.

However, they did not undertake exemplary violence to consolidate post-revolutionary society, but to precipitate the revolution itself.

Whereas anarchists hoped to bring on a broad, decentralized revolution of the masses, the program of communism developed in a wholly different direction. As Hannah Arendt observed, compared to the terror of the French Revolution, the ideological and political purges of Bolshevik terror, both before and after the Russian Revolution, were framed in relation to "historical necessity" as an inevitable chain of events. Vladimir Lenin famously formulated the theory of a vanguard party committed to its ideological vision, ruthless in its disciplined "liquidation" of political opponents – whether the Russian aristocracy or proponents of alternative programs such as the communist anarchism of Alexander Berkman or the "evolutionary socialism" of Eduard Bernstein. Lenin's Bolshevik vanguard took on the character of a revolutionary sect, selective in its membership, committed to Marxist theory as the basis of revolution, collectively planning and carrying out coordinated charismatic action that would patiently build toward the "revolutionary moment" and then lead the wider movement to victory.[37]

The Soviet Revolution of 1917 yielded a new era, no doubt, but of what? Some Slavophiles steeped in Russian Orthodox traditions saw the revolution as a fiery apocalypse that divided the old era from the new.[38] However, initial efforts to establish communism were confused and difficult to pursue, for they took place in the midst of both the "Red Terror" aimed at annihilating the bourgeois ruling class and intelligentsia and a bloody civil war that lasted until 1923 (fueled in part through foreign involvement by capitalist core nation-states). Moreover, communism as a new mode of life was subject to resistance from a population steeped in traditional ways of life. By 1920 the Soviets began to embrace rapid modernization through five-year plans, electrification, and the promotion of a communist work ethic committed to increasing productivity so as to "gain time." As Soviet novelist Valentin Kataev described the process in his novel of Soviet working life, *Time, Forward!*,

> increase in the productivity of one machine automatically entails the increase of the productivity of others indirectly connected with it. And since all machines in the Soviet Union are connected with each other to a greater or lesser degree ... the raising of tempos at any given point in this system inevitably carries with it the unavoidable – however minute – raising of tempos of the entire system as a whole, thus, to a certain extent, bringing the time of socialism closer.[39]

However, the post-apocalyptic utopia was never realized; communism became a future imaginary, a mirage divorced from the Soviet present. Stalinist dictatorship displaced Marx's theorized dictatorship of the proletariat, while Marxist critics like Leon Trotsky embraced a position similar to that of the anarchists immediately after the revolution who viewed the bureaucratization of the party as the evaporation of any prospects for utopia. A jacobinist vanguard party would not tolerate debate or dissent by the likes of Trotsky, and he was expelled from the Soviet Union in 1929 and assassinated in Mexico by a Soviet operative in 1940.

"Materialism entailed losing touch with matter, and substituting for it the schema which had been projected onto it," one scholar has suggested.[40] Yet this striking divergence between ideology and material reality took hold as a result of a political struggle concerning how to implement the revolution. The Soviets sought to build a new institutional structure of society through development of a revolutionary bureaucracy rather than a legal-rational one, and they implemented a stunning program of economic industrial development undergirded by a "charismatic-rational" orientation toward time. But the Soviet ethic of diachronic time compression never took hold in the countryside, where millions died in famine precipitated by the forced collectivization of agriculture. And even in the cities, charismatic commitment to hyper-efficiency began to erode. Faced with threats of failure, in the 1930s, Stalin initiated a new jacobinesque reign of terror. The Soviets initially directed purges at those who most threatened Stalin's revolutionary program – the old-guard Bolsheviks who could challenge party dogma on the basis of revolutionary memory, and rationally oriented managerial elites deemed to lack Marxist revolutionary commitment. But these were only the beginnings. Purges swept across Soviet society, resulting in the recorded executions of 681,692 victims in 1937–8 alone. Jacobin pretenses died as well.[41] The show trials of the 1930s forfeited any claim for a connection between truth, virtue, and violence. A façade of ideology justified brutality devoid of anything beyond the will to dominate.[42] For a time, the Soviet Union continued to achieve historically unparalleled economic development, but ultimately the regime became overextended economically and ethnically.[43] Repressive and totalitarian, the Soviet state failed to sustain its legitimacy among the (still) alienated and ethnically diverse masses, and it decayed from within, until its collapse in 1989.

China's revolutionary path was different, but it was influenced by developments in Russia and the West. China possessed an ancient civilizational vision of the cosmos without any Western dualist disjuncture between the natural and the supernatural. In the Chinese philosophy of Confucianism, the material world *is* the cosmos – on earth, in its harmonious order under the emperor. The apocalyptic has no obvious position in this worldview. However, realities experienced by Chinese people were often at odds with the harmonious ideal, and discrepancies perceived between ideal and reality could be invoked to justify social uprisings. During the first millennium, BCE, the *I Ching*, or book of changes, identified "revolution" as a possible archetypal conduit of transformation, and Lao Tzu's *Tao Teh Ching* pointed to one avenue of "the way" as a "turning back" that benefits from "weakness" to restore balance. In turn, during the first millennium of the modern era these ideas became focused into a "Taiping Tao" (Way of Great Peace) that anticipated messianic deliverance from destruction and the dawn of a golden era. These radical ideas may have influenced sporadic uprisings in China during the second millennium CE. Christian missionaries became occasionally active in China from the end of the thirteenth century onward, and eventually Christian and Chinese ideas converged. Notably, in 1836 a man named Hong Xiuquan found the word *Taiping* used in Bible tracts that had been given to him. Hong Xiuquan came to believe himself to be the younger brother of Jesus. He associated Taiping with the Kingdom of Heaven, not after death, but on earth. In order to establish that kingdom, he employed a Christian theology of apocalypse to launch the Taiping Rebellion, which lasted from 1850 to 1854.[44] Despite Taiping's direct challenge to Confucianism, its attractive program of agrarian communism, its rapid spread, and the deaths of some twenty million people, the rebellion failed, in part because its millenarian program remained mired in nepotism, corruption, and poor leadership.

The real opening for those who wanted to crush Confucianism and open China to modernizing social change came in 1911 with the collapse of the Qing dynasty in the Xinhai Revolution. But the route was a long one. After 1911, traditional regional warlords inherited parts of the decentralized military apparatus of the empire, and they remained powerful for decades. The nationalist Kuomintang party – initially, under Sun Yat-sen, and after his death in 1925, under Chiang Kai-shek – tended to position itself as the heir, not the opponent, of Confucianism. However, it failed to consolidate the Republic amidst conflicts with warlords and the Chinese Communist Party (CCP) – the serious anti-Confucianists. The

Communists took inspiration in part from the 1919 May Fourth Movement, which had precipitated a sort of Chinese renaissance and a critique of all tradition, including the Confucian triad of obedient subjugation – of the subject to the emperor, the son to the father, the wife to the husband. By 1927 the Communists grew powerful enough to respond to the Koumintang's Shanghai Massacre purge and execution of Communist Party members within it. The CCP launched a low-intensity civil war that would last for a decade. Subsequently both the Koumintang army and the Communist guerrilla forces became caught up with fighting the invading Japanese during World War II.[45]

In this extended period, the Chinese Communists charted a distinctive path of revolutionary struggle. The 1919 May Fourth Movement came in the wake of diverse ideas that had spread from Europe, including communism, naturally enough, but also pragmatism as well as anarchism – in both its apocalyptic strategy of trying to precipitate revolution through exemplary and ruthlessly violent martyrdom, and its more communitarian movement of mutual aid. The latter inspired groups of intellectuals like the Heart Society to almost religious obedience to twelve commandments, including abstention from alcohol and tobacco, renouncement of their family name, and atheism. The Communists drew most heavily on Marxist theory, and the Soviet Union tried to direct the Chinese Revolution. But the Soviets played a double game of supporting both the Koumintang and the CCP. Moreover, Soviet efforts were often shaped by Marxist abstraction and their own interests, and distant from events on the ground. The Chinese Revolution succeeded in large part because Mao Zedong, from a rural base, ignored Soviet counsel given to the Communist leadership in the cities. Mao, in the early years, was more influenced by anarchist Petr Kropotkin than by Marx, and he radically recentered revolutionary theory in relation to mobilization of peasant masses. On this platform he consolidated a distinctly modern form of strategic guerrilla warfare focused through the capacity to strike and withdraw quickly, and oriented toward destroying enemy troops rather than winning and defending territory. Variations on this approach would become the basis of twentieth-century revolutionary insurgencies in countries such as Cuba, Vietnam, and Angola.[46]

As important as guerrilla warfare was, however, the CCP did not fetishize it. When the People's Liberation Army took territory, they indicted landlords and established "Liberated Territories" where peasants pursued terrible mob vengeance against landlords. The final establishment of the People's Republic of China during the conflict between 1947 and 1949 came in part as a product of conventional warfare in battles and sieges of cities. Finally, even the bourgeoisie began to hope for a resolution without the Nationalist regime. As one historian concluded, "There was the expectation, then, of Armageddon, but also the hope of an absolutely new beginning. Nationalist China ended in chaos and apocalypse."[47]

Yet the apocalypse did not end with victory. Rather, the CCP turned its efforts toward securing the revolution and the dictatorship of the proletariat. True to the jacobin precedents of revolutionary rule in France and the Soviet Union, from 1949 through the early 1950s the party under Mao launched a brutal purge of counter-revolutionary elements, resulting in the execution of at least 700,000 people and perhaps as many as five million. Then came efforts at centralized, bureaucratically managed state planning to promote modernization through the five-year plans, followed by the Great Proletarian Cultural Revolution beginning in 1966, which Mao encouraged in order to purge any remaining bourgeois tendencies in China and reassert his own power in the bargain.

In all these episodes, the costs in human lives were enormous: whether by neglect or ignorance of the situation, perhaps twenty to seventy million people died in the famines, floods, and mass starvation precipitated by the ill-founded approach to land reform and agricultural development during the Great Leap Forward of 1958 to 1963. In turn, hundreds of thousands, and perhaps millions more, died at the hands of the youthful Red Guards empowered during the Cultural Revolution (the luckier targets of the struggle against "revisionism" only submitted to purges, resettlement, and "reeducation"). This terrible revolutionary debacle has often been attributed to totalitarian rule, or to its opposite, a rigid, hierarchical bureaucracy. But these arguments recently have come into question. On the one hand, the Cultural Revolution, although promoted by Mao, far exceeded any elite CCP control in the spread of its hyper-McCarthyesque campaigns to police enemies of the revolution.[48] On the other hand, the Chinese Communist state was hardly the paragon of a modern legal-rational bureaucracy. Instead, the Communist regime under Mao operated as a "counterbureaucracy" staffed through political appointments that trumped professional expertise and undermined efficiency.[49] Only with the slow rise of Deng Xiaoping to *de facto* power following the death of Mao in 1976 did China pull back from its jacobinist program of revolutionary terror to chart its distinctive market "socialism with Chinese characteristics," with one-party rule, substantial state ownership of the means of production, and state enterprises competing in a wider market economy without price controls.

*Anticolonial messianic movements, terrorism,
and guerrilla warfare*

Beyond their own revolutions, both the Soviet Union and China worked to promote anti-capitalist revolutions in the Third World, where insurgent guerrilla warfare against colonial and neo-colonial powers yielded protracted struggles during the Cold War – in Cuba, Algeria, Vietnam, Angola, Peru, and the relatively brief but terrible debacle of the Khmer Rouge's Kampuchea (Cambodia) from 1975 to 1979 – the most extreme and tragic attempt to wipe the slate of history clean, pursued through mass execution of a million people or more, leaving the surviving people to build the new world.[50]

However, even prior to the spread of communism, less developed countries were hardly strangers to nationalist and anticolonial struggles. As the case of Taiping in China shows, revolutionary politics could grow out of a this-worldly millenarian religious movement. In the nineteenth and twentieth centuries, such movements challenged both traditional social orders and colonial domination, typically from Western powers. Millenarian movements shared a hope that the tribulations of this world would be brought to an end by decisive events that ushered in the new era. But a variety of tendencies emerged among "religions of the oppressed."[51] Faced with overwhelming domination by external powers, some movements – such as U.S. black liberation efforts in the face of slavery – wove in redemptive religious motifs drawn from the religion of the colonizers. Nineteenth-century black ministers often depicted the collective suffering of their people as part of a larger religious redemption by movement to a promised land, perhaps to be achieved by using the "underground railroad" to escape to the North, or after the Civil War, through migration in the "black exodus" from the Old South to Kansas, or, in the visions of many blacks – from the early nineteenth century to the symbolic political movement led by Marcus Garvey early in the twentieth century – in schemes to head "back to Africa." Also in the U.S., the basically peaceful native American Ghost Dance movement possessed an apparent power that disconcerted the U.S. Army troops charged with enforcing a reduction of reservation lands allotted to the Sioux tribe, resulting in the 1890 eruption of violence at Wounded Knee, where 25 U.S. soldiers and 153 Sioux were killed.[52]

Others, more firmly under colonial administration, also sought this-worldly redemption – in escape to a promised land (the Ras Tafari movement that began in Jamaica and posits a promised land in Africa), or in the anticipation of a new era of abundant wealth (Melanesian cargo cults, where envy of Westerners' manufactured goods during World War II led to efforts to acquire the objects of obsession via a variety of magical procedures, including the construction of imitation airstrips meant to attract the airplanes that would provide deliveries). Elsewhere, mystical and apocalyptic motifs of armed struggle infused messianic movements such as the 1905–6 Maji Maji resistance in Tanganyika, armed insurrection of the Joazeiro movement in Brazil early in the twentieth century, and the 1950s Mau Mau Rebellion in Kenya, where spirit-mediums directed some strategic operations and claimed that magical potions would turn bullets into water.[53]

Sociologist of religion Bryan Wilson argued in the 1970s that violent opposition to colonialism typically had little to do with religion *per se*. Nevertheless, Wilson acknowledged that reactions to colonialism sometimes entailed religious calls for supernatural aid, and that prophetic charismatic leadership under fundamentally religious auspices sometimes organized the resistance.[54] In such instances, it has not always been just the poorly educated and dispossessed who participate; rather, a millenarian leader can sometimes transcend differences of social status and mobilize a broadly anticolonial or nationalist movement.[55]

Most of the strongly religious nineteenth- and twentieth-century apocalyptic movements against colonialism were overwhelmed militarily. Yet as we have seen, communist and anarchist movements incorporated distinctly apocalyptic elements. And in the twentieth century, nationalist movements sometimes took on broadly apocalyptic features of insurgency, and with more than occasional success.

No doubt the society with the deepest apocalyptic roots is Israel, sought as the promise of a restoration of land to God's chosen people following the diaspora in the first and second centuries CE, after failed Jewish revolts against the Romans. The goal of a Jewish state was pursued in part through Zionist acts of terrorism from 1944 until the establishment of Israel in 1948. Consolidation of territory included the establishment of utopian communal kibbutzim, and it was sustained in the face of counterrevolutionary resistance by Palestinian refugees who had lost their homes and lands in the struggle.[56]

The quest for Israeli statehood and its subsequent defense against opponents differ dramatically from the more messianic apocalyptic rebellions and anarchist and communist insurgencies, for Israel ultimately prevailed through support by Western powers, which followed the lead of the United Kingdom, where religious and geo-political interests had helped to shape a Zionist movement among Christians since the mid-nineteenth century.[57] With statehood, Israel managed to temper potentially jacobinist possibilities of Zionist ideology through the consolidation of a constitutional regime oriented toward Enlightenment social values of progress and democracy, albeit not on an equal basis for Palestinian citizens of Israel, much less Palestinian refugees. Resistance by Palestinians and their allies ensued. Following the kidnapping and massacre of eleven Israeli participants in the 1972 Olympics in Munich by the Palestinian group "Black September," the Israeli government estab-lished a counterterrorist hit squad called "Wrath of God" that tar-geted Palestinian terrorists and guerrilla leaders. Whereas the German authorities negotiated with the Red Army Faction over exchanging prisoners, the Israeli government set an example by refusing such negotiations, and its antiterrorist teams staged daring rescues, for example, of the hostages that ended up at Uganda's Entebbe airport in June 1976 as the result of a joint hijacking under-taken by the Red Army Faction and the Popular Front for the Liberation of Palestine.[58]

The diverse warring apocalyptic movements that arose in the two centuries following the terror of the French Revolution do not fit into a single mold. The utopian futures projected by such move-ments range across conventional political distinctions between the left and the right: they include both conservative attempts to estab-lish a synchronic worldly utopia on the basis of a religious or ethnic community and progressive attempts to establish a secular, diachronic worldly utopia. Moreover, the kinds of violence range from the largely instrumental economic actions of social bandit groups to magically infused pursuits of the millennium in cargo-cult groups, and on to more strategically oriented apocalyptic war, both by anarchist propaganda of the deed as exemplary violence, and in the increasingly organized and disciplined cadres of value-rational movements that draw on terrorism, guerrilla warfare, and other strategies in the direct pursuit of territorial political power.

Despite these differences, commonalities have given rise to some mixed formations. Social banditry, for example, can be an important basis of support for value-rational apocalyptic movements, justified through a revolutionary ideology of expropriation. Also, as Eric Hobsbawm noted, a transition from one formation to another can occur as a movement enters a new phase, for example, "when a millenarian movement turns into, or is absorbed by, a modern revolutionary movement." Yet such a transition, Hobsbawm argued, does not alter the movement's basic rejection of the existing social order or the anticipation of a promised but vague utopia: it simply shifts the apocalyptic ideology from a more religious to a more secular and modern (anarchist, fascist, communist, socialist, nationalist) form.[59]

Historically, the general tendency has been away from mystical and exemplary anarchist eruptions, and toward more disciplined strategic forms. The most militant apocalyptic movements thus embody the same strategic temporal orientation that is to be found in war more generally. The specific strategy is open. Militant apocalyptic movements often draw on strategies of terrorism and guerrilla warfare, and these would be the favored "weapons of the weak" employed by insurgent groups more generally, including less apocalyptic (but often religious) militant nationalist movements.[60] Insurgent groups that follow Mao's model act strategically, but they do not fetishize any particular strategy, and they will wage conventional warfare if circumstances favor success. As was widely noted in think-tank studies that proliferated following the spread of Marxist-led Third-World movements in the 1960s, insurgents can gain decisive advantages by developing effective relationships with populations in the territories where they operate, especially if leaders affirm a revolutionary struggle that promises an apocalyptic reversal of fortunes. The most effective movements, from social bandits to revolutionaries, demonstrate tangible benefits to both existing and potential supporters, and the more revolutionary movements structure these benefits in policies such as land redistribution that anticipate broader post-revolutionary programs. In order to mobilize even wider support, insurgent movements often field parallel "above-ground" political movements. Above or underground, insurgent movements have their bureaucratic and policy sides, while they encounter bureaucratically organized government forces employing a range of tactics that includes guerrilla warfare. The revolutionary movement, like the bureaucratic state, operates in diachronic time, and the two meet in direct conflict in strategic time.[61]

Developments of terrorism, revolution, guerrilla warfare, and anticolonial struggle have consolidated what may be called "secular-sacred" apocalyptic struggle as a dominant feature of modern insurgency. It would be possible simply to note the commonalities across a diverse range of instances, and leave the matter at that. However, the continuities suggest a greater coherence. Relative to other kinds of strategic temporality (e.g., economic competition, political conflict, conventional war), when there is a strong ideological construction of crisis by an "ideological primary group," members of the group become bound together by "the sacredness inherent in the acceptance of the ideology."[62] If the ideology depicts a situation so dire that violent actions oriented toward achieving ideological goals become imbued with a sacred legitimization, the group comes to approximate an "apocalyptic warring sect." As utopianists under this dispensation see it, the end of (present) history can come only by inaugurating an intensive strategic conflict in unfolding historical time to hasten the dawn of the new age. In the nascent utopian formation of such a sect:

> The members of the sect come out of the quiescent masses to act in historical significance far out of proportion to their actual numbers. … The successful execution of actions related to missions and contingency plans depends on interpersonal trust, the development of high proficiency at various technical and strategic skills, and acts of commitment and bravery which place mission ahead of personal survival.[63]

Apocalyptic war, for its protagonists, is sacred violence. Even in a basically secular movement, strategic actions become strongly infused with transcendent "religious" meanings. In either religiously sacred or secular-sacred apocalyptic war, participants give up their previous lives. They undergo a *metanoia* – a rebirth to the cause that ideologically can end only in victory or death in the pursuit of victory. Either way, true believers seek a "revolutionary immortality" though founding the new era that is to endure for all time.[64] Thus, writing in 1869 for the revolutionary group Narodnaya Rasprava ("People's Vengeance"), the Russian radical Sergei Nechaev declared in "Catechism of a Revolutionist," "the revolutionist is a doomed man. He has no interests of his own, no affairs, no feelings, no belongings, not even a name. … He is an implacable enemy of this world, and if he continues to live in it, that is only to destroy it more effectively." Or, as a placard read at a 1914 rally of

the Industrial Workers of the World that featured Alexander
Berkman speaking in New York's Union Square, "They who Die for
a Cause NEVER DIE. Their Spirit Walks Abroad."[65]

The dialectic of fundamentalism and counterculture through the Cold War

From the nineteenth through the latter twentieth century, secular-
sacred apocalyptic war animated revolutionary anarchists, communists, and anticolonial movements. During the second half of
the twentieth century, self-conscious religious apocalypticism
reemerged on two broad fronts – in developed societies, especially
the U.S., and in Islamic societies (on Islam, see chapter 6). In the
U.S., some theologians during the 1960s, mirroring Nietzsche, pin-
pointed the "death of God" in the purported collapse of any sacred
framework of modernity. Others hoped for a rebirth of the sacred.
But even as theologians announced God's death, the sacred was
being resurrected – in oddly contradictory ways. The theologians
correctly anticipated the increasing absorption of meaningful life
into the sphere of consumption organized under the sign of commodity fetishism. But they did not anticipate the (largely American)
apocalyptic dialectic between evangelical Christianity and the
counterculture. I conclude the present chapter by considering each
in turn: major developments of the apocalyptic in North America
before the twentieth century, the twentieth-century rise of apocalyptic fundamentalism that culminated in the politicization of the
"Christian Right," and, finally, apocalyptic developments (largely)
within the American counterculture.

American apocalyptics through the nineteenth century

North America was settled in part by people who, acting under
apocalyptic auspices, sought to escape Europe and establish one or
another Zion in the New World. Thus came the Pilgrims to New
England in 1620 (with more radical Puritans arriving in the 1630s),
German Pietists and Mennonite and Amish bearers of the Anabaptist legacy to Pennsylvania, Huguenots to South Carolina, and
during the nineteenth century, schismatic Lutherans to Missouri.[66]
    The Pilgrims, sometimes invoking the ancient Jews, pursued a
redemptive quest in time by moving through geographic space,
from perceived persecution in England to the promised land they

sought to establish in North America. For the colony's governor, John Winthrop, one reason for founding this "plantation in New England" was apocalyptic: "who knows but that God hath pro vided this place to be a refuge for many whom he means to save out of the general [European] calamity; and seeing the church hath no place to fly into but the wilderness, what better work can there be than to go before and provide tabernacles, and food for her, against she cometh thither." The Puritan "errand into the wilderness" collapsed by the 1650s, bringing to an end their project of establishing a theocratic state in the New World.[67] But the echoes of this apocalyptic moment have continued to reverberate across centuries of American history.

That apocalyptic speculations animated religious life in pre-revolutionary America is beyond doubt. But the valences shifted over time, and in multiple directions. During the "First Great Awakening" – the explosion of religious revivalism in the 1730s and '40s – Puritans waxed strongly millennialist in their sermons. The Calvinist and Congregationalist Puritan Jonathan Edwards, perhaps the greatest revivalist preacher of his day, came to the conviction that his original calculation of 1866 as the date when the papal Beast would be slain was incorrect: "we cannot reasonably think otherwise, than that the beginning of this great work of God must be near."[68]

Antichrist continued to loom in eighteenth-century New England, though its locus shifted. The British "corrupt system of tyranny and oppression" widely became viewed as the Beast described in Revelation 13: 14. This millennial theology did not drive the Revolutionary War for independence from the United Kingdom, nor did theocratic visions find their ways into the ensuing constitutional construction of the U.S. However, after the revolution some preachers treated independence as a step in the achievement of God's final millennial plan. Thus, in 1783, Ezra Stiles, president of Yale University, preached on "The United States Elevated to Glory and Honor."[69]

Questions about the relation of religion to political power have animated civic debate ever since the founding of the United States out of the thirteen colonies. The Constitution's first amendment affirmed that "Congress shall make no law respecting an establishment of religion, or prohibiting the free exercise thereof," and the resulting freedom of religion has underwritten an enduring American culture of revivalism and theological innovation. An oversimplification, but a useful one, is to map post-Revolutionary War American religious history in relation to a distinction that became increasingly important in the latter eighteenth century, between "premillennial" versus "postmillennial" doctrines concerning the end times. Ideal-typically, *premillennialists* interpret various passages in the Book of Revelation to anticipate Christ's second coming *before* his reign of a thousand years with the souls of those beheaded. *Postmillennialists*, in contrast, expect the *Parousia* only *after* the millennial reign of a thousand years. The former interpretation can produce much more immediate and intense expectations of Christ's appearance, whereas postmillennialism leaves a long stretch of time for "preparation" and "making the world ready," either by conversion or through a social ministry.[70]

Postmillennialists tended toward the "Old Light" suspicion of revivalistic enthusiasm, and they eventually sometimes posited the "Manifest Destiny" of the U.S. as God's chosen nation that would prepare the world for Christ's Second Coming. Thus, myriad inventions and technical progress of the nineteenth century were "taken up in the Divine plan as means to a spiritual end," one Congregational minister affirmed in 1869 as he contemplated the expected completion of the American transcontinental railroad: "Not a railroad is swung by God into its orbit, that he does not put to work on this upward mission." For postmillennialists, the day of God's final judgment recedes into the future, and an ideology of progress through worldly effort informs a religious version of the Enlightenment. Sometimes, notably in the nineteenth-century antislavery movement and the Civil War, militant struggle might be required for progress.[71] More typically, the "social gospel" animated liberal and progressive Protestants to work in the secular world to solve social problems and build the good society. Postmillennialists who subscribed to the social gospel no longer sought to establish a theocracy, as the Puritans had wanted to do. Instead, they came to dominate the secular political establishment. There, they embraced the broader ideology of "corporate liberalism," working to address the problems of an emerging industrial society by the use of (Christian) sociology and other disciplines to provide comprehensive legal-rational state solutions (e.g., universal education, social work, worker disability insurance, unemployment insurance, and social security). Progressive Protestants turned their efforts toward building the Kingdom of God on Earth, with no end in sight.[72] Thus, by the beginning of the twentieth century, postmillennialism as a distinctive doctrine became submerged in broader politics.

On the other hand, premillennialist ideas about an imminent apocalypse coming *before* the millennium inspired interpretations of events at one or another historical moment as foreshadowing the end times, thus encouraging programs of religious repentance and conversion in anticipation of God's final judgment. Already during the First Great Awakening, Jonathan Edwards preached about "sinners in the hands of an angry God." After the American Revolution, revivalism increasingly channeled the religious energies of people concerned about their prospects for salvation. Early in the nineteenth century, camp meetings during the "Second Great Awakening" swept across frontier regions of the United States. But these meetings were not your stern Calvinist encounters with a God who refused to be influenced concerning salvation. As in the first awakening, religious enthusiasm and dramatic conversions of the unchurched again took hold. At the first of the great camp meetings, in 1801, thousands of farm families streamed into Cane Ridge, Kentucky, where one observer reported ecstatic responses to the religiously charged atmosphere, including "the jerks" and "the falling exercise" ("The subjects of this exercise would, generally, with a piercing scream, fall like a log on the floor, earth or mud, and appear as dead ...").[73]

Especially strong apocalyptic orientations can be found in certain of the communally organized religious groups that sought to come to grips with the displacements and possibilities of rapid social change. Emblematic of the complex amalgams are the Shakers, founded by prophetess Mother Ann Lee, and the Mormon movement, initiated by the prophet Joseph Smith.

Ann Lee was influenced by ecstatic practices of immigrant French Huguenots in England. She came to believe the Second Coming of Christ to be imminent, and migrated to America in 1774. There, she and her followers established a network of communities in New England and the mid-South. The Shakers, so called for their rollicking communal dances (with the two sexes on opposite sides of the room), renounced procreation as unnecessary at the end times. Yet during the last days, they worked industriously and rationally to develop lines of commercial distribution for the products of their communal farms and shops, inventing a number of labor-saving devices in the bargain. Anticipating the apocalypse, the Shakers lived out their lives in communal villages that came perhaps as close as anything to the post-apocalyptic heaven-on-earth that others only dreamed about.[74]

The millenarian trajectory of the Mormons developed quite differently, riven by conflicts with non-believers that precipitated a string of migrations to establish their sacred Zion. Joseph Smith affirmed in the late 1820s that he had discovered golden plates with the Book of Mormon inscribed on them near his home in Palmyra,

New York. He published the Book of Mormon and founded the Church of Jesus Christ of the Latter-Day Saints in 1830, when he was 24. Controversy swelled up around the Mormons, first when they settled in Kirtland, Ohio (gaining converts from the Disciples of Christ, itself a product of Presbyterian schism stemming from the 1801 Cane Ridge revival), and then, when they fled in 1838 to what they hoped would be their promised land in Independence, Missouri. But non-Mormon pioneers in Missouri were not prepared to have a Mormon promised land in their territory, and after protracted violent skirmishes, the Mormons decamped to Illinois, where they established a *de facto* theocratic colony, Nauvoo. There, Smith invoked Old Testament precedents and initiated plural marriage, first for himself in 1841, and then in a private revelation to followers in 1843. As in Missouri, the Latter-Day Saints again met pitched opposition. In 1844 a mob attacked a jail where Smith was being held for his own protection, and killed him. Continuing to face hostilities in Illinois, Mormons under their new leader, Brigham Young, headed out in wagon trains, west along what became the Mormon Trail to the territory of Utah, where they finally succeeded in establishing their Zion. Gradually over the latter nineteenth century, the Mormons accommodated to U.S. government pressures to abandon the practice of polygamy, and Utah gained statehood in 1896.[75]

Other American religious movements often have been shaped by apocalyptic ideas, but without the communal isolation of the Shakers or the violence surrounding the Mormons. The most famous American millenarian movement was initiated by William Miller, a self-taught preacher who embraced the long-standing mathematical tradition of predicting the exact date of the Second Coming, based on careful readings of the Bible. In the 1830s Miller began to build up a substantial group of followers who waited for the decisive event until, after several recalculations, on October 22, 1844, they finally experienced the "Great Disappointment" when Christ failed to arrive. A man named Henry Bear recalled, "I got rid of all my money except eighty dollars; this I laid on the table. ... We now left, as we believed, never to return to that house: and went to one of the advent believer's about three miles distant, where all the Millerites had agreed to meet and await the coming of the Lord within twenty-four hours." Yet the Great Disappointment did not spell the end of anticipation. Some believers reinterpreted the predicted date as the onset of the period when people would be judged concerning readiness to take their places among the saved in the millennial kingdom to follow the Second Coming. From this beginning in apocalyptic anticipation, the Seventh-Day Adventists and other Adventist sects emerged in the latter nineteenth century. Some groups sought to gain a legitimate denominational status within U.S. religion, following a trajectory from sect to denomination.[76] However, in the eyes of truly apocalyptic seekers, Adventist efforts to move to the mainstream compromised their claims to be the bearers of the true faith. Adventism thus has been highly prone to the emergence of splinter sects that reassert the coming of the final conflagration.[77]

Other groups, notably, the Watchtower Bible and Tract Society, or Jehovah's Witnesses, also emphasized their complete readiness, watching and waiting for Christ's return. But the broader movement of American Protestant premillennialism echoed the Millerite concern with personal preparation for the Second Coming while tending to back off from setting any date. In ever more institutionalized ways beginning in the 1860s, religious people searching for salvation through faith and personal perfection fueled the emergence of the Holiness movement out of the Methodist Church, which itself had gravitated away from the camp meetings and toward the social gospel. In the 1890s, Holiness seekers, often materially poor and sometimes distant from the alien, rationalized institutions of an emerging industrial society, sought definitive proof of their own salvation in the Holy Spirit, just like, according to Acts 2, the disciples of Jesus had received on the seventh Sunday after Easter. The vehicle of such proof came with the rise of the Pentecostal movement, initiated in Los Angeles's Azuza Street revival by a Black Baptist minister named Seymour, who promoted the doctrine, originally set forth by the Reverend Charles Fox Parham of Kansas, that a believer's glossolalia – speaking in tongues – was a definitive sign of salvation. While they prayed for redemption at the Second Coming, Pentecostalists often practiced a form of Christian mutual aid that amounted to direct social welfare within communities positioned far outside established channels of social-gospel charity and welfare-state benefits.[78]

Twentieth-century American fundamentalism and the rise of the Christian Right

Occasional tensions between religious groups flared during the nineteenth century, notably when people steeped in U.S. destiny as a Protestant nation engaged in "nativist" anti-Catholic agitations against increasing numbers of Irish and Italian immigrants.[79] However, overall, with the increasing (albeit cyclically uneven) stabilization of society that a growing capitalist economy provided during the nineteenth and twentieth centuries, the apocalypse was largely pacified, either translated into postmillennialist theologies of progress or transmuted into premillennial theologies advanced by religious sects promoting conversion as preparation.

Even from the early nineteenth century, a strong premillennialist theology had been emerging, most notably brought forward by Americans attracted to the doctrines of John Nelson Darby (1800–82), an Irish Protestant who built on earlier nineteenth-century English "dispensationalist" theology. Dispensationalism offered the hope of a coming decisive moment – the "Rapture," as they called the events described most explicitly in Paul's first letter to the Thessalonians (4: 15–17) – when believing Christians would be pulled up from earth to join Christ in the clouds (sparing them the awesome events to come on earth). Finally, with the Jews returning to establish a nation in Palestine, Christ would return to defeat the forces of Antichrist, thus launching the millennium.[80]

During the first half of the twentieth century, conservative Protestants who opposed a whole series of modern developments – Darwin's theory of evolution, socialism, the League of Nations, and so on – began to consolidate a broadly evangelical premillennial fundamentalism centered on biblical inerrancy, the divinity of Jesus, and the promise of Christ's Second Coming.[81] Beyond specific theological doctrines, American fundamentalists in the 1910s and '20s evidenced a "radical patriarchalism" concerned with moral decay in the family and society, spawned under conditions of rapid urbanization.[82] On this strong social basis, contending fundamentalist movements developed in ways both fractious and mercurial, encompassing a conservative orientation toward strong traditional religious community, unevenly accommodated to pre-apocalyptic millennialism.

For their part, mainstream progressives of the (decreasingly explicit) postmillennial persuasion predominated in the first half of the twentieth century. The religious fundamentalism that incorporated strong premillennial ideas tended to operate from the margins of U.S. society, outside mainstream denominations (although Presbyterians and Baptists were far more open to such ideas than were Episcopalians, Lutherans, or Methodists).[83] Thus, the 1925 trial of Tennessee high-school teacher John Scopes for teaching about Charles Darwin's theory of evolution gained so much publicity precisely because it went *against* the grain of both the Enlightenment and enlightened progressive Christianity.

In the 1950s, sociologist Will Herberg thought it reasonable to classify American religious diversity under the broad categories *Protestant, Catholic, Jew.*[84] However, this basic and reasonable division obscures important differences within Protestantism. Prophets and converts to apocalyptically oriented ideas flourished in the Great Depression of the 1930s, and they survived and gained numbers in the post-World War II economic boom, sometimes bearing resentment toward (and a sense of conspiracy about) the established order from which they felt alienated.[85]

Compared to mainline Protestants, evangelicals were interested in actively spreading the word of God and Pentecostals were committed to seeking strong assurance of salvation. Their striking growth in numbers came through congregational colonizations of the "new" middle, working, and service classes in the growing suburbs that accommodated substantial migration from rural areas and small towns. In the "postindustrial" society that was beginning to take hold in the 1960s, U.S. Protestant fundamentalism found new energy in a broad and deep reaction against the civil-rights, Vietnam anti-war, women's, and gay-rights movements and the broader counterculture against conventional and conformist ("straight") American life.

Fundamentalism thrived and grew in part because it developed strong evangelical associations of non-denominational churches, and in part by using the media of popular culture – radio, cable television, books, music festivals, and eventually the internet. Truly, to fight the Devil meant using the Devil's tools. Fundamentalist American Protestants became tremendously successful at reaching out to the broader population with television shows like Jerry Falwell's *Old-Time Gospel Hour* and Pat Robertson's *800 Club*, and books like Hal Lindsey's novel describing the Rapture, *The Late Great Planet Earth* (reportedly, it sold 28 million copies by 1990). Yet like many large social movements, the fundamentalist surge encompassed substantial sectarian differences and radical tendencies. Notably, the so-called Christian Identity movement revived old British ideas long simmering on the fringe in the U.S. – that only whites could be saved. Its adherents found common cause early in the twentieth century with the Ku Klux Klan, and, beginning in the 1970s and '80s, with Christian survivalists who formed isolated paramilitary communal groups to prepare for the battle of Armageddon, fighting against the Trilateral Commission or some other designated Antichrist bent on world domination. It was the culture of this sectarian movement that spawned the actions of Timothy McVeigh in the 1995 bombing of Oklahoma City's federal building. More widely, the idea of establishing America as a Christian nation, once embraced by the Pilgrims, now reemerged in a patriotic "Dominion"-style theology that reaffirmed Americans as God's chosen people.[86]

As the 2008 U.S. election demonstrated, evangelicals are not necessarily politically conservative, or, indeed, politically mobilized at all. Indeed, premillennial Christians might think that Christ's Second Coming leaves little rationale for intervention in the affairs of this world. The latter-twentieth-century political mobilization of what came to be called the Christian Right thus depended on the entrepreneurial efforts of key fundamentalist leaders in alliance with a Republican Party increasingly retooled to use "family values" as a wedge issue to pry Christian voters away from any Democratic Party leanings. Their demographic target population awaited them. By 1978–9, "evangelical" individuals (a somewhat broader category than fundamentalists) could be found across the U.S., but they tended to be especially concentrated in rural areas and the Bible Belt of the Old South. Although these culturally conservative Protestants were only marginally more likely to prefer the Republican to the Democratic Party, they were considerably more likely than other people to think that religious organizations should make public statements about politics.[87]

The political implications of these circumstances are marked by two presidential elections that bookend the initial surge of the Christian Right. When Barry Goldwater became the Republican Party candidate in 1964, he ran as a secular libertarian, and he lost badly. But by 1980, Ronald Reagan gained the enthusiastic support of preacher Jerry Falwell's Moral Majority organization and other supporters among the Christian Right, and he won a landslide victory over sitting Democratic (and evangelical) president Jimmy Carter. Reagan's election marked a basic American political realignment toward the right (Richard Nixon had been militarily a hawk, but he has been described by political sociologist Fred Block as a "big-government conservative"). Reagan, in tune with the elite Republican constituency, embraced an emergent business ideology oriented to "supply-side economics." But he also evoked a folksy, feel-good millennialism with talk of what the Puritan leader John Winthrop had hoped for in 1630, building America as a "city on a hill." The Christian Right became mobilized on the basis of "hot-button" issues like abortion, race-based civil rights, feminism, and gay rights. However, their support ironically empowered the Republican business elite to initiate a neo-conservative economic program that unsettled the lives of many people in the social strata most identified with the fundamentalist movement, and to push to dismantle the welfare state. Welfare provision thus would increasingly become the province of religious communities – precisely the emphasis that had long predominated among Pentecostalists and other conservative Protestant groups. In short, the Republican business alliance with the Christian Right both exacerbated social problems experienced by the party's religious constituents and identified their religious communities as the institutions to deal with such problems.[88]

Apocalyptic counterculture

Invocations of the apocalyptic can be found within various religious traditions from the early days of European colonization of North America through the twentieth century and beyond. The great irony of American history is that the religious movement of Christian fundamentalism – relatively marginalized by the mainline denominations during the latter nineteenth century and the first half of the twentieth century – managed toward the end of the twentieth century to trump the death of God through a strange ideological admixture that juxtaposed millenarian anticipation of the end times and antipathy towards government, and nevertheless came to exercise an extraordinary influence in mainstream American cultural and political life. However, this surge did not occur in isolation from other apocalyptic developments.

Conservative American religion gained energy in the turbulent 1960s and '70s in part as a counter-movement to the second broad channel of apocalypticism in the West – the counterculture and antiwar movements. Indeed, some within the conservative movement – radical elements of the anti-abortion movement and Christian survivalists – eventually mimicked the bombings and assassinations initiated by some groups in the New Left, just as the conservative movement more generally adopted certain New-Left social-movement strategies and tactics.

Broadly construed, the counterculture marked a freeing up of the utopian imagination that resembles nothing so much as the heady years of the Puritan Revolution in mid-seventeenth-century

England, when ordinary people came forward to enact their visions of the new society.[89] As in the English Revolution, the counterculture constituted a radical break with an established social order. As in the English Revolution, both the networks of connection and degrees of tension between countercultural participants and the established order were variable. Indeed, over time, American countercultural practices – from smoking marijuana to eating granola and organic food – diffused more widely, thus blurring the once sharp countercultural boundary into a merely subcultural one. Equally, as the charismatic times of the 1960s and early '70s faded, especially after the defeat of the U.S. in the Vietnam War, most countercultural participants found their ways into everyday life in the broader society.

The American counterculture encompassed both the New Left – itself built upon and connected to the ban-the-bomb, civil-rights, black-power, and feminist movements – and alternative lifestyle movements, the latter taking their most concentrated forms in utopian communal groups. The vast majority of countercultural communal groups were peaceful, and although they often shared a strong interest in transcending the old (modern!) order, their enactments of the new order were ideologically diverse. Anarchist colonies and family-style communes sprang up like mushrooms. "Worldly utopian" groups such as the clockwork secular utopia, Twin Oaks, and the religious community centered in the here-and-now at The Farm in Tennessee sought to consolidate ways of life that could work in society more widely. New-Age meditation groups pursued ecstatic transcendence. And deeply apocalyptic communal groups tended to move beyond end-time theology that followers of the Christian Right culture found so important, to the "other" side, where they enacted one or another post-apocalyptic (though not typically Christian) heaven on earth.[90]

The countercultural potential for sacred utopian violence surfaced in both political and communal arenas, albeit in different ways. Politically, certain apocalyptic warring sects advanced doctrines akin to Huey Newton's Black Panther Party program of "revolutionary suicide" – death to one's previous self within racist capitalism and rebirth to a revolutionary struggle that would end only in victory or death. Groups such as the Weather Underground, the Symbionese Liberation Army, Germany's Red Army Faction (dubbed the Baader–Meinhof gang by German officials), and Italy's Red Brigades plotted exemplary violence, carrying out what amounted to "propaganda of the deed" that they hoped would simultaneously further the Revolution and inspire others to like-minded actions.[91]

A different and rare kind of violence erupted in certain post-apocalyptic sects that prophesied a radical break in history and established radical separation between themselves and the established social order. Such groups construed themselves as having "escaped" the Armageddon unfolding in the doomed wider world to found colonies that would survive and lay the groundwork for the New Age. Established as they were on the "other" side of the apocalypse, such groups were especially likely to claim an autonomous sacred legitimacy that directly challenged the established social order and its institutions. Living in often physical but sometimes mostly cognitive isolation, participants in such groups came to believe that they had "escaped" from the clutches of the old world left behind, sometimes, not least importantly, from their parents.

Collective violence followed one of two basic patterns, or a mixture of the two. On the one hand, conflict between a group and external opponents – who fought for custody of children and promoted public accusations of cultural deviance – could spiral into violence if the sect leaders came to believe that their community's existence was threatened. Thus, 913 people died in the murders and mass suicide orchestrated by Peoples Temple at Jonestown, Guyana, in 1978, when their leader, Jim Jones, argued to assembled followers that they would not be able to continue as a community after sharpshooters had assassinated a U.S. congressman and four others at a nearby airstrip. Similarly, in 1993, members of the Adventist splinter sect the Branch Davidians refused to surrender to U.S. government agents who had placed them under siege after a botched raid of their Mount Carmel compound near Waco, Texas. After the FBI began to bulldoze down walls of the building complex, seventy-four Davidians died in a fiery conflagration. Two other cases approximate the second pattern. The Solar Temple in Switzerland and Quebec, and Heaven's Gate in Rancho Santa Fe, California, carried out collective suicide as what they claimed to be travel from this "spiritually failed" world to a better one. In their vision, participants achieved heaven not on earth, but through orchestrated collective death as rebirth.[92]

Overall, countercultural apocalyptic violence either took the form of attacks instigated from within the broadly secular New Left, or it emerged in relatively self-contained episodes involving isolated communal groups. However, one movement, Aum Shinri-kyo in Japan, demonstrated the broader potential of insurgent *religious* apocalyptic violence against a developed modern state. In the 1990s Aum's inner leadership established a secret organization within its broader, seemingly peaceful group. The inner group operated as an apocalyptic warring sect that pursued the grandiose goal of ending what they saw as neo-colonial domination by the United States so they could rule Japan themselves. Aum Shinrikyo established a far more deadly arsenal than either Peoples Temple or the Branch Davidians: they developed and began to deploy biological and chemical weapons, killing twelve people in a sarin gas attack on the Tokyo subway system. Technologies of violence did not just provide the means to defend themselves during the apocalypse. They became instruments meant to *precipitate* the public disaster that would *be* the apocalypse. Compared with secular New-Left warring sects such as the Weather Underground and the Baader–Meinhof gang, Aum Shinrikyo was distinctly religious. But at least in its grandiose vision, Aum marked a transition from the *asymmetric* efforts of small, geographically isolated communal compounds like Peoples Temple and the Branch Davidians to, as they saw it, defend their existence against a far more powerful and territorially extensive state. Aum's was a putatively *symmetric* struggle as a sect that proclaimed equal legitimacy with the established order that it opposed and used biological and chemical weapons that had previously been controlled by state powers.[93]

Conclusion

From the Reformation onward, modernizing states had become increasingly successful at confining and pacifying religious dispensations of the apocalyptic, or relegating them to the fringes of colonial expansion, for example, in the Mormon wars and messianic anticolonial movements such as the Mau Mau Rebellion. Where the apocalyptic retained importance, it often took a sacred-secular form, both in state exercise of violence based on a myth of national destiny and in insurgent revolutionary movements. Yet the apocalyptic also persisted as an organizing motif in Christian fundamentalism, especially in the U.S., which partly mobilized as a countermovement to the anti-Vietnam War movement and the counterculture of the 1960s and '70s. The antiwar movement included apocalyptic warring sects such as the Weather

Underground and the Symbionese Liberation Army that were resolutely secular in orientation. On the other hand, apocalyptic groups that pursued their communal rebirth in the New Age tended to embrace religious trappings. Some such groups, notably Peoples Temple and the Branch Davidians, came into violent confrontation with forces of the established order seeking to redefine the boundaries of legitimate religion. These events were highly unusual, and they were contained in their scope and consequences. However, in Japan, Aum Shinrikyo reinvoked an old formula of apocalyptic religious war under new conditions. In a dramatic but brief and isolated episode, it fused religiously sacred violence with both powerful modern technologies and secular politics. Its program thus unveiled a possibility that was beginning to take form elsewhere much more strongly, of a wider apocalypse in the Empire of Modernity.

6

Radical Islam and the Globalized Apocalypse

Terrorism is nothing new. However, in the twenty-first century, nineteenth-century "propaganda of the deed" has fused simultaneously with long-standing religious ideologies of apocalyptic war and emergent technological possibilities of mayhem. The attacks of September 11 and the response of the U.S. and its (nervous) allies elevated possibilities of apocalyptic war to a global scale. If theologians of the 1960s could have foreseen the future, they might have pulled back from seeking re-enchantment of the world in the aftermath of what they called the "death of God." With the benefit of hindsight we can see that over the course of the twentieth century strongly religious constructions of apocalypse and secular politics again became intertwined, as they had been during the nearly two centuries when post-Reformation politics reorganized state and religion across Europe.

To be sure, the collapse of the Soviet Union closed the curtain on the apocalyptic specter of the Cold War ending in global nuclear holocaust. Looking back on the tremendous toll in human lives of the twentieth century's revolutionary programs as the second millennium of the modern era drew to a close, people might finally believe that the jacobinist urge to make the world anew through the revolutionary triumph of virtue had been laid to rest. That view, however, turned out to be radically mistaken.

The attacks of 9/11 unveiled a world where the modern project of progress through science and the spread of democratic liberties suddenly seemed far more fragilely established. This was observed in October 2001 by Michael Ignatieff, then a Harvard professor, later the leader of the Canadian Liberal Party:

> What we are up against is *apocalyptic nihilism*. The nihilism of their means – the indifference to human costs – takes their actions not only out of the realm of politics, but even out of the realm of war itself. The apocalyptic nature of their goals makes it absurd to believe they are making political demands at all. They are seeking the violent transformation of an irremediably sinful and unjust world. Terror does not express a politics, but a metaphysics, a desire to give ultimate meaning to time and history through ever-escalating acts of violence which culminate in a final battle between good and evil.[1]

Apocalypse is in part a matter of belief, yet the attacks of 9/11 and events in their wake underscored how modern understandings of the world are themselves undergirded by belief – in the rectitude and legitimacy of the modern trajectory of history. Professor Ignatieff's comment overreaches in one way: even if apocalyptic war is a metaphysical construct, myths can mobilize people to acts of violence that have strategic ends. It is too easy to dismiss messianic apocalypticism as merely a collective religious psychosis.

Alternatively, discussion of the apocalyptic is routinely lumped into the category of "terrorism." This term is notoriously difficult to define in any objective and consistent way. Definitions abound. One simple and straightforward approach is to define terrorism as "asymmetrical deployment of threats and violence against enemies outside the forms of political struggle routinely operating within some current regime."[2] However, official and popular usage hardly heels to this kind of definition. Instead, terrorism is now routinely extended beyond any coherent definition to encompass insurgencies, guerrilla warfare, and, indeed, virtually any political violence not conducted by nation-states. Such a category, already profoundly ideological, reinforces popularly sanctioned worldviews.

"Why do they hate us?" President George W. Bush wanted to know after 9/11. Some critics had the temerity to offer responses that did not satisfy. American critic Susan Sontag received blanket condemnation when she asked in the September 24, 2001 issue of *The New Yorker*, "Where is the acknowledgement that this was not a 'cowardly' attack on 'civilization' or 'liberty or 'humanity' or 'the free world' but an attack on the world's self-proclaimed superpower, undertaken as a consequence of specific American alliances and actions?"[3] At a moment of excruciating public grief, Sontag was exceptionally blunt and contentious. However, the strong efforts in the media and among the public to suppress anyone who dared provide an ideologically inappropriate answer to "why they hate us" suggests that the question largely functioned in a rhetorical way. Justification could not be separated from explanation, and the question's worldview presumed that there could be no legitimate answer, certainly no answer that would justify the loss of the innocent lives of some 3,000 people. Reaction to Sontag's answer (as opposed to grief over the death of innocent people) thus affirmed the sacred "religious" status of the American social and political order as a project beyond ideological critique.

Such a view had some warrant in political philosophy. Surveying the rubble of communism's historical collapse in the early 1990s, political philosopher Francis Fukuyama boldly affirmed not just the end of the Cold War, but "the end of History." In his view, communism and fascism both had been discredited. Islam, though "potentially universal" in its appeal, was beset by modern liberal democratic challenges, and fundamentalist Islamic movements offered little more than reactionary responses to these challenges. "The days of Islam's cultural conquests, it would seem, are over: it can win back lapsed adherents, but has no resonance for young people in Berlin, Tokyo, or Moscow," Fukuyama wrote. He saw no "coherent *theoretical* alternatives to liberal democracy." Assuring himself that capitalist democracy lacked any internal dynamics that would unravel its institutional structures, he traced a Hegelian dialectical progress driven by both science and longings for the recognition of self-worth. This dialectic ultimately would result in global capitalist liberal democracy as the end point of history.[4]

In effect, Fukuyama translated modernity's metanarrative of progress through science and democracy into a universal history. However, he hastened to add that he did not expect historical events – "even large and grave events" – to cease. Moreover, his vision of the overall directional course of history could not be expected to serve as a "secular theodicy": "A Universal History is simply an intellectual tool; it cannot take the place of God in bringing personal redemption to every one of history's victims."[5] Like the most careful postmillennial theologians, Fukuyama demurred from setting any date for the onset of the golden age.

Whether Fukuyama's vision of universal history will hold up is a question that others can only address in the long run, when those of us living today are dead. For the moment, we know all too well, the end of communist jacobinism did not spell the end of apocalyptic political violence. Fukuyama gave short shrift to the appeal of militant Islam, and in this, historical events since have shown, he was mistaken. We thus encounter a basic question – of whether Fukuyama's universal history can serve as a model that captures broad historical tendencies in the century ahead.

Perhaps possibilities of apocalyptic violence have traversed a bridge across modernity. In the eighteenth century, the apocalypse became secularized. Now, at the beginning of the twenty-first century, it is being reconstituted in a new way, ambiguously sacred and secular. The curtains have parted on a new and unprecedented globalized epoch of apocalyptic violence. We have reached a truly "postmodern" moment – not just the cultural one announced by literary theorists and deconstructive philosophers during the last decades of the twentieth century, heralded by the triumph of relativity, the eclipse of Reason, and the decline of objective, non-instrumental science. Beyond those developments, we may be undergoing an epochal shift away from understanding history as the march of progress driven by the bundled development of science and democracy. Apocalyptic religious violence now portends a new structuring of modernity's empire, a new, postmodern apocalyptic epoch, the form of which remains as yet open to the play of events.

For all that was written in the wake of 9/11, we do not well understand the import of the manifold developments. Neither received theories of modernity nor critiques by postmodernists have provided tools for analysis. Instead, their accounts of contemporary society have been eclipsed by events, thus presenting impediments rather than means to understanding. Further, we are in the midst of history unfolding, and thus lack that convenient (but methodologically suspect) retrospective capacity to make sense of events in relation to one or another outcome. The sheer trauma and press of events have left little opportunity for such reflection. Yet precisely when history remains open, it is important to try to understand the possibilities of historical transformation.

I do not recount in any detail here what others have analyzed in considerable and impressive depth – the genealogy of radical Islamic insurgencies and the still-unfolding history of al-Qaida and what George W. Bush referred to as the War on Terror, it when he was U.S. president.[6] Instead, I consider implications based on the apocalyptic aspects of these developments. In the wake of 9/11, the apocalyptic has become a widely invoked trope of both popular culture and serious public commentary. But the almost routine references to the apocalyptic fail to consider what this might mean.

Shallow invocations presume the apocalypse as an off-the-shelf metanarrative of the struggle between good and evil, yet without directly considering modernity in relation to the apocalyptic. Despite all the analyses of Islamist movements and the allied response, analysts have given strikingly little attention to wider stakes concerning the character and prospects of modern society. We have reached an exhaustion of historical imagination that dare not speak its name. The mere apocalyptic labeling of events has eclipsed it.

We thus bear the burden of an only very incomplete understanding of our historical moment on three fronts. First, if contemporary radical Islam is indeed an apocalyptic movement, this characterization should yield some insight about how it operates, and what strategies might succeed against it. Second, as the history of the apocalyptic in the West demonstrates, apocalyptic violence does not typically unfold as one-sided shadowboxing. We are left to confront the question of whether and how allied responses to radical Islam have articulated with and fed apocalyptic dynamics, and with what consequences and prospects. Third, like other conflict that eclipses everyday life, previous major apocalyptic struggles – notably, the Crusades, the Reformation, the English Civil War, the French Revolution, and the range of jacobinist movements of the nineteenth and twentieth centuries – have been accompanied by dramatic social changes – especially in how political powers orient to apocalyptic movements. The questions thus arise: has the contemporary apocalyptic struggle restructured the institutions of modernity – in war, geopolitics, and the administration of the social – and should it? Even to begin to consider these issues in the remainder of this chapter, we need not just to shift *what* we study, but also to reinvent *how* we study. An important step would be to come to terms with the problem of violence in a way that transcends civilizational justifications, either of "just war," "holy war," or "jihad."[7]

9/11, Iraq, and the problem of violence

Much has been written concerning the ethical, ideological, and religious justifications of war.[8] These distinctions are of real significance, especially insofar as they can be deployed successfully to limit war, and to judge its moral status. In these terms, on the basis of the argument that the Taliban provided a territorial base to al-Qaida, ethicists might deem the allied response to the 9/11 attacks by unseating the Taliban in Afghanistan to be just. Notwithstanding this line of argument, there is an irony and a contradiction. The irony is that the U.S. CIA and its ally Saudi Arabia had provided support to the Islamist mujahedeen who pushed the Soviets from Afghanistan, establishing conditions ripe for the rise of the Islamist Taliban state.[9] The contradiction is that in 2001 the U.S. did not pursue a similar campaign to oust the Taliban and al-Qaida from the Northwest Territories of Pakistan, where Osama bin Laden was presumed to have reconstituted his base after the U.S. and its allies routed the Taliban from Afghanistan.

On the other hand, George W. Bush's March 2003 launching of a supposedly "pre-emptive" war against Iraq failed on the face of it to meet any reasonable criteria defining just war. Iraq was not attacking, or even preparing to attack, any other sovereign state. That Saddam Hussein was a ruthless tyrant, especially in the treatment of Kurds and dissidents, was beyond doubt, but the United States had not previously sought to purge the world of such tyrants, and it subsequently has left any number of others of that ilk undisturbed. The pre-emptive justification that Iraq was developing chemical and biological weapons of mass destruction turned out to have been false, and based on politically vetted and "sexed-up" intelligence. Subsequently, *ex post facto* justifications for having initiated the war shifted to claiming an association between the Iraqi regime and al-Qaida, but in the event, Bush's Iraq war for some years provided an opening for al-Qaida to establish a foothold there, when none had existed under the autocratic secular regime of Saddam Hussein.[10]

The reasons that the U.S. initiated the Iraq war remain obscure, complex, and subject to debate. The optimistic view would be that the intensive run-up to invasion of Iraq and the massive U.S. mobilization of its own and other countries' military forces derived from realistic geopolitical strategies, however hidden from view. But other theories abound, notably, that Bush the Younger was psychologically compensating for the failure of Bush the Elder to finish off Hussein during the first Iraq war, or that the invasion was nothing but a blatant scheme to seize oil resources. Perhaps, as political sociologist Fred Block has argued, the effort was neither. In his analysis, the plan emerged from neoconservative circles during the 1990s interested in cementing the Republican domestic coalition through foreign military action. In this scenario, 9/11 precipitated a military buildup and plan to unseat Hussein, but these basic goals already had been in place.[11] However, the press of events on the ground in Iraq unraveled Bush's May 1, 2003, declaration of victory beneath a banner reading "mission accomplished." Attempts to justify the invasion then gave way to claims concerning the consequences: if the U.S. left Iraq without creating conditions of political stability, the result would be an even further exacerbation of what had become a chaotic bloodbath.

Whatever the explanation for the Iraq war, it must be located outside any just-war legitimation. The wider War on Terror was similarly plagued by U.S. actions that, on their face, violated the Geneva Conventions concerning humane treatment of prisoners and torture – actions that U.S. officials at the time justified as necessary responses to the threat of terrorism. Many will conclude, as I have, that a number of Bush administration actions in response to the attacks of 9/11 exceeded Western legal, ethical, and philosophical boundaries. Ethics and just-war principles neither justify nor explain the approach taken by the Bush administration. It thus behooves us to consider the problem of political violence from a different vantage point. A useful point of departure is phenomenologist Maurice Merleau-Ponty's 1947 essay *Humanism and Terror*, a reflection on Stalin's political show trials of the 1930s via Arthur Koestler's novel *Darkness at Noon*.

Against the refusals of others, both communists and anti-communists, Merleau-Ponty addressed questions concerning whether and how humanist values operating under the sign of Reason – specifically Reason embodied in a progressive historical dialectic theorized in different ways by Hegel and Marx – should embrace "historical violence." Merleau-Ponty thus concerned himself with political violence, not the violence of crimes of passion and of criminal self-interest, which lack any larger strategic purpose. His specific focus on communist violence is by now dated. Nevertheless, his analysis suggests striking points. As Merleau-Ponty remarked then, so it is now: "the questions that haunt us are precisely those which we refuse to formulate."

Merleau-Ponty drew a basic distinction between two kinds of historical times. First, he pointed to the "historical *period*" relatively free from political violence – "in which political man is content to administer a regime or an established law." By contrast, he identified the historical "*epoch*" – "one of those moments where the traditional ground of a nation or society crumbles and where, for better or worse, man himself must reconstruct human relations. ..." Under epochal conditions, Merleau-Ponty argued, "the liberty of each man is a mortal threat to the others and [historical] violence reappears." Epochal violence inevitably recurs so long as the dynamic forces of history remain in play, Merleau-Ponty argued, concluding, "We do not have a choice between purity and violence but between different kinds of violence."

Merleau-Ponty's conclusion certainly accords with *realpolitik* and historical experience. But it raises the thorny question of whether and how historical violence can be politically justified as legitimate. Here, a difficulty presents itself: according to Merleau-Ponty, *social* truth is never absolute, only historical. It is framed within one or another particular *ideological* vision of how the world should be. As a consequence, the meaning of violence is never absolute, and the answer to the question of whether violence is legitimate or must be rejected becomes evident only after the fact. Only an outcome of violence, when an ideological frame is effectively asserted or reasserted, defines which (ideologically framed) logic of Reason can operate. Only then can violence be identified as *progressive* in its contribution to Reason, or, alternatively, merely *self-serving*. The end of violence that can be justified through ideologically circumscribed Reason (for Merleau-Ponty, Marxism) marks the end of meaningful history. "After that," he asserted, "there remain only dreams or adventures." The absence of a philosophy of history "would mean in the end ... that the world and our existence are a senseless tumult."[12]

Political violence, in this analysis, is inevitable, at least unless the end of history brings a millennial kingdom. Yet some such violence (for example, the control of land or commodities such as gold, oil, or heroin) is merely strategically "self-serving," while other violence advances Reason, which is to say that it contributes to the *telos* of some vision of a larger purpose of history. Yet what that purpose might be comes into view most clearly only when the dust has settled. The *telos* of Reason, if it is at work, can best be defined with victory.

Merleau-Ponty's high-modernist account of political violence might seem to reflect a particularly Machiavellian sort of results-based or "consequentialist" ethics, for historical violence marks a struggle over the direction of Reason in history in which victory justifies right. However, in his analysis, there are also limits to claims of Reason, beyond which is to be found mere self-interest that lacks any legitimate political justification of violence. The stakes of historical violence thus come down to whether Reason will prevail – and whose Reason it will be – or whether the absence of any justification of violence in Reason portends the eclipse of civilization in the "senseless tumult" of self-interested violence.

As we have seen, apocalyptic violence is either initiated by a countercultural movement that seeks to transcend an established social order through holy war, or it can arise within – and be legitimized by – an ideologically established social order that identifies either an internal or external Other as threatening its vision of the sacred. Each possibility may seek to assert its claim of Reason in history. Sociologist Karl Mannheim reflected deeply on this circumstance in his book *Ideology and Utopia*, published while the Nazi Party held power in Germany in the 1930s. As Mannheim showed, *ideological* supporters of an established social order and *utopian* advocates of a new social order may become locked in struggle over the meaning of history. From the perspective of an ideology prevailing within the established order, *any* utopian vision is fantastic, unrealizable, and morally abhorrent. However, such claims of impossibility presume the continued existence of the present order. For the utopianists, these claims are themselves ideological, and they would lose their force if a transcendent social order were achieved. In other words, an ideology is a utopia about an existing social order, and a utopia is an anticipatory ideological account of an order that does not now exist.[13]

In Merleau-Ponty's analysis, if we seek to gain a deeper understanding of apocalyptic developments that rise to the level of historical violence, it is not helpful to formulate questions from within Western liberalism if doing so either legitimizes or demonizes the violence of historical protagonists. Instead, we must explore the historically situated claims of Reason, or their absence, on the two sides of apocalyptic war. I do so here, first by examining the sources of contemporary jihad and its development in the movement centered in al-Qaida, and then by turning to examinations of how the conflict has been approached by the U.S.-led coalition opposing al-Qaida, and how their project might be rethought.

Political violence and contemporary jihad

Soviet communism crumbled largely "from within," partly due to the kind of self-serving corruption of violence that Merleau-Ponty described in *Humanism and Terror*. Soviet violence lost any claim to a progressive rationale, and a façade of ideology justified brutality empty of anything beyond the will to dominate. It was in the wake of the Cold War that Francis Fukuyama could boldly announce "the end of history." However, Fukuyama failed to anticipate the power of religion, specifically Islamic jihad, to organize violence in a way that rises, as Merleau-Ponty puts it, to the epochal level of historical violence, that is, violence beyond any institutionalized framework of legitimation that shakes the world to the roots of conventional understandings.

The violence of the Islamist movement spearheaded by al-Qaida has partly been shaped by historical situations and opportunities. In the era of decolonization that began with the end of World War II, a number of national liberation movements allied themselves with the international communist movement. Some such movements, for example, the Cuban revolutionaries led by Fidel Castro, were fully jacobin: they used military victory to launch the new utopian society. Other movements (the Christian Serbs' genocide against Muslims in Bosnia during the 1990s, for example) have been less than fully modern in their ideological programs and practices; they built on putatively primordial ethnic ties of solidarity, yielding a reactionary "national-communal" rather than a utopian jacobin program.[14]

Leftist liberation movements went into understandable decline with the end of the Soviet empire. However, communalist nationalist violence increased. The reasons for the development are both complex and controversial. Michael Hechter has offered a general theory, that nationalism obtains its most reactionary solidarity when a negatively privileged group facing powerful external social forces regards collective opportunities to control resources as greater than its members might gain as individuals. In the historical instance, Mark Juergensmeyer has suggested that toward the end of the twentieth century a "postmodern" crisis of "secular nationalism" became focused on uncertainty concerning "what constitutes a valid basis for national identity." More broadly, James Aho described nothing less than an "apocalypse of modernity," in which "the glimmer of two prophecies shows through the fractures of modernity": the postmodern embrace of social reality as "constructed" comes up against fundamentalist quests for certainty in uncertain times.[15]

Whatever the explanation of nationalist political violence, the point remains: national-communal movements are reactionary, and they typically lack any utopian program. To be sure, political scientist Robert Pape observes that religious difference between two parties to a conflict (rather than any specific religion – e.g., Islam – or its content) can exacerbate the potential of escalation to the use of suicide terrorism as a tactic. However, although the cleavages in such struggles often break down along religious lines, Pape has argued that nationalism in the face of occupation deemed "foreign," not religion, is the "taproot" of suicide terrorism.[16] No doubt the nationalists believe they have God on their side, but they do not necessarily undertake war specifically as a sacred religious enterprise. The most striking exception to this principle is, of course, the contemporary jihad of al-Qaida and other radical Islamist groups. But as I will argue, it is a double exception: sacred violence that transcends nationalism.

The strands of contemporary militant Islamism span the Sunni and Shi'a traditions. In Shi'a-dominated Iran, the 1979 revolution against the Shah Mohammed Reza Pahlavi put in place the Islamic Republic headed by Ayatollah Khomeini, and led to the diffusion of radicalism to Shi'ites in Lebanon via the establishment of Hezbollah, the Party of God. For Sunnis, significant developments trace directly to the Islamic movements that emerged at the end of the Ottoman Empire in the early 1920s, notably, the Islamic Brotherhood founded by Hassan al-Banna in Egypt and the Palestinian Jihad against Jews who had come to settle in the Levant under the British Mandate. Subsequently, some organizations grew out of nationalist movements. Many Palestinians had fled to Gaza and the West Bank following the partition of Palestine that came with Israeli statehood in 1948. There, Yassar Arafat's Fatah movement, founded in 1954, came to dominate the secular Palestine Liberation Organization after Israel's decisive victory over its Arab opponents in the Six-Day War of 1967, and the PLO gravitated to the patronage of the Soviet bloc. When the Palestinian Islamic movement Hamas emerged in the 1980s, it initially focused on social services. However, at the end of the Cold War in the early 1990s, the PLO began to seek rapprochement with Israel, and Hamas in effect took over terrorist operations that previously had been conducted under the PLO. In Afghanistan, after CIA-financed Islamic mujahedeen fighters defeated the Soviets in 1989, the fundamentalist Taliban movement eventually brought the ensuing civil war to an end by triumphing over mujahedeen factions, and it instituted a fundamentalist Islamic government under strict Shari'a law. A generalization is not inaccurate: the increasing weakness and eventual collapse of the Soviet Union eliminated the left-based patronage of non-religious national liberation movements. In Sunni Muslim regions as diverse as Gaza and the West Bank and Afghanistan, this development opened the way for Islamist ideology to unify leftist and fundamentalist tendencies in the Muslim world under a new, quasi-jacobin program of jihad that may have been indirectly influenced by Marxist ideas via the leftist Arab insurgencies that Islamism began to displace.

9/11 and al-Qaida

On September 11, 2001, television around the world instantaneously showed New York City's World Trade Center twin towers collapsing after two passenger planes rammed into them. This would have to be the most widely and immediately experienced moment of unimaginable horror that has ever sustained belief in an apocalypse. Just as Walter Benjamin described how an historical present and everyday life could be shot through with "chips of messianic time," so came the enduring image of "9/11" – a brilliantly beautiful morning on the East Coast of the United States punctured by a tableau of terror.[17] If the apocalyptic is sometimes hidden from wider view, here it was full-blown, for all the world to see, over and over again. Finally, a month after the attacks, George W. Bush used a press conference reporting on "the state of our war on terror" to suggest that America would be better served if people returned to the normal patterns of diachronic life:

> We cannot let the terrorists achieve the objective of frightening our nation to the point where we don't – where we don't conduct business, where people don't shop. That's their intention. Their intention was not only to kill and maim and destroy. Their intention was to frighten to the point where our nation would not act. Their intention was to so frighten our government that we wouldn't seek justice; that somehow we would cower in the face of their threats and not respond, abroad or at home.[18]

The American-led confrontation with international Islamist insurgency quickly became a central hinge upon which contemporary history turns. Unfortunately, we can be all but certain today that Islamist organizations are planning more moments of reckoning. Certainly Western governments steel people to anticipate challenges involving not only al-Qaida and its networked allies in various countries but also autonomous groups and, potentially, Islamic nation-states.

An attack on the scale of 9/11 by a stateless entity is historically without precedent, as is a war against such an entity. Indeed, the ensuing events did not constitute anything like a conventional war. Had the world become caught up in an apocalyptic war? The mere suggestion of such a possibility would have seemed completely grandiose until September 11. Yet, as I have suggested in earlier chapters, at certain conjunctures, apocalyptic actions shape the course of history. To be sure, the apocalyptic cannot be reduced to any tidy formula. Apocalyptic war is "socially constructed" or "deconstructed," depending upon the actions taken by various parties to a situation. History, even apocalyptic history, is open-ended, not pre-ordained.

Is any analytic advantage to be gained by comparing contemporary global militant Islamism to the sociological pattern of the warring apocalyptic sect identified in chapter 5? On the face of it, military theorists might not think so; outcomes, they would argue, substantially depend on the assets and vulnerabilities of parties to a conflict. For both guerrilla war in general and terrorism as a specific strategy, maneuvers are dictated by the realities of a situation in which the insurgent party operates as an underground network. In the case at hand, these realities do not depend on whether radical Islamist forms of organization approximate the apocalyptic warring sect as an ideal type. After all, strategic time is the constitutive temporal organization of all kinds of conflict. Thus, there are fluid theoretical lines of transition between how actions are organized in the warring sect as a type and in warring cadres more generally. Yet we also have seen that secular guerrilla war and terrorism are often apocalyptically structured. The significant distinction is not between "secular" and "religious" war, but between secular war and war for a "sacred" cause, even one that is not sanctioned by any established religion. Even secular war, as in the case of the French Revolution, can take on the trappings of a sacred cause, albeit with political content. Inevitably, the transitions between sacred and secular war are fluid.[19]

Nevertheless, compared to secular strategic action that serves no sacred cause, theorization of the apocalyptic warring sect throws into relief three features relevant to understanding the distinctiveness of contemporary militant Islam: ideology, internal organization, and external context.

- The *ideology* of apocalyptic war is diffuse and utopian in its goals, and it warrants actions by *religious martyrs*.[20]
- Organizationally, the *charismatic community of a warring sect* legitimated by an apocalyptic ideology empowers charismatic cells that are more durable, more flexible, and more capable of independent action than other military organizations.
- As a countercultural phenomenon, apocalyptic war is sustained by the connections between warring sects and a wider *oppositional milieu*.

In terms of these three dimensions – ideology, organization, and milieu – al-Qaida and allied Islamist movements are quintessentially warring sects that operate in strategic time in order to precipitate the apocalyptic shift to a millennial age.

Ideology

Religions, dealing in ultimate meanings, bear a claim to exceed merely secular authority. Thus, they remain a potent basis for contesting political legitimacy both within and beyond nation-states. Historically and today, the sociological patterns are clear enough. Religious movements acting to challenge a given social order sometimes arise on the basis of shared commitments to ultimate values that link participants of quite different social backgrounds in a *déclassé* alliance. Alternatively, movements originate in social strata that are negatively privileged politically and economically, or socially ascendant but blocked from power.[21]

Whatever the specific ultimate values in an excluded group, as Max Weber observed nearly a century ago, religion represents a special case of status honor that, for participants, is "nourished most easily on the belief that a special 'mission' is entrusted to them. ... Their value is thus moved into something beyond themselves, into a 'task' placed before them by God."[22] Especially religion under Western monotheism thus develops a possibility of " 'holy war,' i.e., a war in the name of a god, for the special purpose of avenging a sacrilege." In Weber's genealogy, the ancient Hebrew promise that God's chosen people would be elevated "above other nations" provided a legitimating framework. In turn, Augustine affirmed a Christian policy of forced conversion. But, Weber argued, Islam was the first religion to establish a connection between "religious promises and war against religious infidelity" aimed at "the subjugation of the unbelievers to political authority and economic domination of the faithful." However, under traditional Islam, "if the infidels were members of 'religions with a sacred book,' their extermination was not enjoined," for they could make useful economic contributions to Islamic society through tribute or taxation.[23]

In Weber's terms, it is clear that the ideology put forward by al-Qaida in the 1990s promoted a violent sacred struggle to avenge sacrilege. Osama bin Laden's September 1996 "Declaration of Jihad against the Americans Occupying the Land of the Two Holy Mosques" (Saudi Arabia) details a long list of what he deems to be sacrileges. It includes: the stationing of U.S. troops in Saudi Arabia near the holiest Muslim cities; the U.S.-led 1991 war against Iraq after it invaded Kuwait; Israeli control of the city of Jerusalem; and, most generally, the defeat of the Ottoman Empire in the 1920s.[24] These transgressions and the wider hegemony that underwrites them are matters of geopolitics, but they are refracted through a lens of religious meaning.[25] In the ideology of radical Islam, sacrilege requires a specifically religious response of military jihad.

Jihad is a complex Islamic doctrine, subject to varying definitions in both Muslim theological debate and scholarly analysis.[26] Historically, as Weber noted, the ethical and legal routinization of Islam in the centuries after its early and dramatic expansion tended to codify limits to wars against "religions with a sacred book," and to dilute the most militant interpretations of jihad. During the twentieth century, however, certain Islamist movements began to reconstruct the theology of jihad in response to contemporary historical conditions – especially the decline of the Ottoman Caliphate during the nineteenth century, the British consolidation of its power in Egypt through declaration of a protectorate during World War I, and final establishment of secular rule in Turkey in the 1920s.[27]

Already before the end of Ottoman rule, calls for jihad against infidels emerged. Subsequently, a highly radicalized anti-modern construction arose within the Egyptian Muslim Brotherhood that 22-year-old Hassan al-Banna founded in 1928. Al-Banna embraced the strand of fundamentalist Sunni Islamic thought called Salafism, calling for a return to the practices of the first generations of Muslims in the time of Muhammad, and he initiated a push to establish a theocratic state in Egypt organized on the basis of *Shari'a*, or Islamic law. How to establish such a state was a question open to alternative strategic answers, both violent and non-violent. However, some Brotherhood members obtained military experience, and the government of Egypt in turn suppressed the group, arresting around 4,000 members shortly after Egyptian police assassinated al-Banna in 1949 in retaliation for Islamic Brotherhood operatives' assassination of the Egyptian prime minister, Nokrashy Pasha, in December 1948.[28]

One of the key Brotherhood thinkers of the 1950s, widely noted for his antipathy to Western culture, was Sayyid Qutb, who came away from a 1948 sojourn in Greeley, Colorado, with a deep revulsion to the culture of the United States. Qutb reacted especially strongly to patterns of dating among college students and practices of lawn cultivation that he observed. Later, writing while imprisoned as part of Egypt's crackdowns on the Brotherhood, he justified jihad as a holy struggle against what he regarded as decadent, immoral, secular Western thought, including not only democratic capitalist ideology, but also Marxist communism, which Qutb saw as infected with the evolutionary theory of Darwin, and behind that, the inevitably atheistic implications of Western scientism. For Qutb, jihad amounted to a basic obligation of believers, a veritable sixth pillar of Islam. He rejected the prevailing prohibition from invoking jihad against a secular ruler who is a Muslim. The Islamic legal solution was to employ the procedure of having such a ruler declared a *kafir* or apostate. In Qutb's view, secular Muslim states as well as non-Islamic ones were infidel states to be overthrown. Obviously, by this doctrine, Qutb identified himself as an enemy of the Egyptian state, and he was tried and hanged in 1966.[29]

However, another Egyptian, Abd al-Salam Faraj, subsequently explicitly extended Qutb's doctrine in the direction of violence, using the title of his 1981 pamphlet, *The Neglected Duty*, to invoke jihad. Faraj was not a spiritual authority; he was an activist who founded Egypt's al-Jihad. He insisted that military jihad is not subject to codified Islamic legal restraints – for example, prohibiting the killing of non-combatants – and that it does not require a *fatwa*, or religious ruling affirming approval by Muslim authorities. More-over, for Faraj, jihad is not a series of battles between soldiers; it can draw on "deception and deceit, surprise attacks, trickery and large-scale violence." These ideas had consequences. Members of the Egyptian army with connections to al-Jihad assassinated then-Egyptian president Anwar Sadat on October 6, 1981. Six months later Faraj himself was tried and executed for taking part in the plot.[30]

Qutb and Faraj were central figures in the broad movement toward the radicalized theology of jihad as espoused in al-Qaida. A key conduit of these ideas was Ayman al-Zawahiri, a doctor who participated in Faraj's Egyptian al-Jihad movement and served three years in Egyptian prison following the assassination of Presi-dent Sadat. Later, in Afghanistan, he met the wealthy Osama bin Laden, who already had been steeped in Wahhabism, the conserva-tive Salafist ideology officially promoted in his native Saudi Arabia. Along with some 20,000 other Muslims, Zawahiri and bin Laden had come to Afghanistan to join the mujahedeen fighting against the Soviet forces who invaded in 1979.[31] Zawahiri worked as a senior leader of al-Jihad, aiding the mujahedeen. Bin Laden had arrived in 1984. He was a protégé of another militant who had been exposed to Qutb's ideas, the Palestinian-born Abdullah Azzam, who already had met al-Zawahiri while engaged in theological studies in Egypt (and reportedly once toured the U.S. as a recruiter for the Afghan mujahedeen indirectly sponsored by the CIA). When it became clear in 1988 that the Soviets would withdraw from Afghanistan, Azzam envisioned the fight against the Soviets as only the beginning: "jihad will remain an individual obligation until we have reconquered all Muslim lands and reinstalled Islam: we still have ahead of us Palestine, Bukhara, Lebanon, Chad, Eritrea, Somalia, the Philippines, Burma, Yemen, Tashkent, and Andalusia." But pride of place went to Azzam's native Palestine. A new group of committed jihadists began to take shape at meetings in Peshawar, Pakistan, on August 11 and 20, 1988, more or less following a program set by Azzam in issue 41 of the journal *Al-Jihad*, published in April 1988. There, Azzam argued for *al-qaeda al-sulbah* – "the solid base," a term that, in Arabic, carries not just a military connotation, but, more importantly, philosophical, legal, and social ones. "All anti-Islamic plots that are being hatched throughout the world must be foiled," Azzam announced, and he detailed ascetic, egalitarian, and religious guidelines for the "vanguard" that would "translate into reality the great dream of victory." Azzam suspected that the human cost would be high, and he did not shrink from saying so: "History does not write its lines except with blood. Glory does not build its lofty edifices except with skulls." A car bomb loaded with 20 kilograms of TNT killed Azzam on November 24, 1989.[32]

Whether the group that was to become al-Qaida, or "the base," intended to follow Azzam's plan to train Muslims so they could participate in insurgencies against non-Islamic regimes in their own native lands has become a moot question. Azzam's death left an opening for Azzam's protégé bin Laden and Zawahiri to pursue the project that became al-Qaida, with bin Laden providing the financial resources and Zawahiri developing the ideology and program. Under the ideological influence of Zawahiri, bin Laden eventually became interested in directly developing a global network of jihadist fighters. Many such jihadists initially trained in Afghani camps run by al-Qaida. Congruent with Qutb's and Faraj's doctrines, jihad in al-Qaida took the path of *al-jihad al-asghar*, warfare on behalf of the faithful, in which both killing the enemy and being willing to die oneself are religious duties that receive divine blessing. War became a site of martyrdom. As a jihad commander said in the mountains of Pakistan in 2002 after retreating from Afghanistan, "We prefer to die in honor than live in humiliation."[33]

In its utopian vision, bin Laden's movement seeks a post-apocalyptic restoration of the Islamic caliphate, untainted by secular rule or external hegemony. As with other totalistic jacobin programs, the path to that restoration requires a holy war. But there is an important innovation on the ideas of Qutb and Faraj, one that grows out of Azzam, bin Laden, and Zawahiri's project of aiding a wide range of nationalist Islamist struggles. The obvious question they faced concerned how supporting these diverse nationalist struggles could gain coherence as a single enterprise. The answer to this question redefined the enemy.

By the time of his 1996 declaration, bin Laden had become incensed with the U.S. basing of troops in Saudi Arabia after the conclusion of the U.N.-sanctioned and U.S.-led war against Iraq for invading Kuwait in 1990. Bin Laden then would reason, "everyone agrees that 'a crooked stick cannot have a straight shadow' and that there must be concentration on hitting the main enemy who has thrust the [Islamic] nation into whirlpools and labyrinths for decades since dividing it into states and statelets."[34] Previously, Islamic fundamentalists had directed their hostilities toward the "nearest enemy," namely, what they regarded as insufficiently Islamic states that governed territories where Muslims live (Egypt, for example). But by 1997, bin Laden had completely reversed the hierarchy of enemies: "if the United States is beheaded," he asserted, "the Arab Kingdoms will wither away."[35]

Thus, in the mid-1990s the earlier Islamist theology of struggle against the "nearest enemy" became displaced by a broader war directed against *al-Adou al-Baeed*, or "the far enemy," that is, "the Zionist–Crusader alliance and their collaborators," with the United States as the foremost representative of Western hegemony in Muslim states. The transcendent character of the struggle is evidenced by a young Pakistani's comment, "Jihad will continue until doomsday, or until America is defeated, either way."[36]

The specific character of actions reveals something of the warring sect's vision, strategy, and goals. Aside from the bomb placed in a parking garage of New York's World Trade Center in 1993, other actions prior to 9/11 attributed to al-Qaida mainly focused on U.S. government targets – the 1996 bombing of U.S. military families living in Khobar Towers in Saudi Arabia, the nearly simultaneous 1998 bombings of U.S. embassies in Kenya and Tanzania, and the attack on the USS *Cole* in the fall of 2000. But 9/11 repositioned terror as a technique that targeted the established global order itself. True to the warring tradition of jihad within Islam, this struggle is simultaneously a strategic and a sacred one. Its theological/

strategic shift is of the utmost significance, for it has redirected Islamic jihad from subnational and national arenas, where it was relatively "contained," to a global arena, where it becomes oriented to an epochal redirection of world history.[37]

In sum, the *ideology* of al-Qaida and allied movements is quintessentially apocalyptic. Let us consider, then, questions of whether militant Islamist *organization* and *actions* are also apocalyptic, and, in turn, whether *oppositional milieu* makes any difference in the jihadist struggle against the United States and the West.

Organization and modes of action

The temporal structure of jihad, like warring apocalyptic ideology more generally, promises eternal transcendence through victory or death. But the temporal structure of action by the warring sect takes the form of a "Manichean battle between the forces of good and evil."[38] Apocalyptic war is not conventional war, and not just because it typically involves a struggle between networks of underground cells pursuing guerrilla and terrorist strategies. Rather, the kinds of violence undertaken in holy war exceed political conventions of violence in war. Apocalyptic war is sacred terror. In it, strategic actions become strongly infused with symbolically transcendent "religious" meanings.

In the 9/11 attacks, as the "final instructions" to the hijackers show, the plan of action was religiously saturated ("Pray for yourself and all your brothers that they may be victorious and hit their targets," instruction 28 read in part.[39]) The careful religious framing of the 9/11 attacks is striking. Yet the religious yoke of apocalyptic war wears lightly. As Max Weber observed concerning fighters for the faith – from early Muslims and Crusaders to Sikhs and Japanese Buddhists – "even the formal orthodoxy of all these warrior religionists was often of dubious genuineness."[40] Participants in a holy war will be a diverse lot, varying in their religious sophistication and commitment. To be sure, the sources of jihad as a doctrine are to be found in alienated religious thinkers and members of Arab professional classes; the movement did not originate among the poor, the ignorant, or the dispossessed. Still, like medieval Christian crusaders, frontline operatives of al-Qaida and its allies participate in a struggle infused with religious meaning without necessarily being saints themselves.

In the early months after 9/11, the U.S. government was at pains to demonstrate that responsibility for the attacks did not rest with the nineteen hijackers alone, or even with their immediate handlers.

In effect, designating the responsible organization as al-Qaida legit-imated a war against it. Yet this does not provide an adequate basis for understanding al-Qaida as an organization.

There can be no doubt that terrorist actions require tight organization and coordination, but both the strategy of operating underground and the demands of terrorist operations require a *decentralized* and *disaggregated* organization open to reconstitution, rather than a tightly integrated top-down organization. These are general features of the apocalyptic sect that characterize both the funding as well as the structure of al-Qaida. Although its financing remains incompletely understood, al-Qaida evidently engages in the "spoils communism" typical of warring sects, but elevated to a global level. The sources of funds are said to range from Osama bin Laden's personal wealth and business operations to the support by Saudi princes and other wealthy Muslims, Muslim mosques and charities, and perhaps profits from heroin trafficking. Resources flow to diffuse and far-flung elements of the loose network through diverse channels, often disguised as to their nature and address.[41]

As for organization, al-Qaida reportedly became structured in 1998 as a organizational council, the *shura majlis*, led by bin Laden, that would oversee four committees – concerned with military, business, theological, and public-relations activities. A substantial international network of operatives and a broad and informal inter-national coalition of insurgent and terrorist groups claiming affili-ation extended beyond the committees. They have employed highly sophisticated versions of the strategies long used by underground quasi-military cells to avoid detection. Whatever the structure of al-Qaida and its connections to Islamist groups at any given point, their forms have continued to undergo transformation as conditions have changed.[42]

The list of signatories to the 1998 "International Islamic Front for Jihad on the Jews and Crusaders" counted jihad groups in twenty-one countries, from Bosnia and Croatia to the Philippines.[43] The alliance initially was extensive in its reach, and its participants have coordinated actions on a global scale without historic precedent in a stateless insurgent movement (insurgent communism and anar-chism had considerable international communication, but did little to coordinate operations internationally). Al-Qaida enjoyed a phys-ical sanctuary in Afghanistan as long as the Taliban ruled, but the closing of training programs there created something of a jihadist diaspora, relocating a core of operatives to Pakistan and spreading others literally to every continent and region of the world.

Depiction of the network as centralized in a top-down command structure would not well capture either the independent cell structure common to warring sects, the complexities of how the 9/11 attacks were undertaken, or radical Islamist use of the internet to coordinate actions, distribute materials like its *Encyclopedia of Jihad* training manual, and spread jihadist ideology to wider publics.[44] Nor does a centralization thesis adequately take into account the degree to which success of actions depends on commitment to mission rather than authority as a basis of coordination. In the aftermath of 9/11, the counterterrorist efforts of the U.S. and its allies have taken their toll on al-Qaida and they have forced jihadist cells (further) underground. Still, cells capable of independent action and autonomous groups have continued to coordinate with one another and take actions, apparently sometimes on the basis of witnessing public acts and statements, rather than by direct communication. Through 2009 there was a continuing stream of terrorist and guerrilla actions both strongly and weakly associated with al-Qaida, including bombings, military attacks and skirmishes, assassinations of both governmental workers and other Westerners, and continued war in Afghanistan, spilling into a new front in Pakistan's Northwest Territories. Apart from concrete acts of terrorism, preemptive arrests in the U.S., the United Kingdom, and other parts of Europe suggest the existence of "sleeper cells" that could be called upon to conduct further actions. And although, contrary to assertions of the U.S. Bush administration, there is no credible evidence that al-Qaida had any connection to Saddam Hussein *before* the U.S. toppled his Baathist regime in 2003, *after* the U.S.-led invasion, al-Qaida in Iraq – the independent jihadist organization established by the Jordanian Abu Musab al-Zarqawi – initiated a militant Islamist program of terrorism and insurgent warfare in Iraq. As of this writing, developments in Afghanistan, Pakistan, and Iraq demonstrate that far from having been shut down, jihad initiatives of al-Qaida and other groups continue, and in certain regions, increase. Furthermore, the commitment of al-Qaida to attacking the U.S. is, in the words of the U.S. National Intelligence Officer for Transnational Threats, "undiminished."[45]

Oppositional milieu

Finally, let us consider whether the wider *oppositional milieu* of militant Islam further differentiates al-Qaida from both conventional military organizations and terrorist organizations that lack a strong apocalyptic ideology. Conventional military organizations typically receive the patriotic support of their own homeland, but the boundaries between the military and other social actors are clearly demarcated. Terrorist organizations lacking legitimacy among a wider populace may coerce cooperation by individuals and groups in the territory where they operate, but once again, the boundaries between the terrorists and others are distinct.

By contrast, participants in an apocalyptic warring sect are the most highly committed people in a oppositional social milieu that offers both direct infrastructural support and the indirect "moral" support of a much wider population who find themselves sympathetic to the sect's ideology. Sometimes, a state can pin down and eliminate an isolated terrorist organization, but the warring sect with broad countercultural support represents a much more difficult challenge. In these terms, al-Qaida is clearly not a maverick terrorist organization, isolated from any wider public. What is most unsettling for the allied counterinsurgency is that far-flung networks of jihadist groups are themselves intricately connected with complex networks of other militant Islamic organizations, Islamic schools, and Muslim patrons. Beyond these relatively tangible networks, al-Qaida enjoys extensive support within a much broader "apocalyptic" Islamist milieu.[46]

For an apocalyptic thesis to add anything to a more conventional analysis of resources and strategies in conflict, the distinctive features of apocalyptic war must make a difference for the nature of a conflict and its trajectory. The three features I have considered – apocalyptic ideology, decentralized organization, and connection to a wider counterculture – could simply be empirically noted. But they are not independent: they tend to reinforce one another as a coherent overall logic of collective action by groups approximating the apocalyptic warring sect. The lines of transition from strictly strategic guerrilla warfare or terrorist actions may be fluid. However, taken together, the apocalyptic elements undergird collective violence as sacred action in relation to a wider sacred cause, and they thus intensify the attraction of the movement to potential recruits willing to undergo death to previous lives and rebirth of total dedication to the sacred struggle, including willingness to die for the cause.

War, the German military theorist Carl von Clausewitz defined early in the nineteenth century as "the pursuit of politics by other means." Implicit in this definition is the idea that once the probabilities of victory become remote and the costs of continued war insupportable, rational strategists on the weaker side will seek political solutions to end war. Politics is a game of strategy, bluff, and compromise. With war as extreme politics, peace is possible.

Is apocalyptic war different? The alternatives depicted by Michael Ignatieff are stark: total victory or death. Yet as Mark Juergensmeyer describes what he calls "cosmic war," victory would be hard to define, because the goals of apocalyptic war are often murky, grandiose, or both. Given the totalistic revolutionary visions that animate the apocalyptic warring sect, defeat would be unthinkable, yet conversely, during incipient phases of any apocalyptic struggle, the chances of "victory" in a concrete historical sense typically seem slim to non-existent.[47] All the same, in historical circumstances when apocalypse has become conjoined with disciplined organization – initially in the English Civil War, and then in the French Revolution and the communist revolutions of the twentieth century – apocalyptic war could decisively alter the political landscape. Surely the contemporary situation unveils similar possibilities. Thus, a conservative American political analyst affirms the apocalyptic and jacobin character of al-Qaida, calling bin Laden and other radical Islamists the "new Bolsheviks."[48] With the jihad announced by al-Qaida, victory would amount to nothing less than a reconstitution of the global geopolitical order, by the elimination of Western – and especially U.S. – hegemony directly or by proxy in lands that the jihadists deem Islamic.

In the early twentieth century, French social theorist Georges Sorel argued that violence – as a challenge to the ideological construction of the established order – nurtures the myth that change is possible.[49] While the *goal* may seem unreachable, *having* the goal can be consequential. Put differently, apocalyptic violence may be simultaneously strategic and sacredly symbolic.[50] The struggle of al-Qaida not only exceeds conventional political violence (to recall Tilly's definition of terrorism), it positions terror as a technique in an effort to constitute a globalized civilizational struggle. When al-Qaida's program first drew widespread attention after the 9/11 attacks, this goal seemed impossibly remote. Yet precisely the remoteness of this goal – and, indeed, the Western refusal to countenance al-Qaida's program as a legitimate topic of discussion – has enhanced the sanctity of the goal for those drawn to the Islamist cause. And today, future Islamist attainment of the movement's overall goals can no longer be completely dismissed as merely a remote possibility. How, then, has the U.S.-led coalition framed its strategy against al-Qaida, and how might its strategy be reconstructed? It is to these two issues that we now turn.

Apocalyptic war and the established social order in the West

The attacks of September 11, 2001, were abhorrent to modern civilized life. Yet moral condemnation does not provide adequate grounds for understanding the struggle that unfolded between al-Qaida and the U.S.-led coalition. The attacks – taken on their own – succeeded, probably more than those who planned them anticipated, in altering political agendas, economic realities, and social life around the globe. However, as events in Afghanistan, Iraq, Pakistan, and elsewhere played out in the wake of 9/11, it became obvious that jihad alone did not ordain the globalized apocalypse. Instead, in Sorel's terms, the United States (and, in different ways, Britain and other allies), too, framed the struggle in mythic terms.

Early in the twenty-first century, the *New York Times* culture critic forcefully argued that the attacks of 9/11 required a disavowal of postmodern relativism and a reaffirmation of objective truth.[51] And indeed, the intellectual hubbub about postmodernism did subside. Yet matters turned out not to be so simple, for in the face of critics who argued that the U.S. administration of George W. Bush needed to face reality in the Middle East, an administration spokesman asserted his own postmodern claim: "That's not the way the world works any more. We're an empire now, and when we act, we create our own reality."[52]

The Bush administration's War on Terror may seem encompassing as a characterization, but it was not a sufficient basis for understanding the contemporary apocalyptic moment and its implications. There are conventional reasons for saying so. First, war is an inadequate characterization of the struggle, and, second, the contemporary struggle by the U.S. and its allies is not against terror, but against Islamist terrorism. A number of observers thus have questioned whether the phrase "war on terror" makes any sense. But there is a different interpretation: a war *on* terror might suggest the existence of a reality *sui generis* – the terror – that is the object of a "war," similar to the war on drugs, on poverty, or on cancer.[53] However, this analogy does not work. Apocalyptic war does not unfold as a one-sided series of terrorist actions that are met by autonomous exterior efforts to eradicate the problem. Rather, it is an *interactive* process.

The possibilities can be charted between two poles of apocalyptic war. At the *asymmetric* pole, there is a substantial imbalance of power. The central interaction occurs between a relatively small apocalyptic sect and the security forces of a far more powerful established social order. In this circumstance, beyond the initial sacred cause, the sect points to actions by the dominant social order to justify its own acts. In particular, when the established order responds with force, the sect points to this response to promote its claim among a wider countercultural audience to be the authentic vessel of God in a sacred struggle against the evil of the existing social order. For their parts, forces of the established order seek to contain and eliminate the group that claims an autonomous sacred right to engage in political violence, while the group itself seeks not only to achieve its strategic and symbolic goals, but by doing so, to enlarge the popular basis of its support and encourage likeminded people to rise up themselves.

By contrast, in *symmetric* apocalyptic war, both parties are able to assert roughly equivalent claims of legitimacy, typically operating out of different territorial strongholds. The very boundaries of state-like territorial monopolies on power are thus at stake in symmetric apocalyptic war. The struggle of the parties to apocalyptic war is centered on territory and social and political allegiances.

In the asymmetric situation, as my colleagues and I suggested in *Apocalypse Observed*, "States face a delicate situation: they are duty bound to control the acts of strategic apocalyptic war, but to the degree that they do so, they become apocalyptic actors themselves. The problem that states confront is how to act strategically without feeding images of the state as an actor in an apocalyptic drama."[54] All too easily, the established social order itself comes to define its struggle in apocalyptic terms, or its actions lead others to believe that it has joined such a struggle. In effect, the forces of the established social order risk lending legitimacy to the apocalyptic sect. This problem becomes all the more pronounced insofar as the struggle tends toward construction as a *symmetric* apocalyptic war, for in those circumstances, defenders of the established social order find themselves in a position remarkably similar to that of the apocalyptic insurgents. Each side becomes party to a crusade. The implications of this construction become evident if we recall Juergensmeyer's account of the prospects for those who undertake a cosmic war: just as for the insurgents, for the established order defeat is equally unthinkable, yet, conversely, the character of victory in any concrete historical sense is extremely difficult to define.

How, then, has al-Qaida's challenge been met in the West? There is a strong basis to argue that the agenda of the established order *itself* bore trappings of a holy war. Indeed, certain public figures and commentators suggested that Americans *ought* to see the conflict in these terms.[55] Thus, in the early days after September 11, there were echoes of German political theorist Carl Schmitt's friend/enemy distinction that legitimates total war in an apocalyptic vein. President George W. Bush drew a sharp symbolic and geopolitical line in the sand, implicating any individual or group associated with al-Qaida, or providing financial support – including nation-states giving safe harbor to its members – as a party to the larger struggle: "Every nation, in every region, now has a decision to make. Either you are with us, or you are with the terrorists. From this day forward, any nation that continues to harbor or support terrorism will be regarded by the United States as a hostile regime."[56]

Bush also characterized his announced War on Terror as a "crusade," and the Afghan military operation initially was named "Infinite Justice." The Bush administration quickly backed away from these narrative formulations, just as they later dissociated the U.S. government from remarks by then Major-General William Boykin, who appeared in combat fatigues in churches around the U.S., telling his audiences, "No mortal is the enemy. It's the enemy you can't see. It's a war against the forces of darkness." In the wake of driving the Taliban from power in Afghanistan, in January 2002 President George W. Bush also sought to define a more encompassing and coherent enemy than the liminal and difficult to defeat al-Qaida network. To do so, he designated an "axis of evil" that included states deemed to pose a threat to the hegemony of the prevailing global order – Iraq, Iran, and North Korea – even though these states were historically hostile to, or disconnected from, one another. Bush thus invoked an encompassing historical struggle between good and evil, the forces of light and the forces of darkness. Later, in 2005, his broader focus on the axis of evil broke down in the face of a disastrously orchestrated war in Iraq, and Bush used a speech at the National Endowment for Democracy to take aim again at al-Qaida: "In fact, we're not facing a set of grievances that can be soothed and addressed. We're facing a radical ideology with inalterable objectives: to enslave whole nations and intimidate the world." Yet in parts of the Muslim world, Bush's dismissal of al-Qaida's strategic goals overreached. An observer in Pakistan's *The Nation* suggested that Bush confused al-Qaida's tactics with its ideology of reestablishing the caliphate, which, the writer argued, is shared much more widely beyond al-Qaida, and amounts to "Islam's political default setting." Similarly, the American author who wrote under the name Anonymous, a man closely connected to U.S. corridors of power, argued that the United States erred by obscuring the strategic interests of al-Qaida in a smokescreen that dismissed its participants as mere ideologues with weapons.[57]

Likely, Bush's dismissal was strategic: he did not want to lend legitimacy to a non-state organization that carries out horrific acts of terrorism. Nevertheless, it is of a piece with how he framed an ideologically based crusade, especially to the Christian Right as an audience. Thus, historian of religions Bruce Lincoln has identified a "symmetric dualism" between Osama bin Laden and George Bush: "Both men constructed a Manichaean struggle, where Sons of Light confront Sons of Darkness." Neither envisioned any neutral ground. It is important to note that, despite some occasional awkward formulations about a crusade, Bush largely framed the struggle as good versus evil, civilization versus terror, decidedly not Christianity versus Islam. Even so, as Lincoln has shown, Bush was able to "assert the religious nature of the conflict in the same moment that he sought to deny it," by invoking coded significations that millenarian Christians would understand immediately, but most of his audience would miss.[58]

For all Bush's actions that helped define the conflict in apocalyptic terms, it would seem mistaken to focus solely on his individual faith and his connections with the Christian Right. Bush simply signaled his alliance with the millennial tradition in American religion that has long framed American history. Already in 1771, the young Yale College tutor Timothy Dwight could envision America's special role in relation to rest of the world during the end times:

> Through earth's wide realms thy glory shall extend,
> And savage nations at thy scepter bend ...
> Then, then an heavenly kingdom shall descend,
> And every region smile in endless peace;
> Til the last trump the slumbering dead inspire,
> Shake the wide heavens, and set the world on fire.[59]

This distinctly American millennialism carried forward to the nineteenth-century American doctrine of Manifest Destiny: "The word 'empire' – understood in the sense of the prophecies of the 'kingdoms' – was never an evil one to the militant millennialist. A race destined to 'out-populate' the decadent areas, to bring up the old nations, to end wars, could hardly be satisfied with embellishing its homeland."[60] From there, American historian Ernest Tuveson connected the millennialist doctrine directly to the messianic role of the United States in the two world wars and the Cold War.

The irony here is deep: in the 1960s, the Islamic theologian Sayyid Qutb asserted an equivalent scope of jihad. Broadly and positively conceived, the struggle he depicted exceeds mere concern for "defense" of Muslim lands. "Islam," he argued, "being the last divine path for humanity, has an essential right to establish its own system on earth so that all humanity can enjoy its blessings, while every individual enjoys the right to follow his own creed, for 'there is no compulsion in religion'."[61] Today, Islamic jihadists could easily find their counterparts in the U.S. "Pious nationalism," a theologian argued in 2005, continued to drive militant Christian-Right "religious revolutionary romanticists" whose vision nurtured pursuit of American empire.[62] For both neoconservatives in the Bush administration and the Christian Right, a holy war by whatever name replaced the Cold War against the "Evil Empire" (as Ronald Reagan called the Soviet Union), to become the transcendent meaning of history.[63]

In time, the U.S. government backed away from framing its post-9/11 agenda in apocalyptic terms (or sidestepped the question of agenda altogether). Yet the structure of the conflict itself eclipsed public formulations of American intentions. As events after 2001 demonstrated, the War on Terror, even if only implicitly and marginally a "holy war," framed the conflict in terms that mirrored those of al-Qaida and kindred networks. Insofar as rhetoric – and, especially, events on the ground – constructed the conflict in these terms, many people in the Islamic world came to view it as a *symmetric* one between two parties, each claiming good, righteousness, and God on its side, rather than a conflict between a global modern social order in which Muslims share a stake versus a fringe Islamist movement whose acts of terror are to be rejected as un-Islamic.[64]

Here, then, is the possibility of a "clash of civilizations" between the West and Islam that Samuel Huntington anticipated in the 1990s.[65] Huntington's account sometimes has been criticized as empirically incorrect. But empirical description is not the issue: the validity of Huntington's account hinges on the historically open question of whether a non-militant Islam open to engaging modernity and the West will prevail, or whether the forces of Islamic jihad are able to sustain the legitimacy of their struggle among wider publics of Muslims. In the campaign against Islamist jihad, the dilemma faced by the U.S. and its allies thus has been how to deal with warring sectarians without mobilizing *other* Muslims to their cause, and without destabilizing other governments – in Pakistan, the Philippines, Morocco, and Nigeria, for example – by engaging in military actions or establishing bases that, in the eyes of many Muslims, confirm the validity of Osama bin Laden's case against Western hegemony. The key question about any strategy adopted by the allies concerns whether its successes at decimating networks of cells associated with al-Qaida and the Taliban produce the unintended "blowback" consequence of broadening and deepening the pool of support for the apocalyptic warring cause. Unfortunately, military actions in Afghanistan, Iraq, Pakistan, and elsewhere have put the U.S. at risk of radicalizing Muslims in diverse social strata who might otherwise reject jihad.

The most contentious debates in the immediate wake of 9/11 centered on whether quasi-imperialist actions by the West, and specifically, the United States, had somehow "caused" the attacks.[66] But this formulation posed the wrong question. Rather, the issue is whether long-term policies of the West created conditions conducive to (or failed to undermine) a political and social climate in the Islamic world where jihad could gain such wide appeal. In its global extensions, the West has promoted two principles – capitalism and democracy – that sometimes could not be maximized simultaneously. In many situations, democracy has been compromised in favor of access to markets tied to regimes that lack political legitimacy among their populations. The consequences are unfortunate. When foreign powers prop up an authoritarian regime through military and economic aid, this support undermines the need for that regime to bargain with its constituents.[67] Obviously, jihadists do not embrace a Western vision of democracy. The point is this: lack of Western commitment to the construction of political and economic institutions that can claim broad legitimacy in states with large Muslim populations (and more generally) fosters conditions favorable to apocalyptic readings of history. Yet the West stands to lose a great deal if such readings become widespread. The Cold War played out for four decades in the absence of deep religious meanings. By comparison, apocalyptic war framed in strongly religious terms is potentially far more intractable. Crusades and jihad unfold in the *moyen durée*, not *le temps court*, of history.

By driving the Taliban from control of the state in Afghanistan, by targeting and eliminating al-Qaida operatives, and by working to increase security against terrorist actions in their own homelands, the allies initially dented the capacity of al-Qaida to operate effectively, and this accomplishment tends to undermine its claims of legitimacy. But to date, the allies have not contained jihad. Indeed, the Iraq war provided an opening for jihad where none had existed before. Moreover, periods of relative quiescence may not mean much. So long as a sect sustains ideological commitment, it can continue to conduct devastating operations even under extremely compromised conditions. The attacks of 9/11 were undertaken by a small number of operatives, nineteen men directly. The cost of the attacks, variously estimated at less than $500,000, is minuscule compared to the resources estimated to be at the disposal of militant Islamist organizations.[68]

There might be some grounds for thinking that a charismatic movement would either become routinized or fade away, once subsequent historical events eclipsed its dramatic moment. However, as revolutionary movements in the twentieth century demonstrated, the apocalyptic trajectory can take years, even decades, to play out. The warring sect does not necessarily pursue an unfolding sequential series of actions in a concerted campaign, but instead seeks to mount effective actions at strategic moments that have a cumulative effect. In 2005, historian Niall Ferguson maintained, "we all know that another, bigger September 11 is quite likely; it is, indeed, bin Laden's stated objective."[69] Yet the season of dramatic single attacks like 9/11 may have passed for the moment. By the time of his first address to Congress in February 2009, President Barack Obama had committed his administration to withdrawing the bulk of U.S. troops from Iraq by mid-2010. But he also planned to increase U.S. troop levels in Afghanistan by 17,000, to around 53,000, and he promised a "new and comprehensive strategy for Afghanistan and Pakistan to defeat al-Qaida and combat extremism."[70] Thus, the U.S. and its allies were spread across strategic and military theaters from the homeland to Iraq, Afghanistan, and Pakistan. In Lebanon, the Iranian-backed Shi'a Islamic Hezbollah had moved to consolidate its position as a legitimate political participant. The Israeli–Palestinian struggle remained unresolved. And Iran continued to loom as a potential threat to Western interests. Under such circumstances, Islamists might reasonably conclude that compared with pursuit of other strategies, immediate dramatic terrorist actions of the 9/11 type would add no strategic or symbolic advantage.

On the other side, apocalyptic war can hardly be a palatable project for the U.S. and its allies. Ferguson has noted that Osama bin Laden made a sly claim to have achieved a certain kind of victory over the U.S. administration only because the White House pursued a strategy involving "opening of war fronts to keep busy their various corporations. ..." As Ferguson observed, bin Laden was here using the language of Lenin. He continued, "bin Laden has been getting help in 'bleeding America to the point of bankruptcy' from the Bush administration's fiscal policy."[71] It is this strategy that jihadi websites in 2008 asserted to be "the principle cause of the collapse of the economic giant."[72] In terms of the present analysis, bin Laden positioned apocalyptic struggle not as terrorism but as a total war on the institutions of the Empire of Modernity.

The mobilization initiated by the United States and its allies against militant Islamist networks has been enormous. Yet military and diplomatic strategies – the crux of empire in modern theories – may not bring success against an apocalyptically oriented opponent. The warring sect's ideology of revolutionary martyrdom, its organizational decentralization, and its countercultural support make defeating radical Islam through use of military force and geopolitical strategies extremely difficult, so difficult as to have led strategic planners to question whether this goal is an adequate basis for responding to al-Qaida. The War on Terror fundamentally mischaracterized the challenge facing the Western allies.

Policing modernity's empire

We thus face the question of how power operates in the contemporary world, and, specifically, how power centered in regimes of bureaucratic administration strategically counters apocalyptic war. As I have argued, diachronic temporality predominates in the organizing projects that institutionalize modernity, but any contemporary established social order necessarily operates from diachrony outward, across multiple and intersecting temporal horizons. The (incomplete) power of diachronic modernity is implemented in part through efforts at the colonization of the lifeworld, through orchestration of the conditions under which national, religious, and other communities organize, by attempting to delimit and control religious and other (therapeutic, recreational) access to the transcendental, and by containing the apocalyptic.

Perhaps the greatest challenge for the modernizing enterprise is how to harness and regulate channels of the social that operate in strategic temporalities of action and build upon one another in history. On the one hand, the possibility of modernity has been predicated upon war and the building of colonial empires –

enterprises centered in strategic temporality that "make" history. Moreover, the dynamism of modernity depends on economic, legal, and political forms of conflict and competition that operate in relatively pacified frames of strategic temporality. Functionally, regulated strategic temporality in markets, law, and political processes is essential to the complex formation of modernity. Yet compared to social action centered in other temporal constructions, strategic temporality is inherently more volatile. Thus, despite all the ideological promotion of the *laissez-faire* operation of the free market, unregulated economic activity has demonstrated its potential to be disastrously destabilizing. It is due to such circumstances that there are modernizing institutions centrally concerned with orchestrating the peaceful transfer of political power within nation-states, and that business interests even from the early twentieth century frequently have called upon private, state, international, and other entities to regulate economic competition. Even more problematic for modernity is interstate war, which may serve the interests of a nation-state's historical destiny and even benefit certain industries and overall economic development, but which nevertheless threatens to overturn the ever precarious achievements of modern society.

Modern state containment altered war's status. Its change was evocatively signaled by the 1949 U.S. terminological relocation of military organization from the Department of War to the Department of Defense. Whereas "war" was occasional and largely strategic, "defense" is a permanent activity, orchestrated through diachronic management of diverse enterprises, a number of them not directly oriented to military conflict. With the emergence of what in the 1950s U.S. President Dwight Eisenhower described as the "military-industrial complex," war changed. To tweak Carl von Clausewitz's formulation, it became the game-theoretic extension of administration by other means.

Bureaucracy and war are at odds with each other as bases of action, for war, like politics, depends on leadership and the formulation and execution of strategy, both of which are alien to the bureaucratic mentality. "Defense" thus uncomfortably brings more bureaucratic military planning, logistics of recruitment and training, procurement, supply, and service into relationship with operations of fighting units. This already awkward relationship is further challenged by guerrilla warfare in general and even more so by apocalyptic conflict, where diachrony confronts not only the volatility of strategic temporality but also the sacred quest for eternity on the part of the warring sect.

The overall strategy of the U.S. and its allies in the conflict with radical Islam certainly includes a strong military component, but it cannot adequately be construed as "war." Indeed, the characterization that the Bush administration adopted was at odds with the Peace of Westphalia, which from 1648 presumed war as either civil war or war between nation-states, a formulation both reinforced and altered by Carl Schmitt's conceptualization of total war, still between sovereigns. In both Westphalian and Schmittian terms, a war cannot involve an external non-state entity.

In reflections after 9/11, social theorist Jürgen Habermas connected Schmitt's doctrine to the totalitarianism of the twentieth century, arguing that it in effect had been repudiated by post-World War II international judicial proceedings that held nation-states and their operatives accountable for crimes of war. A contradiction noted by philosopher Jacques Derrida thus calls for resolution: George W. Bush clearly invoked a Schmitt-esque friend–enemy distinction that legitimates total war, but the U.S. and its allies confront an enemy amorphous at best, which lacks state sovereignty and is not contesting civil control of territory within a single state, and thus falls outside Schmittian definitions.[73] Bush is no Derrida, and so he may have missed this point. However, there is an alternative possibility, that despite the optimism of Habermas's account, total war now has become relocated, as the prerogative of the super-sovereign Empire of Modernity, undertaken through the leadership of its military hegemon (today, the U.S.), no longer only against ("rogue") nation-states, but, potentially, against the external Other that exists beyond the social boundaries of empire and its mappings of territorial sovereignty.

Not surprisingly, in the climate of ambiguity about whether the U.S. was at war against a non-state entity, the U.S. came into confrontation with its own constitution and with other Western nation-states over a series of legal issues that fall outside modern U.S. and international regulation of warfare – issues concerning "extraordinary rendition" of captives to states where torture is routinely used as an interrogation technique, the use of Chinese communist interrogation techniques at the U.S. prison in Guantánamo, Cuba, the legal classification and treatment of "non-state combatants," the abuse of prisoners at Abu Ghraib prison in Iraq, suspension of habeas corpus both for American citizens taken as prisoners in counterterrorism operations and, more generally, for non-state combatants held in U.S. prisons, including at Guantánamo.[74]

The legal issues are profound, and disturbing to constitutional government. To the degree that these issues emerge because of confusion generated by the Bush formulation of a War on Terror, it will be useful to retheorize that conflict in order to clarify its character. My argument, simply stated, is that the contemporary conflict against militant Islamism is best understood as a project of "policing," when policing is understood to take place in relation to the Empire of Modernity that has emerged with globalization over the last several decades. Geopolitical theorist Martin Coward has provided the intellectual framework for this argument. Proceeding from the analysis by Michael Hardt and Antonio Negri, he understands empire as a regime along the lines depicted by Michel Foucault in his poststructuralist concept of "governmentality," concerned with the diffuse operation of power in relation to individuals who are no longer simply political subjects, but bodies governed in time and space.

In the Empire of Modernity, a new ethos of "security" transcends any merely political definition. The challenge it faces is how to counter threats to the administratively defined order from any quarter. With national sovereignty increasingly enmeshed within a broader web of sub- and super-national projects of governance, empire is no longer centered in a nation-state and its territorial dependents. Rather, the Empire of Modernity constitutes something like the overall field in which liberal governance of the social operates. It is the field of the fully diffused diachronic that operates both within and across domains of state sovereignty. Modernity's empire reaches around the globe. However, it has boundaries both geographic and social. The most basic one divides barbarian zones where the Other refuses to accord legitimacy to empire, versus what Coward calls empire's "zone of pacific civility." Internally, policing organizes the social order both within nation-states and on an increasingly global basis. But empire must also be defined at its boundaries. Thus, a second kind of policing occurs at liminal and contested zones where empire finds "its universality and civility questioned" by "barbarian others." Insofar as the Empire of Modernity is directly challenged, it can only be sustained through violence, but blood is only shed to achieve peace. Rather than pursuing military victory, the Empire of Modernity deploys policing strategies that define the otherness of its enemies and their location in "zones of incivility." On this basis, Coward argues, it is possible to maintain "the fiction of the universal civility of Empire by excluding the alterity that might expose such a fiction."[75]

In the conflict between the U.S. and its allies and radical Islam, this dual policing strategy operates on multiple fronts. At the core of the strategy is a combination of police-like work to apprehend network participants and interrogate them. On the basis of a secret 2004 U.S. Government order authorizing attacks against al-Qaida in Syria, Pakistan, and other countries, its forces use this intelligence on a quasi-military basis to hunt down additional operatives, capturing them if possible, but targeting them for remote assassination (e.g., by a tactic reaffirmed by the Obama administration, of using unmanned missile-firing Predator aircraft) if direct capture is deemed unfeasible.[76] However, many tactics lie relatively distant from any direct conflict with radical Islamists – tightening security, controlling immigration, cutting off flows of financing, and aggressively gathering and filtering intelligence. Beyond these relatively conventional tactics lie the more diffuse (post)modern Foucauldian policing practices of governmentality aimed at the biopolitics of organizing and disciplining people in lifeworldly space – that is, both elite "nation-building" efforts toward the consolidation of national politics in Afghanistan and Iraq, and strategies of governance that regulate and facilitate everyday life through state and NGO development projects. Whether it is possible to defeat Islamist warring sects through surveillance, combat, policing operations, and efforts to eliminate the financial resources of their networks remains an open question. How to attain a longer-term goal – of discrediting terrorism – remains underspecified.[77]

Just as certainly as the Empire of Modernity is best served by seeking to defeat the apocalypse through governmentality, its Islamist opponents see governmentality as a key target. We only need to note the strategies of al-Qaida operatives and their allies generally, and the insurgents in Afghanistan, Iraq, and Pakistan specifically, to understand this point. In a conventional war, attacking aid workers, journalists, representatives of NGOs, and tourists would amount to senseless and barbarian violence and a clear violation of the Fourth Geneva Accord concerning treatment of noncombatants. Certainly this is the incontrovertible view within the established social order. But the Islamist war against the Empire of Modernity challenges governmentality in all its forms, military and otherwise, manifestly in the destruction of the World Trade Center, but also in actions against the postmodern simulacratic world as a tourist destination, generalized source of entertainment, and domain available for colonization by Western culture – from Christian missions to NGOs and universities, to McDonald's.[78]

Under these conditions, especially to the degree that the contemporary conflict approximates a symmetric apocalyptic war in which each side mounts its own claim to the legitimate exercise of violence, the tidy formula of policing modernity's empire comes under pressure. The very boundaries of an empire's state-like monopoly on legitimate violence are thus at stake in symmetric apocalyptic war. In Coward's terms, to attempt a decisive war against the Other is to "risk exposing the universality of imperial rule as a fiction."[79] This precept perhaps sheds some light on the Bush administration's early and continued reluctance to pursue al-Qaida into the tribal regions of the Northwest Territories of Pakistan, despite strong evidence of this as the location of its redoubt. Only in 2008, when Taliban power grew and terrorist actions planned and initiated from within Pakistan accelerated, did the U.S. reverse course, yielding what on the ground sometimes looked very much like a war.[80] The stability and legitimacy of the Pakistani regime are thus opened to doubt, as Coward would anticipate.

Soon after 9/11, one commander in the Hezbul Mujahadeen, Kiramat Ullah, was quoted as saying, "we would be very happy if America attacked Afghanistan, because now all Muslims are divided. If America attacked, it would unite the Muslim world."[81] Like most utopian visions, the goal of a united Islam has the quality of a fantasy. Although the allies fulfilled the apocalyptic wish for a counterattack in Afghanistan, it did not unite the Muslim world. The subsequent 2003 U.S.-led invasion of Iraq and decimation of Saddam Hussein's Baathist regime brought to the surface previously contained crosscutting Iraqi political cleavages – Sunni against Shi'a, Islamist versus non-militant, religious opposed to secular. But over and above these consequences, the geopolitical agenda pursued by the U.S. and its allies further radicalized and mobilized segments of the Muslim population already predisposed toward apocalyptic views.[82] Certainly with the 2003 invasion of Iraq, events reinforced their views. The U.S. strategy, in one 2002 private intelligence assessment, was heavily weighted toward unrelenting gathering of intelligence and overwhelming use of force. The calculation at the time must have been that the U.S. did not need to bother to worry about whether its actions might legitimate the Islamist view that the U.S. is a "crusader" state. In this calculation, overwhelming military force was supposed to "render perception immaterial."[83]

For the West, an Orwellian prospect is unveiled by symmetric apocalyptic conflict: jihad and the "war" against it fuel one another in ways that erode civil liberties within the Empire of Modernity and consolidate an international security state and an increasingly integrated and internationalized apparatus of surveillance. Globally, Empire's struggle against Islamist militants brings to the fore a militarized network of international relationships rather than fostering conditions for pursuit of any positive agenda directed toward political stability, social and economic development, and dealing with pressing global problems of poverty, disease, ecological degradation, and global economic crisis. To the extent that the U.S. established the struggle against terrorism as the dominant axis of international relations, states and NGOs became subject to goal displacement away from any agenda of addressing serious world problems. In all this, the social fabric of the Empire of Modernity is substantially, and no doubt permanently, altered, and to what end?

An apocalyptic "war" can only be won, if at all, with ruthless brutality and relentless pursuit, which tend to reinforce the apocalyptic mentality; even victory would produce memories for the seedbed of a future apocalyptic moment.[84] All-out efforts to win such a war more likely fuel it, whereas countering jihad centrally requires undermining rather than enhancing its utopian appeal to wider Muslim audiences. Reversing the radicalization of substantial numbers of Muslims is more likely to result from fundamental policy shifts toward the Middle East and Islam, and not simply by pursuing the elusive goal of political stabilization in Afghanistan, Iraq, and Pakistan.

An apocalyptic analysis suggests that the Empire of Modernity faces a different but similarly formidable task. The challenge posed by al-Qaida and its allies must be redefined both for the *realpolitik* of power circumstances and material interests within the Empire of Modernity and for those who embrace the Enlightenment vision (if not its spotty record of actualization to date). The challenge is not how to "win" an apocalyptic war. Military and diplomatic strategies – the bases of the empire-building state in modern theories – may not bring success against an apocalyptically oriented opponent. The established social order is strategically better served by forsaking a struggle in apocalyptic time, and thus breaking the cycle of violence in which apocalyptic warriors point toward attacks by the U.S. as vindication of the righteousness of their own cause. For the Empire of Modernity, the challenge is to act outside of, and thus move the historical moment *beyond*, the time of apocalyptic war, by undermining the plausibility structures of apocalypse – precisely in the regions where the reach of modernity's empire is particularly problematic. How to do so is a central world-historical challenge at the beginning of the twenty-first century.

Contemporary Muslim societies also face basic alternatives, either finding ways to accommodate Islam to non-Islamic institutions, or reasserting Islam as the crucible that will envelop the social order, including its modernized features. The Empire of Modernity is not in a position to force that choice. But sentiments in the Muslim world will be affected by Western policies – from strategies of fighting terrorism, to dealing with the Palestinian–Israeli debacle, to war with Iraq, to political alliances with client regimes, to repression versus grudging acceptance of Islamic parties in politics. The question, starkly posed by Michael Ignatieff, is whether, in the Muslim world, the United States will look like Louis XVI looked in France in 1789.[85]

Conclusion

All significant war is "apocalyptic" in the broad sense that it involves strategic action in historical time directed toward ending a traumatic crisis through victory. But apocalyptic religion imbues conflict with sacred meaning and a quest for world-historical transcendence. An apocalyptic holy war differs from conventional war in its organization, in the relation of its cadre to a broader population of supporters, and in the difficulty for an established social order of achieving victory in the apocalyptic time of war. The stakes of apocalyptic war grow dramatically when an established order becomes a symmetric participant in conflict with apocalyptically oriented opponents, as did the administration of U.S. President George W. Bush.

Histories of our era will be written and rewritten from different future times and vantage points. Just as historians in the British tradition sometimes have struck "balance sheets" weighing the positive accomplishments versus the terrible human costs of British colonialism, future historians will be asking whether Bush's War on Terror accomplished any good that could outweigh its cost – in human lives, in the alienation of Muslims from the world order, in the fraying of relationships among Western allies, in the decline of American moral authority around the globe, in its consequences for the U.S. society and economy.[86] In this chapter, I have approached the problem of historical assessment in a different way, by following phenomenological philosopher Maurice Merleau-Ponty's argument that historical actors themselves strike the balance sheets of history.[87]

As Merleau-Ponty saw in communism and its adversaries, we must recognize in current geopolitical struggles that there are multiple sources of sacred violence – coming from radical Islamists, but also from the West, especially the United States. And like Merleau-Ponty, we must recognize that whether any of this violence is "progressive" is an historically open question, not one that can be answered simply by referencing transcendent values of Western liberalism or any putative "essential" violent character of Islam.

Let us revisit Merleau-Ponty's concern with the relation between violence and history. Historical violence, Merleau-Ponty held, is inescapable unless we reach the "end of history," which remains, at this juncture, only a fantastic possibility. We will not reach the end of history – or of violence – any time soon. The question is whether violence in history will be justified by meaning, direction, purpose. In Merleau-Ponty's terms, with 9/11 we entered a new "epoch" – according to his definition, a period of violence with distinctive and significant historical stakes. In this epoch, with its clashes between groups embracing opposing ideologies, any ultimate "meaning" of the violence from both sides remains undefined, awaiting the "objective" moment when victory and the return to (a different) normalcy will define "truth." History, its agents and witnesses, and their failures and successes will answer questions about the meaning of 9/11, Islamic jihad, and the Empire of Modernity's policing of terror. The question is, how? Will violence turn out to have been "progressive" in its consequences for the advancement of (one or another ideologically defined form of) Reason in history, or merely "self-serving"? Only by limiting violence to the pursuit of a transcendent purpose, or Reason, Merleau-Ponty argued, can we avoid a grim dystopian world of adventurism and a "senseless tumult," or what might amount to "the new dark ages."

7

The Last Apocalypse?

The apocalypse of the twenty-first century, like other decisive epochs, is yielding a transformed world. Yet *how* social formations and their geopolitics become reconfigured is a matter still in play. In the present book, I have explored how the apocalyptic has been shaped, contained, rechanneled, and reasserted in relation to modernity, and, conversely, how modernity has been affected by apocalyptic epochs. This analysis shows that when an apocalyptic epoch is world-historical in its import (as with the Protestant Reformation), institutional transformations of nation-states and the world order can be deep, substantial, and irreversible. How, then, might we understand the fate and character of contemporary society and our future prospects in light of the apocalyptic? Is it possible to transcend the apocalypse? What is our fate? These questions take us beyond history, and they have no definitive answer, but we can at least consider them. I will first reflect on the significance of apocalyptic narratives in general, and then retrace my historical analysis of the apocalyptic in relation to the West. In turn, I will follow the implications of this configurational history, first, for formulating a revisionist account of modernity, and then in relation to challenges of the apocalyptic in the future.

Apocalypse as narrative

Apocalyptic time, I have argued, is an extreme form of historically contingent temporality, in the most general terms, oriented toward a decisive end that is held to inaugurate a theoretically timeless tableau of heaven. One way or another, the apocalyptic brings the sacred into conjuncture with history. However, the apocalypse has no single story, unless God finally unveils the answer to the puzzle of the ultimate end. Multiple historical sources collectively yield an expanding field of narrative possibilities. The many texts created over the centuries are open to interpretation by one or another prophet who (again!) finally comes forward in the last days to reveal what was previously hidden. Prophetic narratives, when brought into the vivid present, can become framed within specific temporal structures of apocalyptic action. Some people who hear a prophetic story will find it compelling. Living at the end of history, they will feel a special sense of their own destiny, to have been chosen to take part in the decisive events whereby the ultimate meaning of human existence is to be resolved by the events that unfold.

The occasion of prophecy is open, and open-ended in its meaningful construction of "the times." A given narrative in the apocalyptic genre may locate "the end" at a fixed point in objective time, or key it to the coming of specified human or divine actions. In one story, the meek and the poor in spirit will pass through the wrenching crisis that marks history's end, to gain redemption in a post-apocalyptic world. Under such a reading, life is lived as an act of pre-apocalyptic preparation for "the end." However, preparation, based as it is on prophecy, can take diverse forms. Believers may simply repent, live piously, and spread the word, converting others before the day of God's judgment. But it is also possible that prophecy will call for believers to engage in action to end an era of corruption, injustice, and evil, even to undertake a "holy war" to bring on the new era. Alternatively, those who follow prophecy may seek to "escape" the apocalypse to a post-apocalyptic world, either eternal, or on earth, where they are to survive and repopulate the world with God's chosen people, who will manifest God's will to create the new Zion themselves, after the plan that has been revealed.[1]

No matter what the open-ended possibilities of the apocalyptic as a genre, any actual apocalyptic narrative will be specific in its invocations. In turn, any apocalyptic narrative that emerges at one point in historical time may have consequences – both in actual events and in subsequent constructions of historical memories – that delimit or encourage the development of later apocalyptic ideas along one line rather than another. The apocalyptic arises under conditions that are, as social scientists like to say, path-dependent. Since their ancient origins, the horizons of generic apocalyptic narrative possibilities have widened over historical time, historical moments with their challenges and opportunities have shaped apocalyptic possibilities, and the genre and its elements have diffused (or, in some cases, independently developed) until, today, apocalyptic narratives are available to invoke anywhere, around the globe.

It would be reductionist to suggest that the apocalyptic is some sort of *Geist* or spirit – the driving force of a universal history. Instead, I have used a temporalized historical phenomenology to illuminate important axes of social development. The apocalypse is not a universal omnipresent reality or "thing" any more than is the diachronic. Rather, we have found, the apocalyptic encompasses forms of temporal enactment that, when and where they arise, envelop the meaningful lives of some, or, occasionally, great numbers of, people. Yet we would be mistaken to treat apocalyptic phenomena as imaginary or unreal. They have the same ontological status as other socially constructed realities, in that individuals in concert with one another can act meaningfully in relation to them. Thus, apocalyptic social realities can be considered in empirical terms in just the same way as "bureaucracy" and "community."

The apocalyptic cannot simply be relegated to treatment as a "variable" that is "caused by" or "explains" (or fails to explain) other social phenomena – economic development, war, family structures, and so on. Rather, sometimes, radically alternative forms of social enactment are constituted through apocalyptic narratives, narratives that inherently traffic in *de facto* sacred questions of ultimate meaning. People make sense of their circumstances in various ways, and how people do so can be consequential for how events unfold. These sorts of relations between ideas, interests, and situation have been evocatively described by Max Weber in his famous railroad metaphor. After acknowledging that "material and ideal interests" govern conduct, Weber continued, "Yet very frequently the 'world images' that have been created by 'ideas' have, like switchmen, determined the tracks along which action has been pushed by the dynamic of interest. 'From what' and 'for what' one wished to be redeemed and, let us not forget, 'could be' redeemed, depended upon one's image of the world."[2] Meaningful temporalities of enactment – apocalyptic ones among them – do not "cause" action: they set the alternative tracks of meaning along which action unfolds.

The apocalyptic and Western historical development

The present study has traced one genealogy – centrally focused on apocalyptic conjunctures with emergent modernity in the West. Given the protean character of the apocalyptic and the manifold historical moments when apocalyptic developments have occurred, other relevant genealogies could have been followed. I could have gone much more deeply into the history of Islamic jihad and followed Jewish traditions that included such figures as the sixteenth-century self-proclaimed messiah, Sabbatai Sevi. Outside the monotheistic world, it would be possible to explore apocalyptic strands in Buddhism and elsewhere. My more delimited interest has been to provide a configurational history that identifies key historical shifts of modernity's development, aligned along the axis of the apocalyptic.

The apocalyptic emerged in the ancient world, a world where "history" as we variously understand it had not yet become a generalized form of social self-understanding. Before the rise of the ancient kingdoms and empires, a philosophical archeology suggests, life was basically experienced in the here-and-now, tempered by collectively orchestrated rituals that ordered life and shaped experience of the transcendent. Beyond the here-and-now and the rituals that encompassed it lay the awe of eternity. With the emergence of kingdoms and empires came history as the succession of wars and conquests. However, ancient accounts tended to reframe historical events in relation to eternal structures of myth. With the rise of empires, the content of the eternal shifted in scope, but the synchronic time of the immediate present continued to organize different but connected experiences – of the immediate *Umwelt* that people directly experience; of the world as socially communed in relation to myth and the sacred; and of the transcendent horizon of the eternal "now" beyond any social construction. Historically, over the last four millennia, other social temporalities built out from, enveloped, and shifted the organization of the synchronic. But the basic possibilities of synchronic temporality remain in place today, and in some regions of the world, they predominate.

The rise of the apocalyptic traces to ancient Zoroastrianism, and to the great monotheistic religions – Judaism, Christianity, and Islam. Zoroastrianism, with its imagery of a battle between the Lord of Wisdom and the god of falsehood and disorder, anticipated an ultimate victory of truth and light. The ancient Israelites developed a sense of historical destiny as Yahweh's chosen people, who, when challenged by subjugation under alien powers, formulated prophetic hopes for a dramatic reversal of collective fortune. How might this occur? Zealots sought to achieve military victory over the oppressors in the name of Yahweh; communal groups such as the Essenes endeavored to fulfill the Covenant with Yahweh in their daily way of life while quietly waiting for history to take its toll on the forces of darkness; many anticipated the coming of a redemptive messiah. Christians came to believe that Jesus was that messiah. However, with the suppression of the Jerusalem Church dominated by Jews, Christian theology pushed in two sometimes intertwined directions – toward personal transcendence of history by connection to eternal salvation, potentially for all humankind, or toward alternative formulations of how and when the apocalypse would yield redemption of the faithful at the end of history. In turn, despite many continuities among the monotheistic traditions, what we may call Islamic apocalyptic emerged independently of specifically Jewish or Christian antecedents, as triumphalist holy war meant to bring ever more territory under theocratic rule committed to the fulfillment of Allah's purposes. Overall, with the formation of the three great monotheistic religions – Judaism, Christianity, and Islam – protean narrative possibilities of the apocalyptic yielded new ideas about the character of history. In turn, in what would become the West, in the second millennium CE, historical and apocalyptic dynamics increasingly transpired in the context of emerging modern diachronic temporalities and the rationalized logics of action that accompany them.

The apocalyptic developed on various fronts. Five configurational shifts are notable. First, beginning in the eleventh century, the Roman Church gained sufficient organizational capacity to begin a centuries-long apocalyptic triumphalist movement to establish the predominance of Christendom in relation to those whom it defined as Other – both externally via the Crusades against Muslim infidels, and internally against "heresy" through regional crusades, the Inquisition, and religious pacification and conversion.

Second, in a social climate riven by hardship and calamity, the Crusades spread an ethos of apocalyptic fervor among the popular classes. This fervor became erratically mobilized via long-standing heterodoxical tendencies and Christian theological discourses that began to consolidate a generalized medieval template of the apocalyptic social movement. The most revolutionary of such movements promised an end to exploitation of the poor by landowners and the church, and they fed the flames of peasant rebellions and small-scale holy wars, which feudal powers allied with the church duly suppressed.

The third configurational shift, during the Reformation, emerged when some secular authorities cast their lot with religious reform movements, in part to forestall the success of even more radical apocalyptic movements. There were dual consequences. On the one hand, national Reformation movements themselves often took on an apocalyptic aura, as a struggle against Rome as "the Beast." On the other hand, in Catholic as well as Protestant countries, the state took over the previously religious function of regulating religious legitimacy within its borders, thereby largely containing, pacifying, and ultimately undermining the apocalyptic within societies increasingly oriented toward "modernizing" personal discipline and social order. The eventual exception in the West was the United States, where millennialism continued to flourish under modernizing conditions.

Fourth, in the wake of modernizing containment and pacification, the motifs of apocalyptic war became relocated from the lineages of religious apocalyptic, and into the sphere of secular politics – in particular, quasi-sacred nationalist, anticolonial, and anticapitalist movements. The most significant development was the fusion of apocalyptic war with diachronic discipline, strategic temporality, and technologies of modern warfare, yielding apocalyptic insurgent strategies ranging from anarchists' terrorist "propaganda of the deed" to guerrilla warfare.

Fifth, the collapse of the Soviet Union meant the eclipse of communism as a global secular-apocalyptic movement, and the end of its support for anticapitalist nationalist struggles, especially in underdeveloped and developing countries. Modernity had raised the secular apocalyptic to a global level. However, the ascendancy of modernizing projects had not brought the death of God and the end of religion, least of all in apocalyptic domains. Instead, at the end of the twentieth century, al-Qaida and its allies shifted Islamic jihad from nationalist struggles against the "nearest enemy" to a global struggle against the "far enemy," embodied in the United States. In turn, the Bush administration took the occasion of the 9/11 attacks to launch a multipronged countermovement against a so-called "axis of evil." Apocalyptic war unfolded in a symmetric if not always explicit fashion, and it came to occupy the ideological space previously taken up by the secular yet apocalyptic Cold War.

The apocalyptic introjection of the sacred into history originated before modernity, but the apocalyptic became modern, and now, modernity has become apocalyptic. Although sometimes unmitigated disasters (Hurricane Katrina, for example) are colloquially deemed "apocalyptic," and sometimes apocalyptic episodes may be triggered by economic or social traumas, the ones that I have traced in this book center on an opposition between a typically superordinate administratively organized power versus a people deemed either to be Other or God's chosen ones, depending on vantage point. The people or the power, or both, may cast their struggle in apocalyptic terms – as triumphant war against the godless Other, an encounter with a dangerous and powerful Antichrist, a plan to bring on apocalyptic crisis, or an effort to survive it and make way for the new age. In apocalyptic enactments, either the power or the people construe themselves as the vehicle of historical destiny that bears a sacred purpose.

From the times of Zarathustra's followers onward, a persistent thread runs through to the modern world: empire is either a sacred cause that must triumph in the name of God, or it is Antichrist, to be endured, escaped, or resisted. Who "the people" are and on what basis their status-group solidarity is organized are historically open and emergent possibilities. The outcomes of epochs when the apocalyptic becomes the central axis of history are similarly contingent and open. But apocalyptic confrontations have their consequences – even when the reverberations are relatively contained, as with the 1978 murders and mass suicide at Jonestown, Guyana, and certainly when they rise to the level of serious confrontations over political power and its limits, as in the Puritan Revolution.

The diverse strands of the present analysis suggest that the relationship between the apocalyptic and modernity is neither constant nor evolutionary. Rather, stepwise historical developments along multiple fronts – religious, geopolitical, social organizational – come into conjuncture or dialectical opposition with one another, yielding manifold novel ways that the apocalyptic and modernity intersect. Governmentality operates to contain the religious apocalyptic, but secular states and insurgent movements harness the apocalyptic to their own purposes. Militant apocalyptic movements, with the English Revolution and the Terror of the French Revolution as templates, draw the apocalyptic away from purely messianic and magical motifs of divine transformation, and into ever more chilling engagement with modernizing social organization and technological possibilities, brought to bear in strategic time. Today, in this kind of climate, fraught with potential for historical crisis, millennialism diffuses into popular culture with supercharged energy, not only in pop religious novels such as *Left Behind* and a whole range of popular movies like *28 Weeks Later* and *Southland Tales*, but also in mainstream dystopian post-apocalyptic novels such as Cormac McCarthy's *The Road* and Jim Crace's *The Pesthouse*.[3]

The differences from non-fictional analyses are not so substantial. Michael Ignatieff describes a possible worst-case scenario of defeat by terrorists.

> It would not be like invasion, conquest, or occupation, of course, but rather would entail the disintegration of our institutions and way of life. A succession of mass casualty attacks, using weapons of mass destruction, would leave behind zones of devastation sealed off for years and a pall of mourning, anger, and fear hanging over our public and private lives. … We might find ourselves living within a national security state on permanent alert, with sealed borders, constant identity checks, and permanent detention camps for suspicious aliens and recalcitrant citizens.[4]

Thus, even scholars and politicians give serious consideration to what life might be like if the modern social order were to unravel.

The end of history and the retheorization of modernity

After 9/11, Francis Fukuyama's affirmation of the eventual "end of history" in the triumph of Western market neoliberalism inevitably came to be seen as both ideologically narrow and wildly naïve. Certainly he had been mistaken to write off the significance of Islam. However, 9/11 did not cancel Fukuyama's end of history in the superficial way that much criticism has supposed. After all, in *The End of History and the Last Man*, Fukuyama emphasized that he did not anticipate the end of historical events, or, in the near term, the final triumph of market neoliberalism. Rather, democratic market capitalism lacked any credible utopian alternative. It was on the upswing, and it would triumph … in the long run.[5] To put this scenario in Maurice Merleau-Ponty's terms, violence would no longer rise to the level of history, and it would be managed through government. Such a world could be envisioned in a dystopian version as a sort of Foucauldian triumph of governmentality, or, more optimistically, in a Habermasian world. In the latter model, conflicts would be resolved through dialogue and negotiation in the public sphere, or by following administrative or juridical procedures, rather than by violence.

The end of history anticipated by Fukuyama may be taken as either utopian or dystopian, but it is not radically at odds with theories about the directions of emergent social order that were advanced in the twentieth century. However, granting the subtlety of Fukuyama's account leads to a deeper critique. 9/11 brought an end to history, but not the end that Fukuyama anticipated. It ended the viability of modern *historical accounts* of history, including Fukuyama's universal history, for it exposed – yet again – the inadequacy of the model of historical time on which most conventional modern history – including Fukuyama's metanarrative – is based: the modern objective (typically linear, sometimes dialectical) model of historical time that produces either a whiggish or a radical teleological metanarrative of modernity's triumphal development in the face of setbacks. Equally, 9/11 ended the postmodern fragmentation of history into pieces: suddenly, unfolding events became anything but fragmented. They became globally interconnected.

The cancellations of both modern and postmodern models of history will not end the production of modern or postmodern historical *accounts*, any more than Fukuyama's end of history put to an end the unfolding of events. However, if history is neither linear nor fragmented, how then might we construe it?

One fruitful approach is to retheorize modernity as a set of relations between diachronic and other, not particularly modern, social phenomena. This approach can be pursued by shifting from holistic linear theories to a more modest approach. Late in the eighteenth century, Immanuel Kant wanted to write a universal history, but he struggled with a basic modern recognition (later embraced as postmodern), that it is impossible to represent the world as such. The alternative that he embraced was to represent the world from a particular vantage point, in relation to values that he specified.[6] In the present study, I have followed a neo-kantian strategy by exploring what history comes into view when we focus on the apocalyptic in relation to the emergence of Western modernity. The core logic of this approach, based on recognition of multiple temporalities, in turn offers a way to theorize complex hybrid formations of modernity while avoiding the totalizing strategies fashionable in nineteenth- and twentieth-century social theories.

S. N. Eisenstadt has moved toward retheorizing modernity by advancing the thesis of "multiple modernities," thus acknowledging that there is no single *telos* of modernity. Even in an ever more globalized world, European societies may move in certain directions, Asian countries in other directions, and so on. Eisenstadt's thesis disabuses us of the ideological notion that even a globally integrated world society would tend toward any single modern pattern. But his analysis is also important because it raises the next questions – how are the various social formations through which modernity operates structured, in themselves and in relation to each other? How might we conceive of the overall field of the social that I have described as the increasingly globalized Empire of Modernity?

The temporal structures of modernity

My historical phenomenology of multiple temporalities has set certain markers along a pathway toward describing the temporally hybrid Empire of Modernity (see chapter 5).

- First, I argued that multiple forms of temporally structured action are constitutive of any given social formation. Thinking about modernity as a complex hybrid of multiple and overlapping temporal forms of action can displace the simplistic and ideologically saturated binaries of modernity and tradition, advanced and underdeveloped society.
- Second, I have put the presumed coherence of modernity in question by translating the analysis of modernizing projects by Peter Wagner into a phenomenological register, in order to suggest that such projects operate in temporally disparate social fields where actions are not wholly subsumed by a modernizing ethos.
- Third, such recognition of the multiple temporalities in play under the sign of modernity offers a way of transcending the radical opposition in social theory between accounts of administrative legal-rational *modernity* versus accounts of the strategic conflicts of *imperialism* as bases of social order.

As is now widely understood, "modernity" is uneven in its development, incomplete in its manifestations, and hybridically connected to other social forms in its organization.

The postmodern turn thus was not only a sociocultural transformation or a fanciful theory of high intellectuals. It marked the end of the social theory of modernity as an illusion of totality – of a coherent social order that can contain and organize its parts. Yet both postmodern history "in fragments" and postmodern theory are inadequate to the challenges of our day.

Both take our inability to "represent" the social in an objective, quasi-positivist way as the rationale for shifting to discursive approaches that emphasize a multiplicity of narratives. The narratological turn that began in the 1970s was important, for it signaled a concern with the play of multiple stories and scripts, social actions, and their agency in temporally unfolding social processes. Time and narrative, as a number of scholars have recognized, are deeply bound up with each other.[8] Now, this postmodern emphasis on narrative can be connected via phenomenology back to earlier modern theoretical interests in understanding society. The present study of phenomenological history identifies multiple types of social temporality, and it links each of alternative social temporalities to different kinds of social actions that, it turns out, are historically emergent in relation to one another in what we conventionally call modern society.[9] Yet precisely because it is possible to identify multiple temporalities, and thus multiple streams of action with their own forms of (and limits to) agency, a temporal phenomenology does not reduce the social to a totality with an evolutionary or dialectical *telos*. The meanings of actions, and thus the outcomes of events and the directions of change, remain open to the play of agencies in relation to the conditions of action.

The typology of temporalities that I proposed in figure 2.1 provides a basis to sketch a phenomenological theory of the social. Most centrally, what I have termed the Empire of Modernity has developed through a centuries-long series of projects and initiatives centered in interacting diachronic and strategic times. The shape and span of the resulting social order are plastic and subject to myriad institutional patterns, new formulations, and reconstructions. Multiple modernities can be described as alternative complex weblike compositions of various temporalities and their interconnections with fundamentally alternative and often conflicting temporal forms of social activity. In the future, inquiry should examine the Empire of Modernity as a shifting set of ordered relationships among multiple forms of temporality – themselves spatially differentiated by the different compositions of temporality across and within different social regions and societies. In any such project, it would be important to emphasize that even when social life is centrally ordered along one temporal dimension – the diachronic – social actions complexly move across multiple temporal registers on a moment-to-moment basis.[10] Here, I offer an initial ideal-typical sketch of various temporal forms as loci of different yet interconnected institutional orders of social life. This sketch, exploratory though it is, has the merit of demonstrating how a phenomenology of the social can reframe a series of modern theoretical conundrums.

The diachronic axis of modernity

To begin with, as Peter Wagner argued, modern society depends upon forms of "discipline" that order social activity, but simultaneously must orchestrate conditions of "liberty" that underwrite the potential of individuals to act autonomously in pursuing their own interests – albeit in socially appropriate ways.[11] The central venue from which modern disciplining emanates is the realm of diachronically organized action.

I have described diachronic temporality as the medium of social action organized along legal and rational lines, in which the flow of events becomes subject to routinization and calculation. Here, if Weber's sociology of legal-rational authority is restricted to considering the state, bureaucracy, and legitimacy, its focus is too narrow. Weber's legal-rational typification must instead be understood to extend the legitimate exercise of power outward to the entire range of diachronic operations in the social. In this, it merges seamlessly with Michel Foucault's argument that governmentality is diffuse in its exercise. The diachronic is not just about power and bureaucracy; more broadly, it encompasses the ordering and coordination of social activity in any domain.

In these terms, the diachronic is emergent, not fixed. Social theorists long have heralded the rise of modern "clock" time; however, they have tended to fall into a trap of reification.[12] The task instead is to investigate manifold constructions of diachronic temporality. In the first place, diachronic time encompasses the ever more precise measurement of duration and the "disembedding" of units of time that can be moved around on schedules.[13] Moreover, because diachronic time makes possible the projection of alternative future events, it puts into play the planning of the future, such that any given present is no longer simply a "here and now," but also the realization of a (past) projected future and the anticipation of events to come, already plugged into diachronic schedules. The "present" becomes decentered. Both the technologies by which decentering occurs and the directions that it takes are historically open. Thus, medieval objective representations of time depended on one or another regulated clockwork mechanism, and subsequent social orientations to time for centuries mimicked this clockwork mechanical repetition. Yet clockwork or "machine time" itself undergoes development. For example, the computer has radically reconstructed diachronic temporalities in relation to a network of relationships among software subroutines of computer activity, some intersecting exactly with other subroutine activities, others only loosely coupled. In a more socially direct way, the internet has made possible ever tighter and more extensive social coordination via shared calendars. In turn, computer and internet changes represent only one complex among an enormous range of scientific, technological, cybernetic, and biological/genetic/information systems of temporal interlinkage and development, in relation to governmentality and organization of the "posthuman" social. As Bruno Latour has emphasized, the social is not constituted independently of the complex extra-human (but not simply "natural") networks in which it is enmeshed.[14]

"The times" indeed are a'changing, but not simply as "historical" times, in the way that Bob Dylan envisioned in the 1960s. Instead, we continue to witness ever novel constructions of the diachronic that underwrite ever novel integrations of technology and "nature" across divergent spheres of lifeworldly social activities. This expansion transpires through the differentiation of multiple diachronic worlds – quintessentially of government agencies, business corporations, and, increasingly, diachronically centered social-movement organizations and non-governmental organizations (NGOs). Each has its: distinctive temporal horizons; administrative arrangements; opportunities of power by way of legitimacy, decrees, laws, patents, property rights, and popular support or acquiescence; claims of jurisdictional span for goal-oriented operations of administration and policing; and capacities of resource mobilization. In the world where diachronic temporality predominates, social systems both proliferate within organizations interfacing with their environments, and differentiate in relation to one another. Typical problems that arise stem from mismatched jurisdictional claims and conflicting procedural protocols of systems that overlap with one another as environments, for example, internationally, in conflicting state and NGO claims of jurisdiction and application of standards, and within states, in lack of standardization of administrative data transfer among multiple jurisdictional agencies, e.g., in health-care provision. In short, the diachronic world emblematic of modernity is not "the" system, but a pluralized welter of interconnected, overlapping, and sometimes contradictory "systems."[15]

The spread of the diachronic could be traced along diverse paths. Surely, as I have argued at various points, one of the most significant developments centers on the multiple and emergent relationships between diachronic and strategic temporalities. On this front, operations within the diachronic time of rational bureaucracy have subordinated legitimate strategic violence to administrative (and judicial) regulation. The upshot is (incomplete) diachronic organization, administration, and regulation of how strategic violence is deployed in contending nation-state territorial empires, in interstate war, and in the broader supra-national governmentality of the Empire of Modernity. Along a different route, diachronic governmentality has spread in part through operations in strategic time, for example, in the extension of operations and regulative frameworks to bring various kinds of order to zones of lifeworldly activity that previously lay beyond its effective policing – from crime and non-legitimate violence, to the play of strategic action in economic activities such as "markets."

The interrelations between actions framed in diachronic and strategic temporality are facilitated because both these temporal orientations are centered on unfolding sequences of events. Disjunctures and aporias, when they occur, tend to arise because of the difference between the diachronic emphasis on repetition and calculability, versus the emphasis in strategic temporality on one-off actions meant to shape the future course of events. Simply put, manufacturing and governmental administration depend on certain temporal enactments, chess and war on radically different ones. Nevertheless, when harnessed in relation to one another, the diachronic and the strategic enhance the prerogatives of social power, on the one hand, for administration, governmentality, and empire, and, on the other, in the fusion of diachronic discipline with apocalyptic war that first emerged in the Puritan Revolution. Ultimately, administrative initiatives within the Empire of Modernity seek to monopolize, regulate, or contain strategic action deemed illegitimate, whether crime, insurgency, or terrorism, whereas contending nation-states within the Empire of Modernity may threaten or deploy force in order to attain or affirm dominance within one or another sphere of influence.

The interfaces, disjunctures, and aporias between the diachronic and the synchronic are quite different. Here, Habermas's theory of lifeworld colonization and Foucault's model of governmentality capture the overall dynamic, in which diachronically organized action is undertaken to organize the here-and-now according to goals external to the social actors who are the object of its organization and discipline. The operations of colonization and governmentality toward the lifeworld are diverse. They encompass not only education, labor market regulation, social welfare administration, health services, and the like, but also policing of families and sexuality, and the mediated permeation of lifeworlds through popular entertainment, marketing and advertising, mass media and the internet, the orchestration of consumption and leisure (and consumption as leisure), and the design of social lifeworldly spaces that Baudrillard dubbed "simulacra" (such as shopping malls, fast-food restaurants, and tourist destinations) to mimic the imaginaries of consumer desire. As we move through daily life in the here-and-now, we routinely interface with external diachronically ordered systems and agents of governmentality.[16]

Modernities in the shadows of the diachronic

Yet for all the power and seeming pervasiveness of diachronic colonization and governmentality, it is inherently incomplete. Rationalization, Max Weber already understood at the beginning of the twentieth century, has its limits.[17] Indeed, everyday life extends far beyond the administrative, normative, and ethical categories that would contain it.[18] Just as surely as some Mormons continue to practice polygamy, somewhere out there are persons claiming to be Christians who nevertheless engage in practices of Wicca. Elsewhere, people who are incarcerated still constitute important aspects of their lives beyond the panoptic gaze. What is true in prisons surely is also the case in less totalistic lifeworlds, where people both "game" the systems they encounter and constitute novel forms of activity "outside" colonization. Indeed, these possibilities would seem to flourish under modernizing conditions.

In his recent magisterial reflection on the secular, Charles Taylor has depicted a broad shift that opens up the here-and-now. If secularization has any predominant implication, Taylor argues, it is that the individual self becomes "buffered" from the play of cosmic forces, spirits, and magic. Borrowing from Weber, Taylor asserts that people can become autonomous because the world has become "disenchanted." Yet autonomy implies that people have the freedom to develop meanings on their own. Modern people are engaged in fashioning their own selves. These kinds of activities do not imply equality among individuals, a freedom beyond social constraint, or forms of selfhood that break radically from available cultural tool-kits. However, theorists such as Peter Berger argue that self-fashioning is a central project of modern persons, who cast, narrate, and enact their own biographies. The details of these processes are subject to debate, but a basic implication is straightforward. As Peter Wagner argued, the very character of modern social institutions implies that no matter how much liberty is circumscribed, agency cannot be completely delimited.[19] Modern society inherently spills beyond the boundaries of diachronic rationalization; it has been built up upon a regulation and disciplining of the here-and-now that must remain incomplete. On the one hand, diachronically centered modernity thrives upon this (incomplete) subordination of other temporally centered spheres. On the other hand, a diachronic totalization is precisely the "iron cage" nightmare of technocratic and fascistic modernity that theorists from Weber to Habermas have decried. Under the latter conditions, the autonomous and buffered modern self would be reduced to the sort of posthuman, postsocial, and postmodern totalitarian life that Yevgeny Zamyatin satirized in his 1920s dystopian novel, *We*:

> Every morning, with six-wheeled precision, at the very same hour and the very same minute, we get up, millions of us, as though we were one. At the very same hour, millions of us as one, we start work. Later, millions as one, we stop. And then, like one body with a million hands, at one and the same second according to the Table, we lift the spoon to our lips. And at one and the same second we leave for a stroll and go to the auditorium, to the hall for the Taylor exercises, and then to bed.[20]

Unless the lifeworld remains relatively autonomous, unless communities can develop and affirm their own solidarities, unless a public sphere of free discourse can exist, neither personal life, nor community, nor politics can formulate meanings outside their diachronic orchestrations.

Phenomenologically, then, it becomes possible to locate a series of puzzles concerning modernity's empire in temporal terms. Just to list them is to suggest future tasks of social theory. Collapsing the categories of Habermas and Foucault, theory should consider

systemic governmentality both internally, in relation to its diachronic bases, and externally, in relation to politics. Systemically
ordered governmentality is in principle capable of organizing
modernity not only via social control and promotion of self-discipline, but also in the delimitation of liberties and rights. Here, the
distinction between "democracy" and "dictatorship" sets up a false
opposition, used by Francis Fukuyama and others to assert the
inherent elective affinity between democracy and capitalism. But
once we acknowledge the complex webs of systemic governmentality across zones of temporality, the distinction becomes blurred by
more complex issues: (1) whether, how, and in what social and
spatial regions the Empire of Modernity fosters or regulates
"liberty"; (2) the ways and means by which democratic versus other
kinds of political power "contain" and direct administrative and
corporate governmentalities; and (3) whether individuals, *subcultural* communities, and social strata that form around recognition
of shared interests regard prevailing systemic governmentality as
legitimate, or whether they coalesce into a social movement of
opposition – including those that take some apocalyptic or other
countercultural direction (here, the most significant contemporary
issue in Western countries of integration in subcultural community
versus divergence via countercultural social movement centers on
Muslims). People generally find democracy attractive in principle,
but it is a fragile hybrid that connects the diachronic with both communities and the civil society of individuals in free association with
one another. Under emergent conditions of globalization, as the
transformative departures from state communism in Russia and
China demonstrate, democratic processes versus alternative kinds
of administrative and corporate power remain open to ever novel
complexities. More generally, the devolution of national sovereignty into multiple, often overlapping sub- and super-national
jurisdictions only differentiates the possibilities of governmentality.
On an entirely different front, capitalism increasingly has substituted privately owned quasi-public spaces (e.g., shopping malls,
vacation destinations) for public spaces, yielding a proliferation of
private sovereignties to which the consuming public is subject. The
overall consequences of such developments are clear. Democracy is
not the ultimate basis of power even in democracies, nor is it inherent to modern nation-state formation. Instead, democracy comes
into play at specific sites and nexuses within nested and overlapping complexes of systemic governmentality that are not inherently
democratic. Law, regulation, policy, and "best practices" rather

than representative government *per se* are the operative principles of systemic governmentality in the Empire of Modernity.

The play of the diachronic also spills beyond strategic politics narrowly construed, into domains of synchronic communities. Like the lifeworld here-and-now that is both essential and antagonistic to modernity, synchronic communities remain strongly resistant to diachronic colonization. The persistence of communities embodies the enduring potential for collective organization in relation to communally experienced social aspirations, and it is thus a central though fragile institutional locus of modern life that precisely on this basis establishes a counterpoint to thoroughgoing rationalization of the social order. As I typified collective synchronic temporality in chapter 2, it is built upon an occasioned ritualization of communion underwritten by religious sacralization. Whether we follow Durkheim or Eliade, whether ritual reaffirms the sacredness of community itself or its traditions, group solidarity is enhanced by the ritualized delineation of boundaries – between the group and the Other, between the sacred and the profane, between what Durkheim described as the positive cult of the sacred to be embraced versus the negative cult of sacred evil, which is taboo. To be sure, with the postmodern efflorescence of "personal religion," "spirituality," and the drug culture, there has been an increase in freelance individual and self-forming group quests for spiritual transcendence in the ecstatic here-and-now, independent of formal religious organizations. Nevertheless, religious congregations have not disappeared. Outside Europe, they thrive in much of the world, and mediation of access to experiences of transcendence is still their stock-in-trade.[21] In addition, the same general synchronic ritual-creating solidarity occurs in a wider range of communities, ethnic groups, nations (and political religions such as fascism that promote aesthetics of nationalism), lifestyle and cultural movements centered on special activities and experiences, social clubs, sports teams, and status groups of all kinds, including those based on positively or negatively privileged class positions. Each offers individuals the potential for experience of catharsis linked to group identity and collective solidarity.

With the rise of modern, mass-mediated culture, communities have increasingly become subject to organization via diachronic procedures of rationalization. Moreover, the synchronic solidarity-producing ritual that facilitates a collective state of nervous excitement – what Durkheim called effervescence – became a very early target of rationalization projects, notably in the Roman Church's medieval formulation of a mass-distributed liturgy and calendar of masses. By the twentieth century, fascist and communist political movements used highly ritualized mass rallies to manufacture the experience of solidarity. In turn, they filmed rallies, thus taking a major step in the direction of producing mediated simulations of synchronicity. Film, television, and the internet, it has turned out, can substitute for the immediacy of synchronic ritual in the vivid present. As with fictional kinds of cultural representation such as theater, when people experience mediated representations of solidarity rituals, they "suspend disbelief" and participate as though they are engaged in the synchronic here-and-now. In short, the collective synchronic is subject to rationalization and simulation in its orchestration. Its basic ritual mechanism that produces solidarity is not of modernity, but it persists within modernity.

As we now know, modernity did not end the salience of race, ethnicity, community, religion, or nation as bases of identity and solidarity. Whereas mid-twentieth-century theorists envisioned a world of equal rights among individuals, later theorists increasingly grappled with the question of how societies could balance equality among individuals with the politics of recognition of identities affirmed on the basis of group membership – especially ethnic identities, gender identities, and religious identities.[22] Not so long ago, democratic theory focused on the question of how legal institutions centered on representation, voting, and extra-systemic actions of (increasingly bureaucratic or otherwise centrally organized) social movements would connect "civil society" or organize the "public sphere" in relation to the formal structures of governance. Now, these questions of democratic structure and political process share the political stage with substantive questions concerning how the state can or should recognize or delimit the rights of various communities of solidarity.[23]

Wider theoretical issues about modernity and its Others are crystallized in the puzzle of secularization. Vigorous debates have emerged about why religions persist and spirituality thrives under modernizing conditions that might seem to promote secularization. The reason for these debates is obvious enough: against the master narrative of secular modernity, religiosity has not faded away into the sphere of private life. Rather, it continues to be a source of identity and social solidarity, and a basis of cultural innovation and collective political action. The debates are nuanced and complex, and today even scholars who identify secularization as a significant social process offer substantially different accounts than those describing a relatively linear historical process that prevailed among functionalist theorists in the middle of the twentieth century.

In his 1985 book, *The Disenchantment of the World*, Marcel Gauchet argued that the modern structuration of religion itself, in particular in its distinctive Western forms, sowed the seeds of its own decline in institutional significance.[24] Yet Gauchet hardly expected religion to disappear. Rather, the institutional decline of religion ironically could be expected to exacerbate issues of existential meaning that are an important basis of religious engagement. The "post-religious" situation thus would be peculiarly open to religious interventions. In a different way, rational-choice sociologists have argued against any thesis of secularization, instead theorizing religion as something like a (relatively dominated or relatively free) marketplace where different groups compete for consumers, who have not ceased to seek salvation.[25] More recently, David Martin has revisited his earlier effort to fit alternative world-regional developments of religion into a general theory of secularization.[26] Now, he seeks to understand the historically uneven character of the process. Precisely under modern conditions, for example, obviously counter-secular tendencies such as ecstatic Pentecostalism nevertheless constitute meaningful responses to particularly modern predicaments of constrained embodiment and routinized meaning. Noting such ironies, Charles Taylor emphasizes the many ways in which religiosity persists – and spirituality grows – under conditions of secularization.[27]

Processes of secularization run parallel to those of rationalization. Many communities, such as those of surfers, music fans, or pyramid-sales movements, will define the sacred in terms outside conventional religion, and the diachronic will colonize ritual as a device to promote organizational solidarity within the state, corporations, and other legal-rational organizations. However, both relatively institutionalized and relatively self-organized communities will continue to offer bases of meaning, identity, membership, and solidarity beyond these confines. Secularization is necessarily incomplete so long as communities continue to define themselves and their participants by differentiating the sacred from the profane, the group from its Other.

Overall, a structural phenomenology reveals the Empire of Modernity as a hybrid composition of social activities unfolding within and across multiple fields of temporality. The implications concerning religion resonate more generally. The diachronic institutions that project modernity are vehicles of secularization. However, diachrony can never subsume either the here-and-now or the collective synchronic temporality of the community. In particular, although synchronic ritualizations of sacred versus profane may be orchestrated by way of diachronic temporality (for example, via the mass media), the core logic of ritual is synchronic. Simply put, the diachronic does not do ritual. Thus, although the diachronic can provide a way of life that either does not entail community or, more likely, organizes the conditions under which subcultural communities exist, short of administratively organized, highly politicized, quasi-religious nationalism, it cannot offer a compelling basis of social organization that substitutes for community or addresses "religious" aspirations of individuals.

The last apocalypse

We can consider the relation between the apocalyptic and the Empire of Modernity for the last time, by looking to the future. Al-Qaida and the War on Terror have raised a distinctive epochal challenge. A number of authors have put forward proposals for defeating al-Qaida or otherwise responding to the challenge of terrorism.[28] But how the contemporary apocalyptic episode will play out, and for how long, are open questions at this moment of writing. On the one hand, much apocalyptic culture does not result in violence, and many violent apocalyptic eruptions are short-lived, their tragedies relatively limited. On the other hand, the contemporary *zeitgeist* brims with the most diverse apocalyptic narratives. Moreover, as we have seen, when the apocalyptic animates state power, diachronic discipline, and politics, it can have sustained historical import. We cannot know the future. Nevertheless, there is a benefit to considering the basic question of how the present historical analysis of the apocalyptic might alter our conception, our social imaginary, if you will, of the world in which we live.

However much modern apocalyptic action draws on diachronic strategies, it is centered in either (1) an intense pre-apocalyptic strategic temporality of preparation, (2) pre-apocalyptic war, or (3) establishing or migrating to an often mythically formulated post-apocalyptic eternity of utopia isolated from the apocalypse engulfing the established social order. Along any of these tracks, the wellspring of the apocalyptic is the solidarity of community, typically of an emergent sectarian group's fashioning, usually improvised by drawing on previously available cultural materials, sometimes seeking to appropriate the solidarity of a larger preexisting group. Ideologically, the apocalyptic conventionally lies beyond the pale of modernity, and one central modernizing project has been to contain it. Yet other modern projects have harnessed the apocalyptic to ideologies promising progress through "necessary" violence – on the one hand, the colonization and pacification of territory for empire; on the other hand, the revolutionary violence meant to facilitate the future establishment of the new utopian social order. With 9/11 and all it came to signify in the War on Terror, secular apocalyptic political religions gave way to a new, postmodern apocalyptic confrontation. Any number of observers used binary logics to struggle with the puzzle of how this could happen under the sign of modernity. The barbarity of religiously inspired apocalyptic terrorism strikes at the core of modern ideals: it must be a medieval throwback that lies outside modernity.[29] Or it has nothing to do with religion: the institutional relationship of modern religion to the secular thus can be preserved. Or alternatively, al-Qaida can only be understood as a quintessential modern organization, no matter how much its sometimes purely symbolic violence may strain our conceptions of modernity.[30]

The present analysis is not centered in binary oppositions, and it does not anticipate the triumph of the diachronic modern. It thus brings into consideration complex relationships and aporias among radically alternative spheres of social life. The central disjuncture it reveals does not concern the problems of political and economic justice of individuals and groups participating in the diachronic sphere. For all that Marx anticipated the core dialectical process driving modern life to be economic, issues of material interest are at least in principle open to containment and resolution within the institutions of the diachronic sphere. On the other hand, modern efforts to subordinate the apocalyptic to secular diachronic purposes of state, to contain religious apocalypticism by regulating the boundaries of legitimate religion, and to police any potentially disruptive messianic versions of the apocalyptic – these are, and are likely to remain, incomplete.

The reasons now seem obvious. The apocalyptic is simultaneously ideologically Other and nevertheless formed today in powerful compositions that draw diachronic organization to strategic actions legitimated – for those who subscribe to them – by sacred purpose. John Gray is right that al-Qaida is modern in its organization.[31] Yet the apocalyptic predates modernity, and the possibilities of the apocalyptic are historically emergent. This point changes our

understanding of modernity, al-Qaida, and other apocalyptic movements yet to come (and they will come). The apocalyptic is ancient
in its provenance, but it is become modern. Apocalyptic narratives
that preceded modernity have been grafted onto modern possibilities of strategic action, social organization, and mediated diffusion
of ideologies and coordination of actions. Not only is al-Qaida
modern, but, more generally, although apocalyptic violence lies
outside the normative institutional framework of modernity,
modernity shapes the conditions under which the apocalyptic
becomes expressed, conditions different from those of, say, medieval times.

One deeply thoughtful Christian, René Girard, argues that the
Book of Revelation describes the apocalypse in terms that are often
missed. It will not be the widely depicted act of God's wrath or
judgment. It will be a cataclysm of human conflict. In this view, we
must either steel ourselves to the coming of much worse along
apocalyptic lines, or find some fundamental alternative to the ritualized religio-political construction of the Other that feeds sacred
violence.[32] The challenge for the Empire of Modernity thus is
whether it is possible to contain the apocalyptic, or to eliminate the
conditions that spawn it in the first place. Yet on the present analysis, this challenge can only be addressed under structural constraints
embedded in the character of modernity as presently constituted.
Monotheistic religions once aspired to universal sanctification of
the social, but that possibility has become eclipsed by global religious pluralism. Unless the sacred is effectively redirected away
from theologies centered on the end of history, until the Empire and
its Others – whatever their future configurations – no longer offer
bases for mutual opposition, if and when some new global sacred
– perhaps some sort of postreligious religion – displaces the present
global religious pluralism, only then will people have witnessed the
last apocalypse.

Whether such a religious development is desirable, "functionally" necessary, institutionally possible, or socially attractive,
whether it can amount to anything more than a mythic horizon, is
the central religious question for the future. In the view of Mark
Lilla, unless we choose differently, we already have embarked on
a post-religious path – ironically opened up by religion. On this
path, to avoid the temptations of political theology, we are better
off ordering society through reason, and thus, necessarily, containing religion. On the other hand, Adam Seligman makes the case that
modernity is incapable of coming to terms with the competing

legitimacies of alternative religious meanings. Thus, to find grounds of a new, deeper mutual religious tolerance, he argues, we must engage religion from perspectives that are themselves authentically religious.[33]

Given global religious diversity, as well as the declining capacity of religious organizations to speak to the "spiritual" quests of individuals in the West, it is difficult to imagine the emergence of some new, universal religion. Such a development would entail a dramatic social upheaval on the order of the Protestant Reformation, which was itself shaped by apocalyptic engagement. On the other hand, absent some new, universal religious movement, the global convergence of an ethic of tolerance of the sort encouraged by Seligman, or the complete ascendency of the Empire of Modernity, perhaps along lines envisioned by Francis Fukuyama, we are left to contend with historical circumstances in which the apocalyptic will remain in play, on a variety of fronts – from the holy wars and messianic anticipations of Islamists, to continued Christian eruptions of millenarian sentiment, to the transreligious preparations for apocalypse tied to the end of the Mayan calendar "long count" cycle of 5,126 years on December 21, 2012 CE.

Clearly, contemporary conditions are dramatically different from those in the wake of the Reformation and the Peace of Westphalia. Whereas states emerged in the seventeenth century as strong territorial entities that, within their borders, could act to contain the apocalyptic, globalization has changed the equation. Now apocalyptic movements may target the Empire of Modernity that builds across state boundaries, as al-Qaida and allied groups have done. It is no longer just states that wrestle with containing the apocalyptic within their boundaries. Instead, given the emergent conditions of nested, overlapping, and crosscutting sovereignties and jurisdictions, containment now necessarily involves multinational and global action. Yet how states, multinational alliances, international organizations, and NGOs are supposed to pursue such containment remains an open, contentious, but largely unspoken question. Clearly the decision of the U.S. administration of George W. Bush to pursue a basically unilateral and fundamentally militaristic strategy undermined support from other states that shared its basic interest in containment, especially in Europe, and even in its closest ally, the United Kingdom.[34]

How globalized apocalyptic confrontations will play out in the future cannot be predicted. But reflection on earlier episodes strongly suggests that this question will be an important hinge upon which a reorganization of the – now global – social order will occur, for that has been the pattern in earlier cases – the Crusades, the Protestant Reformation, the English Civil War, the French Revolution, and the communist movements of the nineteenth and twentieth centuries. Each of these was an historical *break*, an epochal turning point that marked – within its domain – the end of a previously relatively durable social order. Major apocalyptic episodes are traumatic and transformative, both individually and socially. They mix up the deck. Whatever the social order before an apocalyptic eruption, it dramatically shifts – by the reorganization of the social order as it pursues apocalyptic triumph or counters an apocalyptic threat, and sometimes by the emergence from apocalyptic origins of a new dispensation that begins to reorder social life. In the wake of the contemporary apocalyptic epoch, modernity will not ever be the same. The questions that remain are: whether the confrontation itself will in turn fuel endemic apocalyptic violence, whether strategies of containment will yield yet a new seedbed of the apocalyptic, and how confronting the apocalyptic situation will transform the social order.

Any number of observers have reduced the contemporary apocalyptic epoch to the confrontation between Osama bin Laden's al-Qaida and the War on Terror as formulated by the administration of George W. Bush. With the Bush era over, this analysis is put to the test. The Bush administration played the full role that al-Qaida assigned to it, fanning wider apocalyptic flames, bleeding its own economy, and jeopardizing its global power position. The election of President Barack Obama has been greeted around the world – including by some Islamists – as a potential turning point in world affairs away from civilizational conflict. Yet soon after Obama's election, an al-Qaida spokesman dismissed the significance of black Americans like Colin Powell, Condoleezza Rice, and Barack Obama serving in high governmental positions.[35] In this context, it is worth recalling that in medieval and early modern Europe, the bearers of apocalyptic visions did not always reduce the Whore of Babylon to a person. Sometimes they singled out the papacy as an institution, or a particular state. So too today, we ought not comfort ourselves by reducing the apocalyptic to personalities, as important as they can be for the course of history. It would be better for parties of power to ponder whether and how the Empire of Modernity itself establishes or undermines conditions of the apocalyptic.

On this point, contemporary circumstances recall the distinction between *Dar al-Islam*, the house of Islam, and *Dar al-Harb*, the house of war, where Muslims were expected to engage in jihad, thereby expanding the *Dar al-Islam*, eventually to the entire world. Whether the contemporary world order is to be oriented on the basis of an analogous binary distinction between the Empire of Modernity and the Land of War remains an open question. A transcendent culture of tolerance – in an expansive sense – might eclipse the binary.[36] However, if the binary construction remains, within the boundaries of the Empire of Modernity, diachronic administration may continue to sustain its basic legitimacy, even though extreme political and economic inequalities endemic to the Empire of Modernity will continue to generate focal crises of legitimacy. After all, the empire is constituted in part on the basis of a neo-imperialist logic of strategic power rather than simply the rational administration of democratically controlled sovereignties. Thus, even within empire, new visions of the apocalyptic doubtless will arise. Beyond the boundaries of the Empire of Modernity lie "rogue" states as well as failed states unable to monopolize violence within their territories, where empire must engage in war and diplomacy, if not to subsume the alien territory, at least to buffer it. These struggles, too, threaten to rise to the level of what Merleau-Ponty called historical violence.

Today, the Empire of Modernity faces quite different circumstances of the apocalyptic than those of early colonial expansion into "new" territories that seemed to offer virtually limitless resources. Earlier, from the fourteenth century onward, colonial expansion could receive a quasi-apocalyptic legitimation of fulfilling God's destiny, and the pressures of apocalyptic "from below" could be relieved by migration of an apocalyptic movement to its Promised Land. Now, however, even if human settlement will continue to colonize new territories, the efficiency of doing so is declining. Spatial apocalyptic movements can only colonize ever more marginal lands. Moreover, the rapid degrading of earth's environment from the dramatic expansion of human society fosters conditions of incremental environmental collapse such as habitat decline and global warming precisely at a time when the limitations in basic resources (oil, water, air) relative to expanding demand drive an ecological crisis that will potentially fuel apocalyptic social conflict.

New scientific discoveries, engineering developments, and technological applications doubtless will continue to facilitate both increased efficiency of resource development, processing, and use, and, more generally, the administrative capacity of the Empire of Modernity, just as innovations have underwritten expansion of capitalism and state power in earlier centuries. (Unfortunately, they also yield new weapons – tactical nuclear, chemical, and biological ones.) Perhaps colonization beyond earth ultimately will offer new venues of expansion, new relief from the constraining pressures of finite resources. But absent such developments, apocalyptic responses to collective experience of crisis stand every likelihood of being exacerbated by ecological conditions – in part induced by the technical advances and inexorable spread of modernity – just as they sometimes had been triggered by famines and plagues in the past.[37]

History is rarely written without concluding, and conclusion renders retrospective closure on the meaning of events. However, concerning the apocalyptic, postmodern theorist Jean Baudrillard asserts, the end is an illusion.[38] Here, we necessarily conclude without coming to the End. Rather, we end at the beginning. Under the new conditions, the modern binary that divided off the religious from the secular has become eclipsed by social deployments of the deeper binary that religion has long demarcated, between the sacred and the profane. That binary can no longer be regarded as the province of religion, conventionally understood. Instead, with the globalization of the apocalypse, the social world itself has once again become the domain where sacred and profane contend with one another. Not that the world has become reenchanted. Instead, uncertainty has infused the intractable challenges of social life. The sacred, formerly contained by modernizing projects within religious organizations, has escaped into the wider world, where forces seemingly beyond human control threaten to overwhelm the established order of social life. Whether God is dead or alive, or lives in us, we will either find a general basis for affirming the sacredness of existence, or we will descend into a new netherworld where even violence has lost its meaning, where the time of modernity has faded, history as we invented it has ended, the last apocalypse arrived.

Notes

Chapter 1 Seeing through the Apocalypse

1 Poll cited in Nancy Gibbs, "Apocalypse now," *Time*, July 1, 2002. On Hurricane Katrina, see Andrew Gray, "World Stunned as U.S. Struggles with Katrina," Reuters, September 2, 2005, *http://www.commondreams.org/headlines05/0902-04.htm* (accessed February 2, 2009). Weisman (2007). John Seabrook, "Sowing for apocalypse," *The New Yorker* (August 27, 2007): 60–71. On Russia and Georgia, *New York Times* (hereafter, *NYT*), August 17, 2008, and on the economy, September 21, 2008.

2 My interest is in mapping key configurational developments in which the apocalyptic takes on unique meanings and becomes articulated with wider phenomena in ways that become historically significant. One alternative strategy, that of Schmithals (1975), is to base history on an initial treatment of the apocalyptic as a worldview and essence. Another strategy, pursued by Bull (1999), is to probe the deep, transhistorical significance of the apocalyptic through philosophical investigation. These alternative projects are not inherently incompatible.

3 See Hall, Schuyler, and Trinh (2000: 4–10).

4 My usage of apocalyptic as a noun follows Schmithals (1975: ch. 1). O'Leary (1994: 77).

5 Berger (1967: ch. 2).

6 Benjamin (1968: 263).

7 Hall, Schuyler, and Trinh (2000: ch. 1).

8 Not only are there historical, sociological, and comparative studies of apocalyptic events, many of which I cite in the present study, but some authors – e.g., Keller (1996), Lilla (2007), Gray (2007) – have

examined religion (and Keller, centrally the apocalyptic) in relation to modernity and future prospects, thus treating some of the same developments that I trace here. Other authors recently have explored topics such as the history of millennialism (Baumgartner 1999; Kirsch 2006) and holy war (Catherwood 2007). The present study differs from these studies in its focus on a "configurational history" (Hall 1999: 216–20), intended to identify long-term structural changes of apocalyptic phenomena in relation to modern society, as it has emerged, and today.

9   The evidence I present suggests distinctive consequences of apocalyptic developments in the West, but I do not make the case that such developments differentiate historical emergence of what became the West relative to other parts of the world. Such an argument could only be based on a detailed comparative analysis that is beyond the focus of the present study.

10   Gray (2003).

11   Eisenstadt (1999b).

12   Schutz (1967) and Schutz and Luckmann (1973).

13   Hall (1980).

Chapter 2   The Ancient Origins of History and the Apocalypse

1   For a useful discussion of social constructions of time, see Orlove (2003).

2   Schutz (1967), Schutz and Luckmann (1973), and Berger and Luckmann (1966). For a parallel linguistic theorization of temporality, see Wood (1989).

3   Hall (1980); see also Sewell (2005).

4   This is what Wilhelm Dilthey (1976) wanted and C. Wright Mills (1959) demanded. Phenomenology remains largely descriptively focused on delimited lifeworlds. However, Berger, Berger, and Kellner (1973) and Jürgen Habermas (1987) have connected social phenomenology to macro-sociological analysis.

5   For a detailed explication of connections between social organization and temporality in utopian communal groups, see Hall (1978b).

6   On the methodology of configurational history, see Hall (1999: 216–20); an exemplar of the methodology is Mann's (1986) history of social power.

7   On the earliest constructions of temporality, see Gurevich (1976) and Whitrow (1988: 23–4).

8   Lyotard (1991: 113).

9   On storytelling, see the phenomenological account by Young (1987).

10 Traditions are hardly immutable. Bourdieu (1977) focuses his critique of structuralism on processes of their modification.
11 Durkheim (1995).
12 Schmalenbach (1961).
13 Eliade (1959: 27–8, 35 [quotations]). See also Gurevich (1976: 230).
14 To invoke Danièle Hervieu-Léger's (2000) evocative characterization of religion more generally.
15 The relation of religious ritual to everyday life in ancient societies has parallels in contemporary everyday conduct in its ritualized aspects; see Goffman (1967) and Collins (2004).
16 Whitrow (1988: 26–7).
17 Eliade (1959: 119).
18 Eliade (1959: 123).
19 Gurevich (1976: 233). On time in ancient Greece, Whitrow (1988: 37–51). See Löwith (1949: 4–10) for a discussion of Greek historical practice and temporality with similar conclusions to those of Eliade, independently of his structuralist argument, and Patrides (1972: 1–2, 9, 13–15), who cites the difficulties that a Graeco-Roman cyclical view of history posed for Christianity's focus on Jesus's life as a decisive historical event.
20 On Herodotus and Greek history, Merkley (1987, chs. 2–3).
21 Eliade (1959: 28, 42 [quotation]).
22 Needham (1965).
23 Boyce (1992: 29) gives the latest possible date as approximately 1100 BCE.
24 Kreyenbroek (2002: 39).
25 See Boyce (1992: esp. 70, 72, 76–7); cf. Cohn (1993: 79, 94–5, 102, 114).
26 See Lincoln (2007: 80 [quote]).
27 On this point, Cohn (1993: 95) seems to exaggerate Zarathustra's embrace of violence.
28 Brandon (1965: 146), Bultmann (1957: 21 [quotation]), Eliade (1959: 102–12), and Whitrow (1988: 52).
29 Bultmann (1957), Eliade (1959: 102–12), and Cohn (1993: chs. 7–8).
30 Brandon (1965: 106–10, 117–24), Cohn (1993: 132–9), and Hengel (1989: 271–2).
31 Brandon (1965: 134–6).
32 Cohn (1993: 144–58, 157, 158 [quotation]).
33 Yet the transitions are blurred; see Kohn and Moore (2007: 21–2, 24–6). Because recent scholarship emphasizes that Jews as followers of the religion of Judaism included other than ethnic Jews, the conventional use of the term "Jew" to designate those in the ancient world who believed in the God of Israel and practiced some form of Judaic religion is somewhat anachronistic. Nevertheless, no noncumbersome alternative has emerged, and the usage is retained here.

34 There is scholarly controversy over whether this quotation is pre- or post-exile, but, as Cohn (1993: 252 n. 49) observes, it contains the rhetoric of post-exilic writings.

35 Whitrow (1988: 52), DeVries (1975: esp. 345–46), Collins (2002: 71), and Cohn (1993: 168–75).

36 Collins (2002: 74).

37 Hengel (1989: 262, 265, 269 [quotation]). Boyarin (1999) rightly insists that martyrdom cannot be defined transhistorically, as its historical and cultural significance varies; it is precisely to explore such variations that I use the term here.

38 In the view of Hengel (1989: 280).

39 Hengel (1989: 280).

40 Lewy (1974: ch. 2). Whether the Essenes were the inhabitants of the community discovered at Qumran has become a matter of controversy, and one that is somewhat distinct from the equally vexsome question of who the Essenes were, and how they lived; see discussions in Edwards (2004).

41 The degree and direction of influence are complex and disputed; see Brandon (1965: 146), Wilson (2002), and Collins (2002: 72).

42 Whitrow (1988: 53, 56). For a survey of scholarship on the Deuteronomist, see Vogt (2006). In part, conflicts among parties and sects centered on what calendar was to be used to determine when rituals would be observed. The Pharisees kept the predominant Temple ritual schedule to a lunar calendar, while the Sadducees, the Essenes, and believers in the apocalyptic prophecies of *I Enoch* adopted the Hellenistic solar calendar. See Whitrow (1988: 55–6) and Cohn (1993: 180–1).

43 Attridge (2002), who provides a useful introduction to scholarly interpretations of Jesus's ministry.

44 Hengel (1989: 340).

45 Boyarin (2004: 27).

46 Attridge (2002) and Kohn and Moore (2007).

47 This point and the analysis that follows from it are drawn from Brandon (1965: 158–9, 166).

48 Stark (1996: ch. 3).

49 Boyarin (1999).

50 Brandon (1965: 163 [quotation], 167). On Paul, see also Segal (1990).

51 See Frend (1967: 57ff.).

52 On the significance of this formulation, and for a detailing of Hellenistic influences, see Williams (1975). Boyarin (1999) argues against the view that Christian martyrdom superceded Judaic martyrdom; rather, both emerged in a shared milieu. Yet this point does not alter the *claim* advanced about Christ's martyrdom by Paul.

53 Brandon (1965: 159–72, esp. 161 note 1, 169 [quotation]).

54 Bultmann (1957: 36, 151–2).

55 In the analysis of Brandon (1965: 172–9, 175 [quotation]). For a general account, see Fredriksen (2000).

56 As Brandon (1965: 187) asserted. On the changing orientations concerning the apocalypse and the Second Coming, see especially Brandon (1965: 182–8), Cohn (1970: 27–9), and McGinn (1995). On the shifts in historicity, see Löwith (1949: ch. IX), Bultmann (1957: 58–9, 151–5), Brandon (1965: 190–205), Pelikan (1985: ch. 2), and Kohn and Moore (2007: 4–5).

57 Weber (1978: 1164).

58 Bultmann (1957: 53, 155 [quotations]).

59 McGinn (1995: 61).

60 Cohn (1993: ch. 12) summarizes the Apocalypse as text. For lines of scholarship and debates, see Duff (2001: 4–14), who emphasizes the importance of internal disputes among the seven churches of Asia Minor as the context of the Apocalypse's rhetoric and arguments, and Frilingos (2004: 1–6), who points to the Roman Empire as offering the template of spectacle and martyrdom to be found in the Apocalypse.

61 On the precarious basis of this claim, see Thompson (1990: 172–3).

62 Quotations of the Book of Revelation are from the King James version of the New Testament.

63 To invoke the title of the notable study by Festinger, Riecken, and Schachter (1964) of a twentieth-century sect. On use of the Apocalypse to encourage conversion, see Cohn (1970: 27–8).

64 Knox (1950: ch. 3) and Cohn (1970: 25–6).

65 Frend (1967: 57ff.) and Williams (1975).

66 Frend (1967: esp. 41, 220). On choices of private worship or persecution, see Frilingos (2004: 116–18).

67 On Christian collective orchestration of martyrdom, see Riddle (1931). Quotation from the *Martyrs of Lyon, http://www.users.drew.edu/ddoughty/ Christianorigins/persecutions/Lyonstxt.html* (accessed February 4, 2009), emphasis added.

68 For a trenchant critical discussion of the resentment evidenced in the Apocalypse of St. John, see novelist D. H. Lawrence's *Apocalypse* (1932).

69 Löwith (1949: 167) and McGinn (1995: 62). For Augustine's discussion of apocalyptic theology, see *Civitas Dei*, Book XX, *http://www. wischik.com/lu/senses/city-of-god.html* (accessed February 4, 2009). As Landes (1995: 290; 2000: 105) has observed, the strategy of pushing back the anticipated date of the apocalypse to dampen anticipations is a stock-in-trade of opponents of apocalyptic movements.

70 Augustine of Hippo, *Civitas Dei*, Book XIX, chapter 7, *http://www. wischik.com/lu/senses/city-of-god.html* (accessed February 4, 2009). See also O'Leary (1994: 73–6).

71 Brandon (1965: 1940–6), Pelikan (1985: 28–33), and Smolinski (2001: 147–9). On further developments of Christianity in relation to secular powers and the *telos* of history, see chs. 3–4.
72 For discussions, see Blankinship (1994: 11, 13, 279 fn. 3), and Obermann (1955: 272–3). Recently, the debate has centered on arguments, e.g., by Kelsay (2007), concerning the history of jihad, and whether al-Qaida's jihad has any theological basis. As Cook (2005: ch. 2) points out, the debates are often driven by desires either to demonize Islam or to discount its militant aspects.
73 Hillenbrand (1999: 94–9) and Arjomand (2002: 110).
74 Here and below, beyond specifically cited works, I draw on Rodinson's (1974) social and historical biography of Muhammad, and Donner (1981); see also Cook (2005: ch. 1).
75 Rodinson (1974: 163) and Donner (1981: 65).
76 Qur'an II: 187–8 (cf. II: 214, IV: 75–80), in the translation of Arberry (1955).
77 Cook (2005: 83); see also Arjomand (2002: 110).
78 Obermann (1955: 271–8), Rodinson (1974: 171–2, 261–2), and Donner (1981: 76).
79 Rodinson (1974: 223, 273–4).
80 Weber (1978: 473–74). On Augustine, Brown (2000: ch. 21). The degree to which Islamic doctrines of the Qur'an and *Hadith* (interpretive traditions) actually protected communities of Jews and Christians (*ahl al-dhimma*) in practice has been historically variable, as have been interpretations of the theology itself.
81 Donner (1981) and Cook (2005: 79).
82 Arjomand (2002: 109).
83 Cook (2005: 85, 88 [quotations], 89). On Islamic tolerance of heterodoxy, see Anderson (1974: 366), and a detailed study, Lewis (2008). On the subsequent history of millenarian Islamic movements, see Ali (1993).
84 Holt (1980), Hussein (1982), and Rinehart (2006: 58–63).
85 Quoted in Boyce (1992: 150).
86 White (1987).
87 Lyotard (1991: 113).

Chapter 3   Medieval Christendom and Its Others

1 Wong (1997), Pomeranz (2000), Clark (2007), and Goldstone (2008).
2 On secularization, Martin (1978) offered a general theory, then (2005) revised his account. In the past quarter-century, secularization theory has been challenged by rational-choice theorists (e.g., Stark and Bainbridge 1987), and defended for Christian Europe (e.g., by Bruce 2002). Davie (e.g., 2002) has adopted an intermediate

view that asks whether religions tend to operate as public utilities or markets. The most comprehensive discussion, controversial for its faith optimism, is that of philosopher Charles Taylor (2007).

3   For a recent general history, see Karsh (2006).

4   Girard (1986).

5   Roth (1975: 151).

6   Weber (1978: 1153, 1175 [quotes], 1158–1211). Robert Bellah (1970) has argued that the West was particularly open to the proliferation of schismatic sectarian movements led by charismatic divines. Thus, the Reformation opening of a direct, personal relationship between the ordinary believer and God "the Father" enabled people to assert the right to answer to a paternal authority higher than any earthly patriarch.

7   Cohn (1970: 28–33). On the lack of Christian inspiration for the Islamic doctrine of jihad, see Hillenbrand (1999: 94). On Christian justifications of violence in relation to the Crusades, see Riley-Smith (1997: 40–52; 2002: 7).

8   On the Germanic–Roman accommodation, see Anderson (1974: 232ff.), and specifically for honor and religion, Russell (1994: esp. 120–4).

9   For essays concerning apocalyptic developments in the period 950–1050, see Landes, Gow, and Van Meter (2003).

10   Cowdrey (1970: 39, 51) and Duffy (1997: 87–132, 98 [quote]). Cf. Anderson (1974: 134–5), Barraclough (1976: 150–5), Bendix (1978: 27–35), Riley-Smith (1987: 15), Frank (1995: 73–6), Logan (2002: chs. 6–7), Lambert (2002: 38–9), and France (2005: 33–6). On the limits to absolutism in absolutist monarchies, see Henshall (1992).

11   Cohn (1970: 82–3). The demise of the Templars was a blow to any theocratic program, and it sparked deep controversy. See Partner (1982), Riley-Smith (1987: 210–12; 2004), Richard (1999: 200–6, 466–71), and Lambert (2002: 198–9).

12   Le Goff (2005: 83 [quote], 95). Riley-Smith (1987: xxviii [quote], 2–3, 15; 2005: 2–3, 9).

13   Benedict (1975: 43).

14   Cowdrey (1970: esp. 139–41). See also France (2005).

15   On the Crusades, see Riley-Smith (1997), Richard (1999), and France (2005), along with Tyerman's (2004) analytic history. On heresies, see Knox (1950) and Cohn (1970). On the persecution of Jews, see Stark (2001: ch. 3).

16   Karabel (2007) is not wrong to emphasize strategic and economic incentives in the Crusades, but he dismisses their religious basis on the grounds of an unreasonable criterion – that Crusader alliances were not aligned *purely* with religious cleavages. On the historiography of "imperialist" theories of the Crusades, see Riley-Smith (2005: 304–7).

17   I am not concerned here with the long-standing debate about the conditions under which apocalyptic and other dissident religious movements arise, whether they be located in natural disasters, material economic and social conditions, or quests for religious meaning. The general thrust of Le Goff's (1980b: 32) observation still holds: "There is a history to be written which will explain Joachimism as well as many other revolutionary movements involving both the soul and economic status." For alternative explanations, see Engels (1964), Hobsbawm (1959), Cohn (1970), and Barkun (1974), and an overview by O'Leary (1994: 8–10).

18   On Islamic challenges to Europe, France (2005: 16–21). On Urban's goals and Cluniac influence: Cowdrey (1970: 180–6), Riley-Smith (1987: 6–7), and Richard (1999: 19–27). Cohn (1970: 61–5) and Le Goff (2005: 93–7). Contemporary chronicler of the First Crusade, quoted by Richard (1999: 66). On popular apocalyptic sentiment, and the debate concerning whether Urban initially framed his proposed expedition in apocalyptic terms, see Rubenstein (2004). On jihad in relation to the Crusades, Hillenbrand (1999: 103–250; 246 [quote]).

19   Cohn (1970: 72, 75–6).

20   Tyerman (2004: 95–107, 123–4) and Riley-Smith (1987: 37). Logan (2002: 118–20). Paul, *Ephesians* 6: 11–17.

21   Bernard and Innocent II quoted in Partner (1982: 8, 9). See also Aho (1981: 84).

22   Collins (2002: 76); see also Newport (2000:18).

23   Tyerman (2004: 115–17).

24   Riley-Smith (1987: 38–9) and Bull (2002).

25   Cohn (1970: 70).

26   Cohn (1970: 68).

27   Cohn (1970: 63–70).

28   Cohn (1970: 77). On legislation affecting Jews, see *http://www. fordham.edu/halsall/source/300–800-laws-jews.html* (accessed February 11, 2009), which draws from appendices to Parkes (1934).

29   Stark (2001: 124–72).

30   Lambert (2002: 47). Cohn (1970: 61–70).

31   Knox (1950: chs. 3–4) and Brown (2000).

32   Stark (2001: 157–8).

33   Lambert (2002: 31).

34   Paralleling my argument, see Moore (2007), who is less concerned with the rise in heresy accusations than with the consequences. Cf. Le Goff (2005: 83). Peter the Venerable, quoted in Riley-Smith (2002: 20).

35   Riley-Smith (1987: 133–9, 167–73), Madaule (1967), and Moore (2007).

36   Knox (1950).

37 On the Waldensians and Cathars, Knox (1950: chs. 5–6). On the challenges to historical research on heterodoxical medieval movements, Knox (1950: 71–5). For more recent accounts of the Cathar heresy and the Albigensian Crusade, see Madaule (1967) and Lambert (2002: chs. 4, 6, 7).

38 Stark (2001: 122, 167).

39 See Firth (1979: 7).

40 Kaelber (1998: 175–81, 221–24). See also Madaule (1967: esp. 11–55), Knox (1950: 79 [quote]), but cf. Oakley (1979: 27–8).

41 Riley-Smith (1987: 133–9, 167–73), Madaule (1967), and Moore (2007).

42 On Pope Boniface VIII's early fourteenth-century doctrine of the two swords, Frank (1995: 89–92). For a social history of the Inquisition in a small village, see Le Roy Ladurie (1979).

43 Lambert (2002: 45–6) and Logan (2002: 136–45). Cohn (1970: 158, 127 [quote]).

44 Knox (1950: 86–8), Cohn (1970: 156–69), Lerner (1972), and Lambert (2002: 199–207). Oakley (1979: 185 [quote]).

45 Oakley (1979: 185–6).

46 Lambert (2002: 4, 40).

47 Joachim of Fiore, *Liber de Concordia*, quoted in Daniel (1992: 85). Cohn (1970: 109), echoing Löwith (1949: 159), credits the Joachim model of the three ages with reverberating down through the ages to Hegel, August Comte, Marx, and the concept of the Third Reich. See also Lambert (2002: ch. 11, esp. examples of Joachim's figures, figures 2, 3), and the account of Reeves (1969: pt. 3).

48 Daniel (1992: 86–7).

49 Löwith (1949: 156–7), Cohn (1970: 108–11), Oakley (1979: 186–9), and Daniel (1992).

50 Cohn (1970: chs. 6–7; 121, 122, 123 [quotes]). On apocalyptic versus naturalistic interpretations of the Black Death, Smoller (2000).

51 Cohn (1970: 209–22, 233–4).

52 Anderson (1974: 28 [quote], 45).

53 On the worldly papacy, see Cohn (1970: 82–4).

54 On general discontent with the church, see Huizinga (1954: 178–9). On Wycliffe, the Lollards, and the Hussites, see Oakley (1979: 189–203), Riley-Smith (1987: 233–4), Lambert (2002), and Le Goff (2005: 171–3). On Wycliffe in relation to the Antichrist, see Kemp (1991: ch. 3).

55 Cohn (1970: 80); Luther on penance, *http://www.faithlitchfield.com/resources/luther/archives/2003/10/penance_part_four.php* (accessed February 11, 2009). Luther quoted in Wuthnow (1989: 135). France (2005: 318). For Luther's critique of the church's treasures of merit, see numbers 55–60 of his Ninety-Five Theses, *http://www.ctsfw.edu/etext/luther/theses/* (accessed February 11, 2009).

56   Anderson (1974: 370–4) and Turner (1974: 124–9).
57   Martin Luther, *Table Talk*, § § 1337, 426, *http://www.reformed.org/master/index.html?mainframe=/documents/Table_talk/table_talk.html* (accessed February 11, 2009). See also Firth (1979: 9–22), Barnes (1988), and McGinn (1994: 201–8). The 1526 Treaty of Madrid, between Francis I of France and Charles V of Spain, quoted in Riley-Smith (1987: 242).
58   Bendix (1978: 258). Schribner (1987: ch. 3) argues that oral diffusion through preaching and kin and friendship networks also drove the spread of Reformation ideas.
59   Lewis Namier, quoted in Hechter (1975: 67).
60   Wuthnow (1989: pt. I; 54, 47 [quotes]).
61   Wuthnow (1989: 62).
62   For general accounts of Müntzer and the Peasants' War, see Cohn (1970: 234–51; 239 [Müntzer quote]) and Lewy (1974: 110–16).
63   Lewy (1974: 114).
64   Cohn (1970: 250).
65   On the apocalyptic character of Anabaptist movements, see Williams (1962: 857–60).
66   On Münster, see Cohn (1970: 252–80) and Lewy (1974: 116–29). For a history of Anabaptism, see Williams (1962: 343).
67   Martin Luther, quoted in Engels (1964: 105, 107, 117). On Luther and the Anabaptists, see Knox (1950: 126–35). See Blickle (1998) on the dialectical interplays among Luther, what Blickle terms the "Communal Reformation," the Peasants' War, Müntzer, and the "Princes' Reformation" after 1525.
68   On Calvin, the apocalyptic, and the New Jerusalem, see Rublack (2005: 113), and for the range of interpretations, Warfield (1909: 240–41, n. 11) and de Boer (2004: 259–60). Calvin has often been interpreted as completely (and wisely) non-apocalyptic, not the least by his theological heirs. But Firth (1979: 32–7) offers a more complex reading – that Calvin was highly skeptical of the Book of Revelation but reached parallel ideas about the last days through other biblical routes.
69   For surveys of the Antichrist and the apocalyptic in the Reformation, see McGinn (1994: ch. 8) and Cunningham and Grell (2000: ch. 2).
70   Wuthnow (1989: 67–115) and Anderson (1974: 236–9, 91–3, 67). The Reformation in England and France is considered further in chapter 4.
71   This point is developed in greater detail in chapter 4.
72   Marx (2003: 86, 184–6, 148–53); cf. Gorski (2003: 159–60). On France as holy land, Tyerman (2004: 186).
73   Wuthnow (1989: ch. 4, esp. 119–20, 124 [quote]) and Marx (2003: 103).

74 Marx (2003); see also Gorski (2003: 163); for an earlier analysis of the Reformation and nationalism in Catholic and Protestant states, see Stark (1967: III: 173–94). Larnar, cited in Corrigan and Sayer (1985: 47). For the relation between religion and nationalism in the Dutch case, comparisons to England, and his more general argument about early modern nationalism and its religious alignments, see Gorski (2000). On the English Revolution and Puritanism, see Goldstone (1991: 125–34) and Lewy (1974: ch. 6).

75 Wuthnow (1989: 152 [quote]), 132).

76 Oakley (1979: 212); see also Knox (1950: 88), and, for an argument concerning the continuities between diverse Christian persecutions of the Other, from heretics to the Knights Templar, and witches, see Cohn (1975).

77 Gurevich (1985: 145–6).

Chapter 4 Apocalypse Re-formed

1 Calvin, *Institutes* III: 25: 5, *http://www.reformed.org/master/index. html?mainframe=/books/institutes/* (accessed February 13, 2009). Boyer (1992: 61); see Quistorp (1955) and Firth (1979: 33–7) for Calvin's relation to apocalyptic thinking.

2 Weber (1958).

3 Latour (1993).

4 For an interpretation that locates the secularizing division between the transcendent and earthly affairs in relation to the rise of the diachronic, see Gauchet (1997: 185–7).

5 Augustine, quoted in Crosby (1997: 75).

6 Needham (1986) and Whitrow (1988: 77–80). The medieval Arab technologist Ibn al-Razzaz al-Jazari (died, c. 1206 CE) wrote a compendium describing devices such as the elegant "elephant clock" with mechanical elements; see *http://www.history-science-technology. com/Articles/articles%206.htm#_edn7*; and *http://www.dailymotion.com/ video/x3ndi4_al-jazaris-elephant-clock-from-the_creation* (both accessed February 13, 2009).

7 For a general account, see Gurevich (1985: ch. 4). On time, the church, merchants, and laborers, Le Goff (1980a: 48 [quote]; 1980b). Chobham, quoted in Le Goff (1988: 39).

8 Thompson (1967).

9 Weber (1958), Duby (1968: 173–81), Hall (1978b: 40–1), Zerubavel (1981: 54–5), and Kaelber (1998).

10 Hall, Nietz, and Battani (2003: 99–100).

11 Huizinga (1954: chs. 13–15), Brandon (1965: 196–7), Kaelber (1998: 106–17).

12 Bernard, quoted in Le Goff (1980a: 50).

13   On monasteries and convents versus heterodoxical movements, see the analysis of Kaelber (1998).

14   Calva, quoted in Le Goff (1980a: 51). On sloth, Wood (2002).

15   Barnes (1988: ch. 3, 115 [quote]). On German end-times calculations, see also Cunningham and Grell (2000: 50).

16   Weber (1958). See also Hall (1978b: 40–2) and Zerubavel (1981: 54–6).

17   For accounts of Calvinism in Switzerland and Geneva, see Gordon (1992) and Rublack (2005: 104–45).

18   Baxter, quoted in Thompson (1967: 87). Weber (1958: 157). Needham (1965: 49) is skeptical that linear time was necessary for the emergence of capitalism, since China also had (not widely diffused) linear time measurement; however, he acknowledges that linear time may have been a "psychological function" that promoted capitalism.

19   On magic and incomplete disenchantment, Hill (1972: 70–4) and Rublack (2005: e.g., 152–7, 192–4).

20   Kaelber (1998: 104). Weber (1958).

21   For a general phenomenology of modern temporality, see Ferguson (2006: 112–14). On clocks and watches, Landes (1983) and Whitrow (1988: 112–14, 158–69). On the industrious revolution, De Vries (1994). For a critique, see Clark and Van Der Werf (1998).

22   Biernacki (1995).

23   Bell (1973: 117).

24   Gorski (2003).

25   Löwith (1949: 155, 158–9).

26   Kemp (1991: 106). Hall (1999, esp. chs. 2–3; quotation of Ranke, 36). On Hegel, see also Löwith (1949: ch. 3, esp. 56), Taylor (1979), and Lilla (2007), for whom Hegel is a pivotal figure in accounting for the fading presence of religion in the modern world. Löwith (1949: 67–91) and Manuel (1962) on Comte.

27   Becker (1932: 6); cf. Gurevich (1985: 125).

28   Kemp (1991: 41).

29   Kemp (1991: 78–9). Gurevich (1985: 109) and White (1987).

30   Harbison (1964: ch. 12); see also Walzer (1965: 26, 64–5).

31   On the persistence of magic, see Thomas (1971).

32   Jacob (1976) and Wallace (2004: 198–201).

33   Löwith (1949: 195).

34   Bartlett (1993). External colonialism is well understood. On *internal* colonialism, see Hechter (1975). Aside from the Crusades, the Cistercians' medieval monastic expansion into eastern and northern Europe was a *de facto* colonizing movement.

35   Riley-Smith (1987, ch. 4) and Tyerman (2004: 156–7).

36   Hall (1984). Tyerman (2004: 166).

37   Partner (1997: 160–1), and cf. Tyerman (2004: 175–6).

38   Bartlett (1993: 314). France (2005: 286–99) rightly differentiates between the Crusades and later colonizing exploration, but also confirms continuities.
39   Houtart (1997: 2). Tyerman (2004: 175).
40   Madden (2005: 225).
41   Watts (1985).
42   Hall (1984).
43   Rivera (1992).
44   Swedberg (1993: 51, 52) and Schumpeter (1951).
45   Firth (1979: 223–4). Hill (1971: 69 [quote], 174–5). Williamson (2001: 23, 24). Mather, quoted in Fuller (1995: 47).
46   See chapter 5.
47   On state religious regulation and toleration during the Reformation, see Kaplan (2004). For a political-philosophical history of religion and modernity that develops themes relevant to containment, see Lilla (2007).
48   On the Huguenots and English in Switzerland and Geneva, Walzer (1965: ch. 2). On Bullinger's influence on English exiles, Firth (1979: 80–1) and Cunningham and Grell (2000: 51–6). On the French and Calvin, Reid (2000: 219–21).
49   On the Reformation in England, see MacCulloch (1992), Parish (2000), and Todd (2000).
50   For the period from the English Reformation to the Puritan Revolution, see Parish (2000) and Todd (2000).
51   Corrigan and Sayer (1985: 57).
52   My account draws on Corrigan and Sayer (1985: 56–60; 57 [quote]) and Marx (2003: 56–67).
53   Quoted in Walzer (1965: 118). See also Hill (1972: 129) and Corrigan and Sayer (1985: 59).
54   Zaret (1985).
55   Walzer (1965: 141).
56   Walzer (1965: 268–99). Gorski (2003: 130–1).
57   Goldstone (1991: 126, 128–32). On cottagers and squatters, see Hill (1972: 35–45).
58   Walzer (1965: 268–99; 277 [quote, orig. ital.]). On the New Model Army, see also Hill (1972: ch. 4), and for a more general discussion of Protestants and warfare, Aho (1981: ch. 11). On Alsted and Mede, see Smolinski (2001: 153–8).
59   Hill (1971: 25–9) and Firth (1979).
60   Hill (1971: 62, 124; 1972: 119). On theological developments and shifting venues of the apocalyptic, see Firth (1979: esp. 202–3, ch. 7).
61   Hill (1971: 115–18 116; 1972). On the Family of Love, see also Zaret (1985: 99–105).
62   Sermon of Vavasor Powell, quoted in Lewy (1974: 139).

63   Hobbes's orientation toward Christianity is much debated. Some, e.g., Hill (1958: ch. 9) and Lilla (2007: 74–93), see him as a vague believer at most, who, concerned that religious dissent legitimated political disobedience, developed a politically inspired theology that would keep the masses in check. On the other hand, Pocock (1971) argues that Hobbes arrived at his theology in good faith, and Lessay (2007) offers a nuanced account of Hobbes as an unorthodox covenant-theology Christian.

64   Walzer (1965: 297–8).

65   Kirby (1941). See also Hill (1980: 71) and Stone (1980: 54).

66   "Declaration of Breda," quoted in Marx (2003: 130).

67   Hill (1972: 303; 1980: 60); see also Walzer (1965: 312). Evidence presented by Burns (2001) for the continued importance of apocalyptic discourse among Whig opponents of the monarchy actually suggests how much it waned relative to the period of the Puritan Revolution.

68   Marx (2003: 128–39, 153–61).

69   Stone (1980).

70   Hill (1967: 228).

71   Fukuyama (1992: 260).

72   Stone (1980: 54, 58, 82–3, 95, 96 [quote]).

73   Zaret (1985: 83–9).

74   Hill (1980: 34–45).

75   The following account draws especially on Marx (2003: 86–94, 122–5; 148–53; 168–75).

76   Walzer (1965: 68–92; 92 [quote]).

77   Marx (2003: 56, 90).

78   Henri III, quoted in Marx (2003: 93).

79   For texts of 1682 Gallican Declaration and 1685 Revocation of Edict of Nantes, see Ehler and Morrall (1967: 205–8, 208–13).

80   On France's royal religion, see Van Kley (1996).

81   Knox (1950: 131).

82   Weber (1978: 1164).

83   Mann (1986: chs. 13–14).

84   Bultmann (1957: 59).

85   Postmillennialism as such became more significant in the eighteenth century; see chapter 5.

86   Habermas (1989: 57–67) identifies Britain as the "model case" of the emergence of the public sphere.

87   Zaret (2000).

88   Hill (1980: 54).

89   Hill (1972: ch. 14, 159 [quote]).

90   Hill (1980: 62–4). Little (1991: 129 [quote]).

91   Jacob's (1976: 104–5) account of latitudinarian millennialism mirrors other descriptions of postmillennialism as a source of the modern

ideology of progress, but nevertheless (139–40) rejects the thesis that millenarianism was behind progress.

92 For debates concerning the connection between Protestantism and the ideology of progress, see Smolinski (2001: 157) and views that he disputes directly or by implication – Tuveson (1949), Nisbet (1980: 126–45), and Hill (1980: 59–61). On Voltaire, McGinnis (2008). On August Comte and positivism, see Löwith (1949: 67–91) and Manuel (1962: ch. 6).

93 Becker (1932: 29–31, 49, 122, 129).

94 That is, the liberal-humanitarian utopia described by Mannheim (1936: 219–29).

95 Van Kley (1996: 13 [quote], 365).

96 Tyerman (2004: 186).

97 Walzer (1963: 86 [orig. ital.]).

98 Hobbes (1998: 95–6). Derrida in Habermas (2003: 102–3).

99 Eisenstadt (1999a: esp. 25, 35–6, 41, 42, 49–52, 63, 73, 74). Robespierre, quoted in Carr (2006: 329).

100 On eighteenth-century millenarianism and the prophetresses, Garrett (1975: 17 [quote of early-twentieth century historian Albert Mathiez]). On *ex post facto* apocalyptic characterizations, McGinn (1994: 243–5) and Burleigh (2005: 43).

101 Barnett (2003: chs. 4–5).

102 Parrow (1993: 64).

103 McGinn (1994: 242–3).

104 Joutard (1985). Knox (1950: 357–65).

105 *Unigenitus* bull, *http://www.papalencyclicals.net/Clem11/c11unige.htm* (accessed February 13, 2009).

106 Knox (1950: 372–88).

107 Joutard (1985: 341). Van Kley (1996: 142).

108 Baker (1990: 33, 37–8, 170 [quote]). Van Kley (1996: 122, 135–53). Barnett (2003: 150–2).

109 Lewy (1974: 349–52, 353 [quote]) and Van Kley (1996: chs. 5–6).

110 Quoted in Lewy (1974: 374). On religion in the revolution, see McManners (1969).

111 Burleigh (2005: ch. 3; 81, 92 [quotes]).

112 Higonnet (1998: 324).

113 Baker (1987: 43, 47, 58 [quote, orig. ital.]).

114 E.g., Higonnet (1998: 312).

115 Furet (1981).

116 Furet (1981: 176).

117 Weber (1978: 56, 305–6, 1164).

118 Baker (1990: 37–8), Barnett (2003: 161). Garrett's (1975: ch. 5) account of the Avignon Society is an exemplar of research that could identify millenarian features of the climate in which Jacobinism developed.

119 Garrett (1975: 84).

Chapter 5   Modernity and the Apocalyptic

1   For example, Parsons (1951, 1954).
2   On the modernity of al-Qaida, see Gray (2003).
3   Partridge 1998: 97–8.
4   On sacred violence, see Girard (1986). For more on Walzer (1963: 86), see chapter 4.
5   This view has its own history; see Lewy (1974: 383–4).
6   Luhmann (1982: 302).
7   Simmel (1950: 409–24).
8   Bell (1973: 117).
9   Harvey (1990, pt. III).
10   Bauman (2005, introduction).
11   Kern (1983).
12   On varieties of ecstatic transcendence, James (1985).
13   Wagner (1994).
14   Foucault (1988: 154).
15   On postmodernism, Hall, Neitz, and Battani (2003: ch. 7).
16   Price (2008) focuses on the existential experiences of temporality, exemplified in the French Revolution and the industrial revolution.
17   Foucault (1988).
18   See Adams (2005) and Hall (2008).
19   On individuals' multiple identities under modern conditions, see Bull (1999: ch. 7).
20   On the civil sphere, moral codes, and the tensions of identity politics, see Alexander (2006).
21   Wagner (1994).
22   Habermas (1987).
23   Hamilton (1994: 192, 194, 196).
24   Lenin (1970); Wallerstein (1974).
25   Steinmetz (2005: 340, 351, 357).
26   Hardt and Negri (2000). Steinmetz (2005: 361 fn. 64) criticizes Hardt and Negri's theorization for its seemingly contradictory acknowledgement that the U.S. is the "only remaining superpower." Yet in discussing earlier empire complexes, Steinmetz (2005: 353–6) also acknowledges possibilities of "hybrid empires, mixed hegemonies." In these terms, the Empire of Modernity offers an ideal typical conceptualization that can be used to specify more clearly the hybrid character of empire today as a structuration that includes aspects beyond hegemonic nation-state predominance.
27   Eisenstadt (1999a).
28   Schmitt (1985: 1 [quote]; 1976: 26–8).
29   Arendt (1963: 5). On millennialist ideology in the Nazi movement, Redles (2005). On Nazi genocide, Hiroshima, and 9/11 in relation to one another, see Ray (2005: chs. 3, 4) and Bousquet (2006). On the

rise of nuclear warfare, in part as the road to Armageddon, see, for example, Keys (1961), Martin and Mullen (1983), and Boyer (1992: ch. 4).

30 Marx and Engels (1978: 473); the core of the dialectic as a shift from feudalism to capitalism to socialism is implicit in Marx's 1843 essay, "On the Jewish question" (Marx 1978b: 44–6).

31 Niebuhr (1964: xi). Engels (1964: 98). The apocalyptic affinity of Marx's theory has been noted by otherwise diverse analysts, for example, Löwith (1949: 51), Bultmann (1957: 68–9), and Hobsbawm (1959: 59).

32 Engels (1939: 307). Marx (1978a: 160). For theorization of worldly utopias, see Hall (1978b).

33 Sorel (1961: 148, italics eliminated); in the introduction, Edward Shils describes Sorel's ideas in relation to apocalyptic transformation.

34 For an introduction to anarchism, see Joll (1964). For historical documents reflecting both atheistic and quasi-religious dimensions of anarchism, see Avrich (1973).

35 Hall (1978a).

36 On nineteenth-century anarchism, see Venturi (2001), Pomper (1970), and Carr (2006). On the Haymarket bombing, Avrich (1984: ch. 27). On terrorism's connections to anarchism, see Laqueur (2001) and Chaliand and Blin (2007).

37 Arendt (1963: 95–6). For his strategic thinking, see, e.g., Lenin (1963) Discussions of the "revolutionary moment" thread through Lenin's works. Higonnet (1998: 328–32) and Furet (1999: 64–7) dispute comparisons made between the Jacobins and the Bolsheviks, though they acknowledge that the Bolsheviks themselves claimed Jacobin inspiration. Cf. Besançon (1981: 32–6).

38 Besançon (1981: 278).

39 Kataev (1976: 166). Soviet constructions of revolutionary charismatic mastery over rational time in the vein fictionalized by Kataev are treated in historical depth by Hanson (1997).

40 Besançon (1981: 281).

41 On Soviet bureaucracy, collectivization, and terror, Fitzpatrick (2001 [death toll, 166]). On everyday life under Stalinism, Fitzpatrick (1999). On the internal decline of the Soviet Union, Furet (1999). On Stalinism, "charismatic-rational" time, and the purges, Hanson (1997: 166–70).

42 See Merleau-Ponty (1969), and for more on his analysis of political violence, see chapter 6.

43 Collins (1986: ch. 8).

44 On Confucianism, Fairbank (1992: 51–3). *I Ching* (1967). On the Taiping Rebellion, Spence (1996: xxiii, 30–3, 55–68, 123–5).

45 Bianco (1975) and Dirlik (1989).

46   Bianco (1975: 31, 62, 68, 74, 184–6). On anarchism in China, Price (1974: 122–3, 208–12), Spence (1981: 44–6), Dirlik (1989: 209–16), and Zarrow (1990). On twentieth-century history through the lens of May Fourth, Miller (2004). On Mao and Kropotkin, Zarrow (1990: 232–7). For histories of guerrilla warfare, Laqueur (1998), Asprey (1994), and, for 1939 through the 1980s, Corbett (1986).

47   Bianco (1975: 188, 198 [quote], 185).

48   White (1989: 7) argues that the Cultural Revolution campaigns can only be explained as vast and diffuse, incompletely encouraged from above. On the Cultural Revolution and anarchism, Zarrow (1990: 234–5). For an interpretation of the Cultural Revolution that gives more significance to Mao, see MacFarquhar and Schoenhals (2006).

49   U (2007).

50   On Cambodia, Margolin (1999).

51   The title of Lanternari's (1963) classic study.

52   On blacks in the U.S., Hall (2004: 49).

53   On Ras Tafari and Mau Mau, Wilson (1973: 63–9, 264–8); on African millenarian movements and cargo cults, Lewy (1974: chs. 9, 10); see also the studies of cargo cults by Worsley (1968) and Lindstrom (1993). Mau Mau movement spirit-mediums, Edgerton (1989: 120–1, 140–1) and Weigert (1996: 29–30).

54   Wilson (1973: 68, 222, 228, 234–6, 258).

55   Adas (1979: 184–5).

56   Corbett (1986).

57   Armstrong (1988: 367–71) traces the political side; Barkun (1997: ch. 1) focuses on British Israelism as a religious movement.

58   Corbett (1986: 190–4; 202–3, 215–17).

59   Hobsbawm (1959: 58–9, 59 [quote]).

60   Lewy (1974: pt. III).

61   Buttinger's (1953) case study focuses on shifts between aboveground/underground strategies. On the government and insurgent encounter in guerrilla tactics, Paret and Shy (1962: 44), Galula (1964), and O'Neill (1990).

62   Shils (1968: 70).

63   Hall (1978b: 206–7).

64   As Robert Lifton (1968) wrote of the Chinese Cultural Revolution.

65   Nechaev, quoted in Carr (2006: 18–19). Placard photo, Roediger and Rosemont (1986: 192).

66   The history of apocalyptic movements in the U.S. has been the subject of a number of important studies; see especially Sandeen (1970), Marsden (1980), Boyer (1992), and Fuller (1995).

67   Miller (1956). Winthrop, quoted in Armstrong (1988: 347), who compares the Pilgrims both to the ancient Jews and twentieth-century Zionists. See also Bloch (1985: pt. I), and Zakai (1992), who frames

settlement of both the Virginia colony and New England in relation to apocalyptic time and religious migration, but in different ways.

68 Edwards (1998: 54).

69 McGinn (1994: 237, 241 [quotes]). On eighteenth-century millennialist theologies and their relation to the Revolutionary War, see Davidson (1977: 232–54) and Bloch (1985: pt. II), but cf. Boyer (1992: 73–4).

70 As Davidson (1977: 261–80) points out, toward the end of the eighteenth century this distinction becomes especially important because of increasing synergies between postmillennialist theologies and Enlightenment ideas; cf. Smolinski (2001), who similarly establishes continuities between European and American millennial theologies.

71 On "manifest destiny," and Congregationalist minister, Tuveson (1968: 74 [quote], 91–136). Young (2006) finds an early template of the modern social movement in nineteenth-century American Protestant causes such as the antislavery movement. On apocalyptic themes in the antislavery movement, Fuller (1995: 88–92).

72 Moorhead (1999); see also Vidich and Lyman (1985).

73 Barton Stone, quoted in Ahlstrom (1972: 434).

74 Knox (1950: 558–66).

75 The standard history remains O'Dea (1957). On millennialist themes in Mormonism, Hansen (1967), Tuveson (1968: 175–86), Sandeen (1970: 47–8), and Harrison (1979: 176–92). On the significance of struggles with detractors for Mormon history, Moore (1986: ch. 1). On plural marriage, Foster (1991).

76 Niebuhr (1929).

77 Barkun (1986) traces the movement's myriad connections to nineteenth-century communal utopias; see also Harrison (1979: 192–203). Bear, quoted in Newport (2000: 152–3), who follows the thread forward to the Seventh-Day Adventists, and then to the Branch Davidians.

78 Synon (1971). Hollenwager (1972: 459ff.). Hall (2004: 6, 9).

79 Ahlstrom (1972: 556–63).

80 Boyer (1992: ch. 6) details the fraught and mercurial relationship of Protestant American millennialism to the role of the Jews. Sandeen (1970: xix, ch. 3), who traces the influence of Darby, argues that American fundamentalism is deeply grounded in millenarianism.

81 Weber (1979), Marsden (1980), Boyer (1992: 86–90, 93–100, 183–7), Fuller (1995: ch. 5), and McGinn (1994: 252–62).

82 See Riesebrodt (1993), who compares U.S. Protestant fundamentalism with fundamentalism in Iran during the 1960s and '70s.

83 See Sandeen (1970), who describes an early twentieth-century "informal alliance" between the Presbyterians' Princeton Theological Seminary and millenarianism.

84 Herberg (1955).

85   Ribuffo (1983).
86   On fundamentalism, see especially Balmer (2006), Boyer (1992), Fuller (1995: ch. 6), Wojcik (1997), and Barkun (2003). On the Christian Identity movement, Barkun (1997). Wright (2007) traces the Oklahoma City bombing connections. On the elective affinity between the American Christian Right and racism during the latter twentieth century, see Barkun (1997) and Burlein (2002). On Dominion theology, see the jeremiad of a liberal Presbyterian, Hedges (2007).
87   Hunter (1983: 52, 57, 115; 1987: 59). See also Wilcox (1992), who has conducted a more detailed survey analysis of evangelicals and their politics.
88   Block (2007a: 18 [quote]). Reagan's frequent invocation of a "city on a hill" came as early as 1974, when he was governor of California; see *http://www.conservative.org/pressroom/reagan/reagan1974.asp* (accessed February 19, 2009). Explanations of the rise of the Christian Right range from approaches emphasizing symbolic politics to rational-choice theories; for debates, see Wilcox (1992), Oldfield (1996), and the collections edited by Liebman and Wuthnow (1983) and Smidt and Penning (1997).
89   See chapter 4.
90   Hall (1978b).
91   On the Symbionese Liberation Army as exemplifying the warring sect, Hall (1978b). On the Red Army Faction and the Red Brigades, Corbett (1986: 200–9).
92   The motives of principals and degree of compulsion of participants in these cases were complex and varied; see Hall (2004) and Hall, Schuyler, and Trinh (2000). The Jonestown and Branch Davidian events bear comparison to other historical incidents in which more powerful external adversaries confronted true religious believers, for example, Russian Orthodox Old Believers during the seventeenth century (Robbins 1986).
93   Hall, Schuyler, and Trinh (2000: 106–10).

Chapter 6   Radical Islam and the Globalized Apocalypse

1   Michael Ignatieff, "It's war, but it doesn't have to be dirty," *The Guardian*, October 1, 2001, *http://www.guardian.co.uk/world/2001/oct/01/afghanistan.terrorism9* (accessed February 24, 2009 [ital. added]).
2   Tilly (2004: 5). See also Hoffman (1998: ch. 1) and Smelser (2007).
3   Susan Sontag, "Talk of the town," *The New Yorker* (September 24, 2001), *http://www.newyorker.com/archive/2001/09/24/010924ta_talk_wtc* (accessed February 24, 2009).

4 Fukuyama (1992: 45, 46, 70 [orig. ital.]).
5 Fukuyama (1992: 12, 130). For an exposition of the metanarrative of modernity, see Lyotard (1984).
6 See Cooley (2002), Benjamin and Simon (2003), Coll (2004), Gerges (2005), and Wright (2006).
7 The very terminology of "jihad" is controversial, both for those Muslims who do not embrace the radical Islamist cause, and for Western opponents, who see the label as lending (Muslim) legitimacy to the movement. See Joseph Lelyveld, "All suicide bombers are not alike," *NYT*, October 28, 2001. More recently, language itself has become part of the struggle. See P.W. Singer and Elina Noor, "What do you call a terror(jihad)ist?" *NYT*, June 2, 2008.
8 See, for example, the essays in Kelsay and Johnson (1991).
9 Cooley (2002: ch. 5) and Gerges (2005: 75–7).
10 There has been no evidence of any strategic presence of al-Qaida in Iraq before the beginning of the Iraq war that toppled the regime of Saddam Hussein. See the U.S. Senate Select Committee on Intelligence report, June 2008, *http://intelligence.senate.gov/080605/phase2a. pdf* (accessed February 24, 2009), and Mark Mazzetti and Scott Shane, "Bush overstated Iraq evidence, senators report," *NYT*, June 6, 2008. As the allied military stabilization of Iraq made progress in late 2008, some "foreign fighters" reportedly went to Afghanistan to join the ongoing Taliban resurgence there; see John Burns, "As US gains in Iraq, rebels go to Afghanistan," *NYT*, October 15, 2008.
11 Block (2007b).
12 Merleau-Ponty (1969: 2, xvii, 92, 107, 175, 153, 156).
13 Mannheim (1936).
14 Eisenstadt (1999a: 116).
15 Hechter (1975). Juergensmeyer (2000: 227). Aho (1997: 69).
16 Pape (2005).
17 Benjamin (1968: 263).
18 George W. Bush, press conference, October 11, 2001, *http://edition. cnn.com/TRANSCRIPTS/0110/11/se.21.html* (accessed March 1, 2009).
19 On "sacred terror," see Rapport (1984).
20 It is all too easy to psychologize or instrumentalize the phenomenon of suicide bombers. For alternative approaches, see Sageman (2002) and Pape (2005).
21 Al-Qaida would seem to exemplify the possibility described by Goldstone (1991) of a blocked elite leading a wider *déclassé* alliance.
22 Weber (1946: 276–7).
23 Weber (1978: 473–4). The degree to which Islamic doctrines actually protected communities of Jews and Christians has been historically variable.
24 "Bin Ladin [*sic*] Declares Jihad on Americans," *Al-Islah*, London, in Arabic, September 2, 1996, *http://binladenquotes.blogspot.com/2004/02/*

fbis-document-10-years-of-osama-bin.html (accessed February 24, 2009); alternative source, Rubin and Rubin (2002: 137–42). After the election of Barack Obama, al-Qaida and the Taliban continued to demonstrate strategic pursuit of goals; see Michael Slackman and Souad Mekhennet, "Jihadi leader says radicals share Obama victory," *NYT*, November 8, 2008, and Helene Cooper, "A world of advice for Obama on foreign policy," *NYT*, November 14, 2008.

25 On this point, see, for example, Jeff Goodwin, "The empire strikes back: the geopolitical roots of 9/11," lecture, University of California – Davis Center for History, Society, and Culture, Davis, California, November 12, 2002.

26 See chapter 2 and note 7 above.

27 For sociological histories of the Ottoman Empire, see Anderson (1974: 361–94) and Turner (1974: 124–34). On jihadist ideology, see especially Habeck (2006) and Khosrokhavar (2009).

28 Sageman (2002: 6–7), Cook (2005: 97–9), and Migaux (2007).

29 Attempts to establish a basic factual history of contemporary militant jihadism are hardly settled, but see Sageman (2002: 8–17), Cook (2005: ch. 5), Wright (2006), Migaux (2007), and Eikmeier (2007). On his opposition to Western Enlightenment values and Marxism, see Qutb (2006: 79–84); cf. Habeck (2006: 57–67), Ali (1993: 72), and Lawrence (1991: 147). For an early discussion of Egypt, Qutb, and the Brotherhood, see Lewy (1974: ch. 18).

30 Faraj, quoted in Seligman (2002: 14). Bernard Lewis (2004) notes continuities, as well as differences, between the assassination carried out by the Egyptian Islamic Brotherhood and the practices of the revolutionary Shi'a Assassins sect of the eleventh and twelfth centuries.

31 On Zawahiri, Qutb, and bin Laden: Neil MacFarquhar, "Islamic jihad, forged in Egypt, is seen as bin Laden's backbone," *NYT*, October 4, 2001; Lawrence Wright, "The man behind bin Laden," *The New Yorker* (September 16, 2002): 56–85.

32 Cooley (2002: 69–70), Cook (2005: 129), and Wright (2006: 150–3). Azzam, quoted in Migaux (2007: 315).

33 Migaux (2007: 294, 296–8). Wright reports that Zawahiri's key treatise, *Guide to the Path of Righteousness for Jihad and Belief*, is a bowdlerized text written by Sayyid Imam al-Sharifi (Lawrence Wright, "The rebellion within: An Al Qaeda mastermind questions terrorism," *The New Yorker* (June 2, 2008): 37–53). Jihadist quoted in J.F. Burns, "Americans battling closer to Qaida bunkers," *NYT*, March 6, 2002.

34 "Bin Ladin [*sic*] Declares Jihad on Americans," *Al-Islah*, London, in Arabic, September 2, 1996, *http://binladenquotes.blogspot.com/2004/02/fbis-document-10-years-of-osama-bin.html* (accessed February 24, 2009). On al-Qaida ideology, Anonymous (2004: ch. 4) and Cook (2005: ch. 6).

35 Anonymous (2002: 48–49). The source of the quotation is an interview by Hamid Mir published in *Pakistan,* March 18, 1997, *http:// binladenquotes.blogspot.com/2004/02/fbis-document-10-years-of-osama-bin.html* (accessed February 25, 2009). On the perceived benefits to al-Qaida of shifting to the "far enemy," see Sageman (2002: 18–24) and Eikmeier (2007: 90–1).

36 Pakistani quoted in J.F. Burns, "Bin Laden stirs struggle on meaning of jihad," *NYT*, January 27, 2002.

37 Gerges (2005: 21 [Zionist–Crusader alliance quote]) provides the most detailed analysis of the shift to the "far enemy." Pape (2005: 104) portrays al-Qaida as "less a transnational network of like-minded ideologues ... than a cross-national military alliance of national liberation movements working together against what they see as a common imperialist threat." On the other hand, Cook (2005: 128) argues that the Afghani war against the Soviets "established contacts among a wide variety of Muslim antigovernment and resistance movements and fused them together" into what he describes as "globalist radical Islam."

38 Hall (1978b: 206).

39 "Final instructions to the hijackers of September 11," in Lincoln (2003: appendix A, 93–8 [97, quote]).

40 Weber (1978: 475).

41 Anonymous (2002: ch. 3), Wechsler and Wolosky (2002), and Gunaratna (2002: ch. 2).

42 Gunaratna (2002: chs. 2, 3).

43 Lawrence Wright, "The man behind bin Laden," *The New Yorker* (September 16, 2002): 81. Sageman (2002) depicts al-Qaida as a network structure that vets potential participants via social networks of kin, friendship, and worship.

44 On the planning and execution of the 9/11 attacks, see Judith Miller and Don Van Natta, Jr., "In years of plots and clues, scope of Qaeda eluded U.S.," *NYT*, June 9, 2002; Douglas Frantz with Desmond Butler, "Sept. 11 attack planned in '99, Germans learn," *NYT*, August 30, 2002; Richard Bernstein, with Douglas Frantz, Don Van Natta, Jr., and David Johnston, "On path to the U.S. skies, plot leader met bin Laden," *NYT*, September 10, 2002; and James Risen and David Johnston, "F.B.I. account outlines activities of hijackers before 9/11 attacks," *NYT*, September 27, 2002. On post-9/11 shifts toward even greater decentralization, see Peter L. Bergen, "Al Qaeda's new tactics," *NYT*, November 15, 2002. Gerges (2005: 41–2) notes the difficulties of charismatic succession. Sageman's (2002: 172–3) network analysis suggests that a hierarchical organization may maintain secrecy more effectively, while a network is more resilient at survival. Sageman and Bruce Hoffman are thus in dispute about the structure of al-Qaida, and the relative danger posed by it as a

centralized organization versus autonomously constituted cells (*NYT*, June 8, 2008, "Week in review").

45 Mark Mazzetti, "U.S. analyst depicts al Qaeda as secure in Pakistan and more potent than in 2007," *NYT*, August 13, 2008, reporting a speech by Ted Gistaro, *http://www.dni.gov/speeches/20080812_speech. pdf* (accessed February 25, 2009). The one region experiencing a decline in terrorist mobilization is Southeast Asia, according to U.S. officials; see Eric Schmitt, "Experts see gains against Asian terror networks," *NYT*, June 9, 2008.

46 Charles Kurzman, "Bin Laden and other thoroughly modern Muslims," *Contexts*, Fall/Winter 2002, cites a Gallup Poll suggesting that 15 percent of Muslims regarded the 9/11 attacks as morally justified. In democratic politics, this would be a small percentage. Nevertheless, numerically, it would include millions of people. The taking of such a position, unthinkable in the West, is a gauge of countercultural alienation among a substantial segment of the Muslim population.

47 Juergensmeyer (2000: 162).

48 Frederick Kagan, "The new Bolsheviks: Understanding Al Qaeda," American Enterprise Institute paper, November 16, 2005, *http://www.aei.org/publications/pubID.23460/pub_detail.asp* (accessed February 25, 2009).

49 Sorel (1961). See chapter 5.

50 Hall (2003).

51 Edward Rothstein, "Attacks on U.S. challenge the perspectives of postmodern true believers," *NYT*, September 22, 2001.

52 Bush aide "reality" comment in the summer of 2002 reported by Ron Suskind, "Faith, certainty and the presidency of George W. Bush," *NYT*, October 17, 2004.

53 For example, Derrida, in Habermas (2003: 100–3).

54 Hall, Schuyler, and Trinh (2000: 200).

55 Thus, conservative commentator Daniel Pipes (2002) warned Americans of the need to awaken to a struggle that extends beyond al-Qaida to Islamists more generally. American Christian public figures such as Jerry Falwell and Franklin Graham depicted Islam as militant at its core, and even "evil"; see Michael Wilson, "Evangelist says Muslims haven't adequately apologized for Sept. 11 attacks," *NYT*, August 15, 2002.

56 On Schmitt, see chapter 5. George W. Bush, September 2001 speech; for a transcript, see "President Bush's Address on Terrorism Before a Joint Meeting of Congress," *NYT*, September 21, 2001.

57 Boykin, quoted in Laurie Goodstein, "Church event set for base stirs concerns," *NYT*, April 6, 2003. In relation to the "axis of evil," in October 2008, the Bush administration removed North Korea from its "state sponsors of terrorism" list as part of a deal to encourage

it to continue to dismantle its nuclear weapons program; see Helene Cooper, "U.S. declares North Korea off terror list," *NYT*, October 14, 2008. Speech by George W. Bush, National Endowment for Democracy, October 6, 2005; for a transcript, see *http://www.washingtonpost.com/wp-srv/politics/administration/bushtext_100605.html* (accessed March 1, 2009). Reaction in *The Nation* (Pakistan), by M.A. Niazi, November 4, 2005, *http://www.watchingamerica.com/thenationpk000011.html* (accessed February 25, 2009). Anonymous (2004).

58 Lincoln (2003: 20, 30).
59 Dwight, quoted in Jewett and Lawrence's (2002: 55) detailed history of millennialist imperialism.
60 Tuveson (1968: 132).
61 Qutb (2006: 13).
62 Taylor (2005).
63 On the elective affinity between neoconservatives in the Bush administration and the millennialism of the Christian Right, see Urban (2007) and Lifton (2003). On American millenarian religion, see chapter 5, and on American millenarian responses to 9/11, see Barkun (2003: ch. 10).
64 A similar analysis had been advanced by Jewett and Lawrence (2002: 20–5).
65 Huntington (1996). On al-Qaida, the U.S., and the clash, Anonymous (2002: 261).
66 Edward Rothstein, "Attacks on U.S. challenge the perspectives of postmodern true believers," *NYT*, September 22, 2001. Later, Rothstein depicted unnamed "international commentators and American intellectuals" as arguing that "terrorism is caused by social and economic injustice"; Rothstein, "Cherished ideas refracted in history's lens," *NYT*, September 7, 2002. For a retort, see Stanley Fish, "Postmodern warfare: the ignorance of our warrior intellectuals," *Harper's*, July 2002, 33–40.
67 Tilly (1995).
68 Anonymous (2002: 31).
69 Niall Ferguson, "Sinking globalization," *Foreign Affairs* 84 (2), Mar./Apr. 2005, *http://www.foreignaffairs.org/20050301faessay84207/niall-ferguson/sinking-globalization.html* (accessed March 2, 2009).
70 Barack Obama, Address to Joint Session of U.S. Congress, February 24, 2009, *http://www.whitehouse.gov/the_press_office/Remarks-of-President-Barack-Obama-Address-to-Joint-Session-of Congress/* (accessed March 1, 2009).
71 Niall Ferguson, "Sinking globalization," *Foreign Affairs* 84 (2), Mar./Apr. 2005, *http://www.foreignaffairs.org/20050301faessay84207/niall-ferguson/sinking-globalization.html* (accessed March 2, 2009).

72   Abu Omar al-Baghdadi, leader of the Islamic State of Iraq, quoted in Michael Slackman and Souad Mekhennet, "Jihadi leader says radicals share Obama victory," *NYT*, November 8, 2008.

73   Habermas (2003: 38). Derrida, in Habermas (2003: 100–3).

74   See Scott Shane, "China inspired interrogations at Guantánamo," *NYT*, July 2, 2008; Joby Warrick, "CIA tactics endorsed in secret memos," *Washington Post*, October 15, 2008.

75   Coward (2005a: 863, 845, 865, 866 [quotes]; 2005b). Cf. Hardt and Negri (2000), Joxe (2002), and Reid (2005).

76   David Johnston and David E. Sanger, "Yemen killing based on rules set out by Bush," *NYT*, November 6, 2002; Seymour Hersh, "Manhunt: The Bush administration's new strategy in the war on terrorism," *The New Yorker* (December, 23 and 30, 2002): 66–74; Eric Schmitt and Mark Mazzetti, "Secret order lets U.S. raid al Qaeda," *NYT*, November 10, 2008.

77   On the long-term strategy, Eric Schmitt, "Pentagon draws up a 20-to-30 year antiterror plan," *NYT*, January 17, 2003. Sageman (2002: 175–84) considers the implications for strategies to defeat a social network. Hoffman (1998) focuses on dismantling al-Qaida as an organization.

78   See, for example, Samantha Power, "For terrorists, a war on aid groups," *NYT*, August 19, 2008.

79   Coward (2005a: 863).

80   See Jane Perlez and Pir Zubair Shar, "Confronting Taliban, Pakistan finds itself at war," *NYT*, October 3, 2008.

81   Kiramat Ullah, a commander in the Hezbul Mujahadeen, quoted in Peter Maas, "The volunteer," *NYT Magazine*, October 7, 2001.

82   Already in 2002, survey research conducted in certain countries with majority Muslim populations – Egypt, Jordan, Indonesia, Lebanon, Turkey, and Senegal – revealed majority opposition to the U.S.-led war against terrorism; see Adam Clymer, "World survey says negative views of U.S. are rising," *NYT*, December 5, 2002.

83   STRATFOR, "Emerging Bush doctrine reshaping U.S. strategy," *http://www.stratfor.com/frontpage*, February 26, 2002 (accessed March 1, 2009).

84   Cf. Joxe (2002: 16–17).

85   Writing before 9/11, the scholar of the Islamic and Arab worlds Bernard Lewis (2001) already described the basic alternatives. On the issues posed for the West, see especially Gunaratna (2002) and Ignatieff (2004).

86   Indeed, historians' "what-if" questions are already being posed by journalists; see Dexter Filkins, "Afghanistan and Iraq: what if," *NYT*, February 25, 2009.

87   Merleau-Ponty (1969).

Chapter 7   The Last Apocalypse?

1   Schmithals (1975: 29–49) provides one generic account of the apocalyptic.
2   Weber (1946: 280).
3   McCarthy (2006) and Crace (2007). On apocalyptic elements in fiction, see Rosen (2008).
4   Ignatieff (2004: 153–4).
5   Fukuyama (1992); for his defense of his thesis after 9/11, see Francis Fukuyama, "History is still going our way," *Wall Street Journal*, October 5, 2001.
6   Hall (1999: 37–9).
7   Eisenstadt (1999b).
8   Hall (1999: 72–97).
9   This phenomenological history of multiple emergent social temporalities mirrors Louis Althusser and Étienne Balibar's (1970) structuralist analysis that substitutes for an ideological construction of "history" a manifold hybrid ensemble of temporalities. However, because phenomenological sociology centers analysis in meaningful social action, it affords a thicker account of temporal structurations than Althusser and Balibar attempted. My colleague Ari Adut has pointed me to an account of temporalities that shares certain affinities with my approach, by Krzysztof Pomian (1984). Unfortunately, it came to my attention too late to take into consideration in the present study.
10   For a study that, though it does not name the temporalities, maps actions across temporal registers of the here-and-now (of partisan publics) and the diachronic (of political parties), see Mische (2008).
11   Wagner (1994).
12   See the important study by Price (2008: ch. 4).
13   Lash and Urry (1994: 229).
14   On times and social systems, see Luhmann (1982: 284–6). On computer times, see, for example, *http://www.gnu.org/software/mit-scheme/ documentation/mit-scheme-ref/Machine-Time.html* (accessed February 25, 2009); Ta-Shma et al. (2008). For a general history of modern diachrony and a pre-internet view on computers, see Whitrow (1988: ch. 10; 181–2). On the social in relation to networks, Latour (1993).
15   On systems and their differentiation, Luhmann (1982, 1995).
16   For this analysis, and its sources in critical theory and Foucault, see Hall, Neitz, and Battani (2003).
17   On Weber's view of the limits of rationalization, see Roth (1987).
18   Certeau (1984).
19   Weber (1958). Taylor (2007). On self-fashioning, see also Berger, Berger, and Kellner (1973). Wagner (1994).

20   Zamyatin (1993: 13).
21   Taylor (2007). On varieties of transcendental and other religious experience, James (1985).
22   Fraser (1997).
23   On the public sphere, Alexander (2006). On recognition, the work of Nancy Fraser (e.g., 2000) is central.
24   Gauchet (1997).
25   Stark and Bainbridge (1987).
26   Martin (2005).
27   Taylor (2007).
28   Particularly important is Ignatieff's (2004) ethical and geostrategic analysis of the challenges that liberal democracies face in choosing "the lesser evil" that will safeguard society without compromising democratic institutions or embracing a logic of violence symmetric with those of terrorists. Other viewpoints to consider include the policy discussions of Pillar (2001), Gunaratna (2002: ch. 5), Wintrobe (2006: 251–60), Smelser (2007: ch. 5), and a quite different volume that offers "an indictment of subversive Muslim leaders representing Saudi Wahhabi interests" (Sperry 2005: ix).
29   For a review of characterizations of terrorism using "medieval" tropes, see Holsinger (2007).
30   Gray (2003: 76).
31   Gray (2003).
32   Girard (2008).
33   Lilla (2007). Seligman (2004).
34   Raymond Bonner, "2 British antiterror experts say U.S. takes wrong path," *NYT*, October 22, 2008.
35   Michael Slackman and Souad Mekhennet, "Jihadi leader says radicals share Obama victory," *NYT*, November 8, 2008; Mark Mazzetti and Scott Shane, "Al Qaeda coldly acknowledges victory," *NYT*, November 20, 2008.
36   Seligman's (2004) essay on religion and tolerance provides a thoughtful discussion of the possibilities. For other important approaches, see Appleby (2000) and Juergensmeyer (2002).
37   On ecological crisis and apocalyptic conflict, see Dupuy (2008). On the relation of the apocalyptic to natural disasters, see Barkun (1974).
38   Baudrillard (1994).

Bibliography

Adams, Paula. 2005. *The Familial State: Ruling Families and Merchant Capitalism in Early Modern Europe*. Ithaca, N.Y.: Cornell University Press.

Adas, Michael. 1979. *Prophets of Rebellion: Millenarian Protest Movements against the European Colonial Order*. Chapel Hill: University of North Carolina Press.

Ahlstrom, Sidney. 1972. *A Religious History of the American People*. New Haven, CT: Yale University Press.

Aho, James A. 1981. *Religious Mythology and the Art of War*. Westport, CT: Greenwood Press.

——. 1997. "The apocalypse of modernity." Pp. 61–72 in Thomas Robbins and Susan Palmer, eds., *Millennium, Messiahs, and Mayhem*. London: Routledge.

Alexander, Jeffrey. 2006. *The Civil Sphere*. Oxford: Oxford University Press.

Ali, Shaukat. 1993. *Millenarian and Messianic Tendencies in Islamic History*. Lahore, Pakistan: Publishers United.

Althusser, Louis, and Étienne Balibar. 1970 (1968). *Reading Capital*. London: New Left Books.

Anderson, Perry. 1974. *Lineages of the Absolutist State*. London: New Left Books.

Anonymous (Scheuer, Michael). 2002. *Through Our Enemies' Eyes: Osama bin Laden, Radical Islam, and the Future of America*. Washington, D.C.: Brassey's.

——. 2004. *Imperial Hubris*. Dulles, VA: Brassey's.

Appleby, R. Scott. 2000. *The Ambivalence of the Sacred: Religion, Violence, and Reconciliation*. Lanham, MD: Rowman & Littlefield.

Arberry, Arthur J. 1955. *The Koran Interpreted*. London: Allen & Unwin.

Arendt, Hannah. 1963. *On Revolution*. New York: Viking.

Arjomand, Said Amir. 2002. "Messianism, millennialism and revolution in early Islamic history." Pp. 106–25 in Abbas Amanat and Magnus

Bernhardsson, eds., *Imagining the End: Visions of Apocalypse from the Ancient Middle East to Modern America*. London: I. B. Tauris.

Armstrong, Karen. 1988. *Holy War*. London: Macmillan.

Asprey, Robert. 1994. *War in the Shadows*. New York: William Morrow.

Attridge, Harold W. 2002. "The messiah and the millennium: The roots of two Jewish-Christian symbols." Pp. 90–105 in Abbas Amanat and Magnus Bernhardsson, eds., *Imagining the End: Visions of Apocalypse from the Ancient Middle East to Modern America*. London: I. B. Tauris.

Avrich, Paul. 1973. *The Anarchists in the Russian Revolution*. Ithaca, N.Y.: Cornell University Press.

——. 1984. *The Haymarket Tragedy*. Princeton, N.J.: Princeton University Press.

Baker, Keith Michael. 1987. "Revolutions." Pp. 41–62 in Colin Lucas, ed., *The Political Culture of the French Revolution*. Oxford: Pergamon Press.

——. 1990. *Inventing the French Revolution*. Cambridge: Cambridge University Press.

Balmer, Randall. 2006 (1989). *Mine Eyes Have Seen the Glory: A Journey into the Evangelical Subculture in America*, 4th ed. New York: Oxford University Press.

Barkun, Michael. 1974. *Disaster and the Millennium*. New Haven, CT: Yale University Press.

——. 1986. *Crucible of the Millennium*. Syracuse, N.Y.: Syracuse University Press.

——. 1997. *Religion and the Racist Right*, rev. ed. Chapel Hill: University of North Carolina Press.

——. 2003. *A Culture of Conspiracy: Apocalyptic Visions in Contemporary America*. Berkeley: University of California Press.

Barnes, Robin B. 1988. *Prophecy and Gnosis: Apocalypticism in the Wake of the Lutheran Reformation*. Stanford, CA: Stanford University Press.

Barnett, S. J. 2003. *The Enlightenment and Religion*. Manchester: Manchester University Press.

Barraclough, Geoffrey. 1976. *The Crucible of Europe*. Berkeley: University of California Press.

Bartlett, Robert. 1993. *The Making of Europe: Conquest, Colonization and Cultural Change, 950–1350*. London: Allen Lane.

Baudrillard, Jean. 1994 (1992). *The Illusion of the End*. Stanford, CA: Stanford University Press.

Bauman, Zygmunt. 2005. *Liquid Life*. Cambridge: Polity.

Baumgartner, Frederic. 1999. *Longing for the End: A History of Millennialism in Western Civilization*. New York: St. Martin's Press.

Becker, Carl. 1932. *The Heavenly City of the Eighteenth-Century Philosophers*. New Haven, CT: Yale University Press.

Bell, Daniel. 1973. *The Coming of Post-Industrial Society*. New York: Basic Books.

Bellah, Robert. 1970. "Father and son in Christianity and Confucianism." Pp. 76–99 in Bellah, *Beyond Belief*. New York: Harper & Row.

Bendix, Reinhard. 1978. *Kings or People?* Berkeley: University of California Press.

Benedict, Saint. 1975 (c. 6th century CE). *The Rule of St. Benedict*. Garden City, N.Y.: Doubleday.

Benjamin, Daniel, and Steven Simon. 2003. *The Age of Sacred Terror: Radical Islam's War against America*. New York: Random House.

Benjamin, Walter. 1968 (1940). "Theses on the philosophy of history." Pp. 253–64 in Benjamin, *Illuminations*. New York: Harcourt, Brace, & World.

Berger, Peter L. 1967. *The Sacred Canopy*. Garden City, N.Y.: Doubleday.

Berger, Peter L., Brigitte Berger, and Hansfried Kellner. 1973. *The Homeless Mind: Modernization and Consciousness*. New York: Random House.

Berger, Peter L., and Thomas Luckmann. 1966. *The Social Construction of Reality*. Garden City, N.Y.: Doubleday.

Besançon, Alain. 1981 (1977). *The Intellectual Origins of Leninism*. Oxford: Basil Blackwell.

Bianco, Lucien. 1975. *Origins of the Chinese Revolution 1915–1949*. Stanford, CA: Stanford University Press.

Biernacki, Richard. 1995. *The Fabrication of Labor: Germany and Britain, 1640–1914*. Berkeley: University of California Press.

Blankinship, Khalid Yahya. 1994. *The End of the Jihad State*. Albany: State University of New York Press.

Blickle, Peter. 1998. *From the Communal Reformation to the Revolution of the Common Man*. Leiden: Brill.

Bloch, Ruth. 1985. *Visionary Republic: Millennial Themes in American Thought 1756–1800*. Cambridge: Cambridge University Press.

Block, Fred. 2007a. "Understanding the diverging trajectories of the United States and Western Europe: A neo-Polanyian analysis." *Politics & Society* 35: 3–33.

——. 2007b. "Why is the U.S. fighting in Iraq?" *Contexts* 6(3): 33–7.

Bourdieu, Pierre. 1977 (1972). *Outline of a Theory of Practice*. New York: Cambridge University Press.

Bousquet, Antoine. 2006. "Hiroshima, September 11 and apocalyptic revelations in historical consciousness." *Millennium* 34: 739–64.

Boyarin, Daniel. 1999. *Dying for God: Martyrdom and the Making of Christianity and Judaism*. Stanford, CA: Stanford University Press.

——. 2004. *Border Lines: The Partition of Judeo-Christianity*. Philadelphia: University of Pennsylvania Press.

Boyce, Mary. 1992. *Zoroastrianism: Its Antiquity and Constant Vigour*. Costa Mesa, CA: Mazda Publishers.

Boyer, Paul. 1992. *When Time Shall Be No More*. Cambridge, MA: Harvard University Press.

Brandon, S. G. F. 1965. *History, Time and Deity*. Manchester: Manchester University Press.

Brightman, Thomas. 1615. *A REVELATION of the Revelation that is THE REVELATION of St. John opened clearly with a logicall Resolution and Exposition*

WHEREIN THE SENSE *is cleared, out of the Scripture, the event also of thinges foretold is Disscussed out of the Church-Historyes.* Amsterdam: no publisher listed.

Brown, Peter. 2000. *Augustine of Hippo*, rev. ed. Berkeley: University of California Press.

Bruce, Steve. 2002. *God is Dead.* Oxford: Blackwell.

Bull, Malcolm. 1999. *Seeing Things Hidden: Apocalypse, Vision and Totality.* New York: Verso.

———. 2002. "The roots of lay enthusiasm for the First Crusade." Pp. 173–93 in Thomas F. Madden, ed., *The Crusades.* Oxford: Blackwell.

Bultmann, D. Rudolf. 1957. *History and Eschatology.* Edinburgh: Edinburgh University Press.

Burleigh, Michael. 2005. *Earthly Powers.* London: HarperCollins.

Burlein, Ann. 2002. *Lift High the Cross: Where White Supremacy and the Christian Right Converge.* Durham, N.C.: Duke University Press.

Burns, W.E. 2001. "A Whig apocalypse: Astrology, millenarianism, and politics in England during the Restoration crisis, 1678–1683." Pp. 29–41 in James Force and Richard Popkin, eds., *Millenarianism and Messianism in Early Modern European Culture, Vol. III: The Millenarian Turn.* Dordrecht: Kluwer.

Buttinger, Joseph. 1953. *In the Twilight of Socialism: A History of the Revolutionary Socialists of Austria.* New York: Praeger.

Carr, Matthew. 2006. *The Infernal Machine: A History of Terrorism.* New York: New Press.

Catherwood, Christopher. 2007. *Making War in the Name of God.* New York: Citadel Press.

Certeau, Michel de. 1984 (1980). *The Practice of Everyday Life.* Berkeley: University of California Press.

Chaliand, Gérard, and Arnaud Blin, eds. 2007. *The History of Terrorism: From Antiquity to Al Qaeda.* Berkeley: University of California Press.

Clark, Gregory. 2007. *A Farewell to Alms: A Brief Economic History of the World.* Princeton, N.J.: Princeton University Press.

Clark, Gregory, and Ysbrand Van Der Werf. 1998. "Work in progress? The industrious revolution." *Journal of Economic History* 58: 830–43.

Cohn, Norman. 1970 (1957). *The Pursuit of the Millennium.* New York: Oxford University Press.

———. 1975. *Europe's Inner Demons.* New York: Basic Books.

———. 1993. *Cosmos, Chaos, and the World to Come.* New Haven, CT: Yale University Press.

Coll, Steve. 2004. *Ghost Wars: The Secret History of the CIA, Afghanistan, and bin Laden, from the Soviet Invasion to September 11, 2001.* New York: The Penguin Press.

Collins, John J. 2002. "Eschatological dynamics and utopian ideas in early Judaism." Pp. 69–89 in Abbas Amanat and Magnus Bernhardsson, eds., *Imagining the End: Visions of Apocalypse from the Ancient Middle East to Modern America.* London: I. B. Tauris.

Collins, Randall. 1986. *Weberian Sociological Theory*. Cambridge: Cambridge University Press.

——. 2004. *Interaction Ritual Chains*. Princeton, N.J.: Princeton University Press.

Cook, David. 2005. *Understanding Jihad*. Berkeley: University of California Press.

Cooley, John. 2002. *Unholy Wars: Afghanistan, America and International Terrorism*. London: Pluto Press.

Corbett, Robin. 1986. *Guerrilla Warfare: From 1939 to the Present Day*. London: Orbis.

Corrigan, Philip, and Derek Sayer. 1985. *The Great Arch: English State Formation as Cultural Revolution*. Oxford: Basil Blackwell.

Coward, Martin. 2005a. "The globalization of enclosure: Interrogating the geopolitics of empire." *Third World Quarterly* 26: 855–71.

——. 2005b. "The imperial character of the contemporary world order." *Theory and Event* 8 (1), *http://muse.jhu.edu/journals/theory_and_event/v008/8.1coward.html* (accessed February 25, 2009).

Cowdrey, H. E. J. 1970. *The Cluniacs and the Gregorian Reform*. Oxford: Oxford University Press.

Crace, Jim. 2007. *The Pesthouse*. New York: Doubleday.

Crosby, Alfred W. 1997. *The Measurement of Reality*. Cambridge: Cambridge University Press.

Cunningham, Andrew, and Ole Peter Grell. 2000. *The Four Horsemen of the Apocalypse*. Cambridge: Cambridge University Press.

Daniel, E. Randolph. 1992. "Joachim of Fiore: Patterns of history in the Apocalypse." Pp. 72–88 in Richard K. Emmerson and Bernard McGinn, eds., *The Apocalypse in the Middle Ages*. Ithaca, N.Y.: Cornell University Press.

Davidson, James W. 1977. *The Logic of Millennial Thought: Eighteenth-Century New England*. New Haven, CT: Yale University Press.

Davie, Grace. 2002. *Europe: The Exceptional Case*. London: Darton, Longman and Todd.

de Boer, E. A. 2004. *John Calvin on the Visions of Ezekiel*. Leiden: Brill.

De Vries, Jan. 1994. "The industrial revolution and the industrious revolution." *Journal of Economic History* 54: 249–70.

DeVries, Simon J. 1975. *Yesterday, Today and Tomorrow*. Grand Rapids, MI: William B. Eardmans Publishing.

Dilthey, Wilhelm. 1976. *Selected Writings*. Cambridge: Cambridge University Press.

Dirlik, Arif. 1989. *The Origins of Chinese Communism*. Oxford: Oxford University Press.

Donner, Fred McGraw. 1981. *The Early Islamic Conquests*. Princeton, N.J.: Princeton University Press.

Duby, Georges. 1968 (1962). *Rural Economy and Country Life in the Medieval West*. Columbia, S.C.: University of South Carolina Press.

Duff, Paul B. 2001. *Who Rides the Beast?* Oxford: Oxford University Press.

Duffy, Eamon. 1997. *Saints and Sinners: A History of the Popes*. New Haven, CT: Yale University Press.

Dupuy, Jean-Pierre. 2008. "Rehabilitating the prophet of doom." Paper presented at the Colloquium on Violence and Religion conference, "Catastrophe and Conversion," University of California – Riverside, June 19.

Durkheim, Émile. 1995 (1912). *The Elementary Forms of Religious Life*. New York: Free Press.

Edgerton, Robert B. 1989. *Mau Mau*. New York: Free Press.

Edwards, Douglas, ed. 2004. *Religion and Society in Roman Palestine*. New York: Routledge.

Edwards, Jonathan. 1998 (1830). "The latter-day glory is probably to begin in America." Pp. 54–8 in Conrad Cherry, ed., *God's New Israel: Religious Interpretations of American Destiny*. Chapel Hill: University of North Carolina Press.

Ehler, Sidney, and John Morrall. 1967. *Church and State throughout the Centuries*. New York: Biblo & Tannen.

Eikmeier, Dale. 2007. "Qutbism: An ideology of Islamic-fascism." *Parameters: US Army War College Quarterly* 37 (Spring): 85–97.

Eisenstadt, S. N. 1999a. *Fundamentalism, Sectarianism, and Revolution: The Jacobin Dimension of Modernity*. Cambridge: Cambridge University Press.

——. 1999b. "Multiple modernities in an age of globalization." *Canadian Journal of Sociology* 24: 283–95.

Eliade, Mircea. 1959 (1949). *Cosmos and History: The Myth of the Eternal Return*. New York: Harper & Row.

Engels, Friedrich. 1939 (1894). *Herr Eugen Dühring's Revolution in Science (Anti-Dühring)*. New York: International Publishers.

——. 1964 (1850). "The peasant war in Germany." Pp. 97–118 in *Karl Marx and Friedrich Engels on Religion*. New York: Schocken.

Fairbank, John K. 1992. *China: A New History*. Cambridge, MA: Harvard University Press.

Ferguson, Harvie. 2006. *Phenomenological Sociology*. London: Sage.

Festinger, Leon, Henry Riecken, and Stanley Schachter. 1964 (1956). *When Prophecy Fails*. New York: Harper & Row.

Firth, Katharine. 1979. *The Apocalyptic Tradition in Reformation Britain, 1530–1645*. Oxford: Oxford University Press.

Fitzpatrick, Sheila. 1999. *Everyday Stalinism*. Oxford: Oxford University Press.

——. 2001. *The Russian Revolution*, 2nd ed. Oxford: Oxford University Press.

Foster, Lawrence. 1991. *Women, Family, and Utopia*. Syracuse, N.Y.: Syracuse University Press.

Foucault, Michel. 1988. "The political technology of individuals." Pp. 145–62 in Luther H. Martin, Huck Gutman, and Patrick H. Hutton, eds., *Technologies of the Self*. Amherst: University of Massachusetts Press.

France, John. 2005. *The Crusades and the Expansion of Catholic Christendom, 1000–1714*. London: Routledge.

Frank, Isnard Wilhelm. 1995 (1990). *A History of the Medieval Church*. London: SCM Press.

Fraser, Nancy. 1997. "From redistribution to recognition? Dilemmas of justice in a 'postsocialist' age." Pp. 11–39 in Fraser, *Justice Interruptus: Critical Reflections on the "Postsocialist" Condition*. London: Routledge.

———. 2000. "Rethinking recognition." *New Left Review* 3 (May–June): 107–20.

Fredriksen, Paula. 2000. *From Jesus to Christ*, 2nd ed. New Haven, CT: Yale University Press.

Frend, W. H. C. 1967. *Martyrdom and Persecution in the Early Church*. New York: Doubleday.

Frilingos, Christopher A. 2004. *Spectacles of Empire: Monsters, Martyrs, and the Book of Revelation*. Philadelphia: University of Pennsylvania Press.

Fukuyama, Francis. 1992. *The End of History and the Last Man*. New York: Free Press.

Fuller, Robert C. 1995. *Naming the Antichrist: The History of an American Obsession*. New York: Oxford University Press.

Furet, François. 1981 (1978). *Interpreting the French Revolution*. Cambridge: Cambridge University Press.

———. 1999 (1995). *The Passing of an Illusion: The Idea of Communism in the Twentieth Century*. Chicago: University of Chicago Press.

Galula, David. 1964. *Counter-Insurgency Warfare*. New York: Praeger.

Garrett, Clarke. 1975. *Respectable Folly: Millenarians and the French Revolution in France and England*. Baltimore, MD: Johns Hopkins University Press.

Gauchet, Marcel. 1997 (1985). *The Disenchantment of the World: A Political History of Religion*. Princeton, N.J.: Princeton University Press.

Gerges, Fawaz. 2005. *The Far Enemy: Why Jihad Went Global*. Cambridge: Cambridge University Press.

Girard, René. 1986 (1982). *The Scapegoat*. Baltimore, MD: Johns Hopkins University Press.

———. 2008. "Apocalyptic thinking after 9/11: An interview with René Girard," conducted by Robert Doran. *SubStance* 37 (115): 20–32.

Goffman, Erving. 1967. *Interaction Ritual*. Chicago: Aldine.

Goldstone, Jack. 1991. *Revolution and Rebellion in the Early Modern World*. Berkeley: University of California Press.

———. 2008. *The Debate on the Rise of the West*. New York: McGraw-Hill.

Gordon, Bruce. 1992. "Switzerland." Pp. 70–93 in Andrew Pettegree, ed., *The Early Reformation in Europe*. Cambridge: Cambridge University Press.

Gorski, Philip S. 2000. "The mosaic moment: An early modernist critique of modernist theories of nationalism." *American Journal of Sociology* 105: 1428–68.

———. 2003. *The Disciplinary Revolution*. Chicago: University of Chicago Press.

Gray, John. 2003. *Al Qaeda and What It Means to be Modern*. New York: New Press.

——. 2007. *Black Mass: Apocalyptic Religion and the Death of Utopia*. London: Penguin.

Gunaratna, Rohan. 2002. *Inside Al Qaeda*. New York: Columbia University Press.

Gurevich, Aron Y. 1976. "Time as a problem of cultural history." Pp. 229–45 in Louis Gardet et al., *Cultures and Time*. Paris: Unesco Press.

——. 1985 (1972). *Categories of Medieval Culture*. London: Routledge & Kegan Paul.

Habeck, Mary. 2006. *Knowing the Enemy: Jihadist Ideology and the War on Terror*. New Haven, CT: Yale University Press.

Habermas, Jürgen. 1987 (1981). *The Theory of Communicative Action, Vol. 2: Lifeworld and System*. Boston: Beacon Press.

——. 1989 (1962). *The Structural Transformation of the Public Sphere*. Cambridge, MA: MIT Press.

——. 2003. *Philosophy in a Time of Terror: Dialogues with Jürgen Habermas and Jacques Derrida*, interviewed by Giovanna Borradori. Chicago: University of Chicago Press.

Hall, John R. 1978a. "Marx and the communards: Some reflections on the socialist mode of production and the collective economy at Twin Oaks." Unpublished paper presented at the Conference on Utopias and Communes, University of Nebraska – Omaha, October 12.

——. 1978b. *The Ways Out: Utopian Communal Groups in an Age of Babylon*. Boston: Routledge & Kegan Paul.

——. 1980. "The time of history and the history of times." *History and Theory* 19: 113–31.

——. 1984. "World-system holism and colonial Brazilian agriculture: A critical case analysis." *Latin American Research Review* 19: 43–69.

——. 1999. *Cultures of Inquiry: From Epistemology to Discourse in Sociohistorical Research*. Cambridge: Cambridge University Press.

——. 2003. "Religion and violence: Social processes in comparative perspective," pp. 359–81 in Michele Dillon, ed., *Handbook for the Sociology of Religion*. Cambridge: Cambridge University Press.

——. 2004 (1987). *Gone from the Promised Land: Jonestown in American Cultural History*, 2nd ed. New Brunswick, N.J.: Transaction.

——. 2008. "Patrimonialism under the sign of modernity: The case of the U.S. public domain from colonial times to the late 19th century." Paper presented at the conference, "Patrimonial Politics, Then and Now," Yale University, New Haven, Connecticut, May 9–10.

Hall, John R., Mary Jo Neitz, and Marshall Battani. 2003. *Sociology on Culture*. London: Routledge.

Hall, John R., Philip D. Schuyler, and Sylvaine Trinh. 2000. *Apocalypse Observed*. London: Routledge.

Hamilton, Gary G. 1994. "Civilizations and the organization of economies." Pp. 183–205 in Neil J. Smelser and Richard Swedberg, eds., *The*

Handbook of Economic Sociology. Princeton, N.J.: Princeton University Press.

Hansen, Klaus. 1967. *Quest for Empire*. East Lansing: Michigan State University Press.

Hanson, Stephen E. 1997. *Time and Revolution: Marxism and the Design of Soviet Institutions*. Chapel Hill: University of North Carolina Press.

Harbison, E. Harris. 1964. *Christianity and History*. Princeton, N.J.: Princeton University Press.

Hardt, Michael, and Antonio Negri. 2000. *Empire*. Cambridge, MA: Harvard University Press.

Harrison, J. F. C. 1979. *The Second Coming: Popular Millenarianism, 1780–1850*. New Brunswick, N.J.: Rutgers University Press.

Harvey, David. 1990. *The Condition of Postmodernity*. Oxford: Blackwell.

Hechter, Michael. 1975. *Internal Colonialism*. London: Routledge & Kegan Paul.

Hedges, Chris. 2007. *American Fascists: The Christian Right and the War on America*. New York: Free Press.

Hengel, Martin. 1989 (1961). *The Zealots*. Edinburgh: T. & T. Clark.

Henshall, Nicholas. 1992. *The Myth of Absolutism: Change and Continuity in Early Modern European Monarchy*. London: Longman.

Herberg, Will. 1955. *Protestant, Catholic, Jew*. Garden City, N.Y.: Doubleday.

Hervieu-Léger, Danièle. 2000 (1993). *Religion as a Chain of Memory*. New Brunswick, N.J.: Rutgers University Press.

Higonnet, Patrice. 1998. *Goodness beyond Virtue: Jacobins during the French Revolution*. Cambridge, MA: Harvard University Press.

Hill, Christopher. 1958. *Puritanism and Revolution*. London: Secker & Warburg.

——. 1967. *Reformation to Industrial Revolution*. New York: Pantheon.

——. 1971. *Antichrist in Seventeenth-Century England*. London: Oxford University Press.

——. 1972. *The World Turned Upside Down*. London: Temple Smith.

——. 1980. *Some Intellectual Consequences of the English Revolution*. Madison: University of Wisconsin Press.

Hillenbrand, Carole. 1999. *The Crusades: Islamic Perspectives*. Edinburgh: University of Edinburgh Press.

Hobbes, Thomas. 1998 (1651). *Leviathan*. Oxford: Oxford University Press.

Hobsbawm, Eric. 1959. *Primitive Rebels*. New York: Norton.

Hoffman, Bruce. 1998. *Inside Terrorism*. New York: Columbia University Press.

Hollenwager, W. J. 1972 (1969). *The Pentecostals*. Minneapolis, MN: Augsburg.

Holsinger, Bruce. 2007. *Neomedievalism, Neoconservatism, and the War on Terror*. Chicago: Prickly Paradigm Press.

Holt, P. M. 1980. "Islamic millenarianism and the fulfillment of prophecy: A case study." Pp. 335–47 in Ann Williams, ed., *Prophecy and Millenarianism: Essays in Honour of Marjorie Reeves*. London: Longman.

Houtart, François. 1997. "The cult of violence in the name of religion: A panorama." Pp. 1–9 in Wim Beuken and Karl-Josef Kuschel, eds., *Religion as a Source of Violence?* Maryknoll, N.Y.: Orbis.

Huizinga, Johan. 1954 (1924). *The Waning of the Middle Ages.* New York: Doubleday Anchor.

Hunter, James D. 1983. *American Evangelicalism.* New Brunswick, N.J.: Rutgers University Press.

——. *Evangelicalism: The Coming Generation.* Chicago: University of Chicago Press.

Huntington, Samuel. 1996. *The Clash of Civilizations and the Remaking of World Order.* New York: Simon and Schuster.

Hussein, Jassim. 1982. *The Occultation of the Twelfth Imam.* London: Muhammadi Trust.

I Ching, or Book of Changes. 1967. Princeton, N.J.: Princeton University Press.

Ignatieff, Michael. 2004. *The Lesser Evil: Political Ethics in an Age of Terror.* Princeton, N.J.: Princeton University Press.

Jacob, Margaret. 1976. *The Newtonians and the English Revolution.* Ithaca, N.Y.: Cornell University Press.

James, William. 1985 (1903). *The Varieties of Religious Experience.* Cambridge, MA: Harvard University Press.

Jewett, Robert, and John Shelton Lawrence. 2002. *Captain America and the Crusade against Evil.* Grand Rapids, MI: William B. Eardmans.

Joll, James. 1964. *The Anarchists.* Boston: Little, Brown.

Joutard, Philippe. 1985. "The revocation of the Edict of Nantes: End or renewal of French Protestantism?" Pp. 339–68 in Menna Prestwich, ed., *International Calvinism, 1541–1715.* Oxford: Clarendon Press.

Joxe, Alain. 2002. *Empire of Disorder.* Los Angeles: Semiotext(e).

Juergensmeyer, Mark. 2000. *Terror in the Mind of God,* updated ed. Berkeley: University of California Press.

——. 2002 (1984). *Ghandi's Way: A Handbook of Conflict Resolution.* Berkeley: University of California Press.

Kaelber, Lutz. 1998. *Schools of Asceticism.* University Park, PA: Pennsylvania State University Press.

Kaplan, Benjamin K. 2004. "Coexistence, conflict, and the practice of toleration." Pp. 486–505 in R. Po-chia Hsia, ed., *A Companion to the Reformation World.* Oxford: Blackwell.

Karabel, Zachery. 2007. *Peace Be upon You.* New York: Knopf.

Karsh, Efraim. 2006. *Islamic Imperialism, a History.* New Haven, CT: Yale University Press.

Kataev, Valentin. 1976 (1933). *Time, Forward!* Bloomington: Indiana University Press.

Keller, Catherine. 1996. *Apocalypse Now and Then.* Boston: Beacon Press.

Kelsay, John. 2007. *Arguing the Just War in Islam.* Cambridge, MA: Harvard University Press.

Kelsay, John, and James Johnson, eds. 1991. *Just War and Jihad.* Westport, CT: Greenwood Press.

Kemp, Anthony. 1991. *The Estrangement of the Past*. Oxford: Oxford University Press.

Kern, Stephen. 1983. *The Culture of Time and Space 1880–1918*. Cambridge, MA: Harvard University Press.

Keys, Donald. 1961. *God and the H-Bomb*. New York: Random House.

Khosrokhavar, Farad. 2009. *Inside Jihadism*. London: Paradigm Publishers.

Kirby, Ethyn W. 1941. "The Cromwellian establishment." *Church History* 10: 144–58.

Kirsch, Jonathan. 2006. *A History of the End of the World*. San Francisco: HarperSanFrancisco.

Knox, Ronald A. 1950. *Enthusiasm: A Chapter in the History of Religion*. Oxford: Oxford University Press.

Kohn, Risa, and Rebecca Moore. 2007. *A Portable God: The Origin of Judaism and Christianity*. Lanham, MD: Rowman & Littlefield.

Kreyenbroek, Philip G. 2002. "Millennialism and eschatology in the Zoroastrian tradition." Pp. 33–55 in Abbas Amanat and Magnus Bernhardsson, eds., *Imagining the End: Visions of Apocalypse from the Ancient Middle East to Modern America*. London: I. B. Tauris.

Lambert, Malcolm. 2002. *Medieval Heresy*. Oxford: Blackwell.

Landes, David S. 1983. *Revolution in Time: Clocks and the Making of the Modern World*. Cambridge, MA: Harvard University Press.

Landes, Richard. 1995. *Relics, Apocalypse, and the Deceits of History*. Cambridge, MA: Harvard University Press.

——. 2000. "The fear of an apocalyptic year 1000: Augustinian historiography, medieval and modern." *Speculum* 75: 97–145.

Landes, Richard, Andrew Gow, and David C. Van Meter, eds. 2003. *The Apocalyptic Year 1000*. Oxford: Oxford University Press.

Lanternari, Vittorio. 1963 (1960). *The Religions of the Oppressed*. New York: Knopf.

Laqueur, Walter. 1998 (1976). *Guerilla Warfare*. New Brunswick, N.J.: Transaction.

——. 2001 (1977). *A History of Terrorism*, 2nd ed. New Brunswick, N.J.: Transaction.

Lash, Scott, and John Urry. 1994. *Economies of Signs and Space*. London: Sage.

Latour, Bruno. 1993 (1991). *We Have Never Been Modern*. Cambridge, MA: Harvard University Press.

Lawrence, Bruce. 1991. "Holy war (jihad) in Islamic religion and nation-state ideologies." Pp. 141–60 in John Kelsay and James Johnson, eds. *Just War and Jihad*. Westport, CT: Greenwood Press.

Lawrence, D. H. 1932. *Apocalypse*. London: Martin Secker.

Le Goff, Jacques. 1980a (1963). "Labor time in the 'crisis' of the fourteenth century." Pp. 43–52 in Le Goff, *Time, Work, and Culture in the Middle Ages*. Chicago: University of Chicago Press.

——. 1980b (1960). "Merchant's time and Church's time in the middle ages." Pp. 29–42 in Le Goff, *Time, Work, and Culture in the Middle Ages*. Chicago: University of Chicago Press.

——. 1988. *Your Money or Your Life*. New York: Zone.

——. 2005. *The Birth of Europe*. Oxford: Blackwell.

Lenin, V. I. 1963 (1902). *What Is To Be Done?* Oxford: Clarendon Press.

——. 1970 (1916). *Imperialism: The Highest Stage of Capitalism*. Moscow: Progress Publishers.

Le Roy Ladurie, Emmanuel. 1979. *Montaillou: The Promised Land of Error*. New York: Vintage.

Lerner, Robert E. 1972. *The Heresy of the Free Spirit in the Middle Ages*. Berkeley: University of California Press.

Lessay, Franck. 2007. "Hobbes's covenant theology and its political implications." Pp. 243–70 in Patricia Springboard, ed., *The Cambridge Companion to Hobbes's Leviathan*. Cambridge: Cambridge University Press.

Lewis, Bernard. 2001. *What Went Wrong? Western Impact and Middle Eastern Response*. New York: Oxford University Press.

——. 2004 (1967). *The Assassins: A Radical Sect in Islam*, rev. ed. New York: Basic Books.

Lewis, David Levering. 2008. *Islam and the Making of Europe*. New York: Norton.

Lewy, Guenter. 1974. *Religion and Revolution*. New York: Oxford University Press.

Liebman, Robert, and Robert Wuthnow, eds. 1983. *The New Christian Right*. New York: Aldine.

Lifton, Robert Jay. 1968. *Revolutionary Immortality: Mao Tse-tung and the Chinese Cultural Revolution*. New York: Random House.

——. 2003. *Superpower Syndrome*. New York: Thunder's Mouth Press/ Nation Books.

Lilla, Mark. 2007. *The Stillborn God: Religion, Politics, and the Modern West*. New York: Knopf.

Lincoln, Bruce. 2003. *Holy Terrors: Thinking about Religion after September 11*. Chicago: University of Chicago Press.

——. 2007. *Religion, Empire, and Torture: The Case of Achaemenian Persia, with a Postscript on Abu Ghraib*. Chicago: University of Chicago Press.

Lindstrom, Lamont. 1993. *Cargo Cult*. Honolulu: University of Hawaii Press.

Little, David. 1991. " 'Holy war' appeals and Western Christianity: A reconsideration of Bainton's approach." Pp. 121–39 in John Kelsay and James Johnson, eds., *Just War and Jihad*. Westport, CT: Greenwood Press.

Logan, F. Donald. 2002. *A History of the Church in the Middle Ages*. London: Routledge.

Löwith, Karl. 1949. *Meaning in History: The Theological Implications of the Philosophy of History*. Chicago: University of Chicago Press.

Luhmann, Niklas. 1982. *The Differentiation of Society*. New York: Columbia University Press.

——. 1995 (1985). *Social Systems*. Stanford, CA: Stanford University Press.

Lyotard, Jean-François. 1984 (1979). *The Postmodern Condition: A Report on Knowledge*. Minneapolis, MN: University of Minnesota Press.

——. 1991 (1986). *Phenomenology*. Albany: State University of New York Press.

McCarthy, Cormac. 2006. *The Road*. New York: Knopf.

MacCulloch, Diarmaid. 1992. "England." Pp. 166–87 in Andrew Pettegree, ed., *The Early Reformation in Europe*. Cambridge: Cambridge University Press.

MacFarquhar, Roderick, and Michael Schoenhals. 2006. *Mao's Last Revolution*. Cambridge, MA: Belknap Press of Harvard University Press.

McGinn, Bernard. 1994. *Antichrist*. San Francisco: Harper.

——. 1995. "The end of the world and the beginning of Christendom." Pp. 58–89 in Malcolm Bull, ed., *Apocalypse Theory and the End of the World*. Oxford: Blackwell.

McGinnis, Reginald. 2008. "Violence and conversion: From Voltaire to Girard." Paper presented at the Colloquium on Violence and Religion conference, "Catastrophe and Conversion," University of California – Riverside, June 20.

McManners. John. 1969. *The French Revolution and the Church*. London: SPCK.

Madaule, Jacques. 1967. *The Albigensian Crusade*. New York: Fordham University Press.

Madden, Thomas F. 2005. *The New Concise History of the Crusades*. Oxford: Rowman & Littlefield.

Mann, Michael. 1986. *The Sources of Social Power*, Vol. I. Cambridge: Cambridge University Press.

Mannheim, Karl. 1936 (1929). *Ideology and Utopia*. New York: Harcourt, Brace, and World.

Manuel, Frank E. 1962. *Shapes of Philosophical History*. Cambridge, MA: Harvard University Press.

Margolin, Jean-Louis. 1999. "Cambodia: The country of disconcerting crimes." Pp. 577–635 in Mark Kramer, ed., *The Black Book of Communism*. Cambridge, MA: Harvard University Press.

Marsden, George. 1980. *Fundamentalism and American Culture: The Shaping of Twentieth-Century Evangelicalism: 1870–1925*. New York: Oxford University Press.

Martin, David. 1978. *A General Theory of Secularization*. Oxford: Blackwell.

——. 2005. *On Secularization: Towards a Revised General Theory*. London: Ashgate.

Martin, David, and Peter Mullen, eds. 1983. *Unholy Warfare: The Church and the Bomb*. Oxford: Basil Blackwell.

Marx, Anthony W. 2003. *Faith in Nation: Exclusionary Origins of Nationalism*. Oxford: Oxford University Press.

Marx, Karl. 1978a (1845). "The Germany Ideology," part I. Pp. 147–200 in Robert Tucker, ed., *The Marx–Engels Reader*, 2nd ed. New York: Norton.

——. 1978b (1843). "On the Jewish question." Pp. 26–52 in Robert Tucker, ed., *The Marx–Engels Reader*, 2nd ed. New York: Norton.

Marx, Karl, and Friedrich Engels. 1978 (1848). "Manifesto of the Communist Party." Pp. 473–500 in Robert Tucker, ed., *The Marx–Engels Reader*, 2nd ed. New York: Norton.

Merkley, Paul. 1987. *The Greek and Hebrew Origins of Our Idea of History*. Lewiston, ME: Edwin Mellen Press.

Merleau-Ponty, Maurice. 1969 (1947). *Humanism and Terror*. Boston: Beacon Press.

Migaux, Philippe. 2007. "The roots of radical Islam." Pp. 255–313 in Gérard Chaliand and Arnaud Blin, eds., *The History of Terrorism: From Antiquity to Al Qaeda*. Berkeley: University of California Press.

Miller, Perry. 1956. *Errand into the Wilderness*. Cambridge, MA: Harvard University Press.

Mills, C. Wright. 1959. *The Sociological Imagination*. New York: Oxford University Press.

Mische, Ann. 2008. *Partisan Publics: Communication and Contention across Brazilian Activist Networks*. Princeton, N.J.: Princeton University Press.

Mitter, Rana. 2004. *A Bitter Revolution*. Oxford: Oxford University Press.

Moore, R. I. 2007. *The Formation of a Persecuting Society*, 2nd ed. Oxford: Blackwell.

Moore, R. Laurence. 1986. *Religious Outsiders and the Making of Americans*. New York: Oxford University Press.

Moorhead, James H. 1999. *World without End: Mainstream Protestant Visions of the Last Things 1880–1925*. Bloomington: Indiana University Press.

Needham, Joseph. 1965. *Time and Eastern Man*, occasional paper no. 21. London: Royal Anthropological Institute of Great Britain & Ireland.

——. 1986 (1960). *Heavenly Clockwork*, 2nd ed. Cambridge: Cambridge University Press.

Newport, Kenneth G. C. 2000. *Apocalypse and Millennium*. Cambridge: Cambridge University Press.

Niebuhr, H. Richard. 1929. *The Social Sources of Denominationalism*. New York: Holt.

Niebuhr, Reinhold. 1964. "Introduction." Pp. vii–xiv in Niebuhr, ed., *Marx and Engels on Religion*. New York: Schocken Books.

Nisbet, Robert. 1980. *History of the Idea of Progress*. New York: Basic Books.

Oakley, Francis. 1979. *The Western Church in the Later Middle Ages*. Ithaca, N.Y.: Cornell University Press.

Obermann, Julian. 1955. "Early Islam." Pp. 237–310 in Robert C. Dentan, ed., *The Idea of History in the Ancient Middle East*. American Oriental Series no. 38. New Haven, CT: Yale University Press.

O'Dea, Thomas. 1957. *The Mormons*. Chicago: University of Chicago Press.

Oldfield, Duane. 1996. *The Right and the Righteous: The Christian Right Confronts the Republican Party*. Lanham, MD: Rowman & Littlefield.

O'Leary, Stephen. 1994. *Arguing the Apocalypse*. Oxford: Oxford University Press.

O'Neill, Bard. 1990. *Insurgency and Terrorism*. Washington, D.C.: Brassey's.

Orlove, Benjamin S. 2003. "How people name seasons." Pp. 121–40 in Sarah Strauss and Benjamin S. Orlove, eds., *Weather, Culture, Climate*. London: Berg.

Pape, Robert. 2005. *Dying to Win: The Strategic Logic of Suicide Terrorism*. New York: Random House.

Paret, Peter, and John Shy. 1962. *Guerrillas in the 1960s*. New York: Praeger.

Parish, Helen. 2000. "England." Pp. 225–36 in Andrew Pettegree, ed., *The Reformation World*. London: Routledge.

Parkes, James. 1934. *The Conflict of the Church and the Synagogue*. New York: JPS.

Parrow, Kathleen. 1993. *From Defense to Resistance: Justification of Violence during the French Wars of Religion*. Philadelphia, PA: American Philosophical Society, Transactions vol. 83, pt. 6.

Parsons, Talcott. 1951. *The Social System*. New York: Free Press.

———. 1954. *Essays in Sociological Theory*. New York: Free Press.

Partner, Peter. 1982. *The Murdered Magicians: The Templars and their Myth*. Oxford: Oxford University Press.

———. 1997. *God of Battles: Holy Wars of Christianity and Islam*. London: HarperCollins.

Patrides, C. A. 1972. *The Grand Design of God*. London: Routledge & Kegan Paul.

Partridge, Robert B. 1998. *"O Horrable Murder": The Trial, Execution and Burial of King Charles I*. London: Rubicon Press.

Pelikan, Jaroslav. 1985. *Jesus through the Centuries*. New Haven, CT: Yale University Press.

Pillar, Paul. 2001. *Terrorism and U.S. Foreign Policy*. Washington, D.C.: Brookings Institution Press.

Pipes, Daniel. 2002. *Militant Islam Reaches America*. New York: Norton.

Pocock, J. G. A. 1971. "Time, history, and eschatology in the thought of Thomas Hobbes." Pp. 148–201 in Pocock, *Politics, Language, and Time*. New York: Atheneum.

Pomeranz, Kenneth. 2000. *The Great Divergence: China, Europe, and the Making of the Modern World Economy*. Princeton, N.J.: Princeton University Press.

Pomian, Krzysztof. 1984. *L'Order du Temps*. Paris: Gallimard.

Pomper, Philip. 1970. *The Russian Revolutionary Intelligentsia*. New York: Thomas Crowell.

Price, Alex. 2008. *Modernity, Reification and Vacuity: An Investigation into the Conditions of Freedom*. Coventry, U.K.: Ph.D dissertation, Department of Sociology, University of Warwick.

Price, Don. 1974. *Russia and the Roots of the Chinese Revolution, 1896–1911*. Cambridge, MA: Harvard University Press.

Quistorp, Heinrich. 1955. *Calvin's Doctrine of the Last Things*. London: Lutterworth Press.

Qutb, Sayyid. 2006 (c. 1960). *Basic Principles of the Islamic Worldview*. North Haledon, N.J.: Islamic Publications International.

Rapport, David. 1984. "Fear and trembling: Terrorism in three religious traditions." *American Political Science Review* 78: 658–77.

Ray, Gene. 2005. *Terror and the Sublime in Art and Critical Theory: From Auschwitz to Hiroshima to September 11*. New York: Palgrave Macmillan.

Redles, David. 2005. *Hitler's Millennial Reich*. New York: New York University Press.

Reeves, Marjorie. 1969. *The Influence of Prophecy in the Later Middle Ages: A Study in Joachimism*. Oxford: Oxford University Press.

Reid, Jonathan A. 2000. "France." Pp. 211–24 in Andrew Pettegree, ed., *The Reformation World*. London: Routledge.

Reid, Julian. 2005. "The biopolitics of the war on terror: A critique of the 'return of imperialism' thesis in international relations." *Third World Quarterly* 26: 237–52.

Ribuffo, Leo. 1983. *The Old Christian Right: The Protestant Far Right from the Great Depression to the Cold War*. Philadelphia, PA: Temple University Press.

Richard, Jean. 1999 (1996). *The Crusades, c. 1071–c. 1291*. Cambridge: Cambridge University Press.

Riddle, Donald W. 1931. *The Martyrs: A Study in Social Control*. Chicago: University of Chicago Press.

Riesebrodt, Martin 1993. *Pious Passion*. Berkeley: University of California Press.

Riley-Smith, Jonathan. 1987. *The Crusades, a Short History*. London: Athlone Press.

——. 1997. *The First Crusaders, 1095–1131*. Cambridge: Cambridge University Press.

——. 2002. *What Were the Crusades?*, 3rd ed. San Francisco: Ignatius Press.

——. 2004. "Were the Templars guilty?" Pp. 107–24 in Susan J. Ridyard, ed., *The Medieval Crusade*. Woodbridge, U.K.: Boydell Press.

——. 2005. *The Crusades, A History*, 2nd ed. London: Continuum.

Rinehart, James F. (2006). *Apocalyptic Faith and Political Violence*. New York: Palgrave/Macmillan.

Rivera, Luis N. 1992. *A Violent Evangelism: The Political and Religious Conquest of the Americas*. Louisville, KY: Westminster/John Knox Press.

Robbins, Thomas. 1986. "Mass suicide before Jonestown: The Russian Old Believers." *Sociological Analysis* 47: 1–20.

Rodinson, Maxime. 1974 (1961). *Mohammed*. New York: Vintage.

Roediger, Dave, and Franklin Rosemont. 1986. *Haymarket Scrapbook*. Chicago: Charles H. Kerr Publishing.

Rosen, Elizabeth K. 2008. *Apocalyptic Transformation*. Lanham, MD: Rowman & Littlefield.

Roth, Guenther. 1975. "Socio-historical model and developmental theory: Charismatic community, charisma of reason, and the counterculture." *American Sociological Review* 40: 148–57.

——. 1987. "Rationalization in Max Weber's developmental history." Pp. 75–91 in Scott Lash and Sam Whimster, eds., *Max Weber, Rationality, and Modernity*. London: Allen & Unwin.

Rubenstein, Jay. 2004. "How, or how much, to reevaluate Peter the Hermit." Pp. 53–69 in Susan J. Ridyard, ed., *The Medieval Crusade*. Woodbridge, U.K.: Boydell Press.

Rubin, Barry, and Judith Colp Rubin, eds. 2002. *Anti-American Terrorism and the Middle East: A Documentary Reader*. Oxford: Oxford University Press.

Rublack, Ulinka. 2005. *Reformation Europe*. Cambridge: Cambridge University Press.

Russell, James C. 1994. *The Germanization of Early Medieval Christianity*. Oxford: Oxford University Press.

Sageman, Marc. 2002. *Understanding Terror Networks*. Philadelphia: University of Pennsylvania Press.

Sandeen, Ernest. 1970. *The Roots of Fundamentalism: British and American Millenarianism 1800–1930*. Chicago: University of Chicago Press.

Schmalenbach, Herman 1961 (1922). "The sociological category of communion." Pp. 331–47 in Talcott Parsons, Edward Shils, Kaspa D. Naegele, and Jesse R. Pitts, eds., *Theories of Society*, Vol. I. New York: Free Press.

Schmithals, Walter. 1975 (1973). *The Apocalyptic Movement*. Nashville, TN: Abingdon Press.

Schmitt, Carl. 1976 (1932). *The Concept of the Political*. New Brunswick, N.J.: Rutgers University Press.

——. 1985 (1922). *Political Theology: Four Chapters on the Concept of Sovereignty*. Cambridge, MA.: MIT Press.

Schribner, R. W. 1987. *Popular Culture and Popular Movements in Reformation Germany*. London: Hambledon Press.

Schumpeter, Joseph. 1951. *Imperialism and Social Classes*. New York: Augustus M. Kelley.

Schutz, Alfred. 1967 (1932). *The Phenomenology of the Social World*. Evanston, IL: Northwestern University Press.

Schutz, Alfred, and Thomas Luckmann. 1973. *The Structures of the Lifeworld*. Evanston, IL: Northwestern University Press.

Segal, Alan F. 1990. *Paul the Convert*. New Haven, CT: Yale University Press.

Seligman, Adam. 2004. *Modest Claims: Dialogues and Essays on Tolerance and Tradition*. Notre Dame, IN: Notre Dame University Press.

Seligman, Charles. 2002. "Religious visions and sacred terror: The case of Islam." Paper presented at the annual meetings of the Society for the Scientific Study of Religion, Salt Lake City, Utah, November 2.

Sewell, William H., Jr. 2005. *Logics of History*. Chicago: University of Chicago Press.

Shils, Edward. 1968. "The concept and function of ideology." Pp. 66–76 in David Sills and Robert Merton, eds., *International Encyclopedia of the Social Sciences*, Vol. 7. New York: Macmillan.

Simmel, Georg. 1950. *The Sociology of Georg Simmel*. New York: Free Press.

Smelser, Neil. 2007. *The Faces of Terrorism*. Princeton, N.J.: Princeton University Press.

Smidt, Corwin, and James Penning, eds. 1997. *Sojourners in the Wilderness: The Christian Right in Comparative Perspective*. Lanham, MD: Rowman & Littlefield.

Smolinski, Reiner. 2001. "Caveat emptor: Pre- and postmillennialism in the late Reformation period." Pp. 145–69 in James Force and Richard Popkin, eds., *Millenarianism and Messianism in Early Modern European Culture, Vol. III: The Millenarian Turn*. Dordrecht: Kluwer.

Smoller, Laura A. 2000. "Of earthquakes, hail, frogs, and geography: Plague and the investigation of the Apocalypse in the later middle ages." Pp. 156–87 in Caroline Walker Bynum and Paul Freedman, eds., *Last Things: Death and Apocalypse in the Middle Ages*. Philadelphia: University of Pennsylvania Press.

Sorel, Georges. 1961 (1908). *Reflections on Violence*, with an introduction by Edward Shils. New York: Collier.

Spence, Jonathan. 1981. *The Gate of Heavenly Peace: The Chinese and Their Revolution, 1895–1980*. New York: Viking.

———. 1996. *God's Chinese Son*. New York: Norton.

Sperry, Paul. 2005. *Infiltration: How Muslim Spies and Subversives Have Penetrated Washington*. Nashville, TN: Thomas Nelson.

Stark, Rodney. 1996. *The Rise of Christianity*. Princeton, N.J.: Princeton University Press.

———. 2001. *One True God*. Princeton, N.J.: Princeton University Press.

Stark, Rodney, and William Sims Bainbridge. 1987. *A Theory of Religion*. New York: Peter Lang.

Stark, Werner. 1967. *The Sociology of Religion: A Study of Christendom*. New York: Fordham University Press.

Steinmetz, George. 2005. "Return to empire: The new U.S. imperialism in comparative historical perspective." *Sociological Theory* 23: 339–67.

Stone, Lawrence. 1980. "The results of the English Revolutions of the seventeenth century." Pp. 23–108 in J. G. A. Pocock, ed., *Three British Revolutions: 1641, 1688, 1776*. Princeton, N.J.: Princeton University Press.

Swedberg, Richard. 1993. "On the relationship between economic theory and economic sociology in the work of Joseph Schumpeter." Pp. 42–61 in Richard Swedberg, ed., *Explorations in Economic Sociology*. New York: Russell Sage Foundation.

Synon, Vincent. 1971. *The Holiness Pentecostal Movement in the United States*. Grand Rapids, MI: W. B. Eerdmans.

Ta-shma, Paula, Guy Laden, Muli Ben-Yehuda, and Michael Factor. 2008. "Virtual machine time travel using continuous data protection and checkpointing." *ACM SIGOPS Operating Systems Review* 42: 127–34.

Taylor, Charles. 1979. *Hegel and Modern Society*. Cambridge: Cambridge University Press.

——. 2007. *A Secular Age*. Cambridge, MA: Harvard University Press.

Taylor, Mark Lewis. 2005. *Religion, Politics, and the Christian Right: Post-9/11 Powers and American Empire*. Minneapolis, MN: Fortress Press.

Thomas, Keith. 1971. *Religion and the Decline of Magic*. New York: Scribner's.

Thompson, E. P. 1967. "Time, work-discipline, and industrial capitalism." *Past & Present* 38: 56–97.

Thompson, Leonard L. 1990. *The Book of Revelation: Apocalypse and Empire*. New York: Oxford University Press.

Tilly, Charles. 1995. *Coercion, Capital and European States, A.D. 990–1990*. Cambridge, MA: Blackwell.

——. 2004. "Terror, terrorism, terrorists," *Sociological Theory* 22: 5–13.

Todd, Margo. 2000. "England after 1558." Pp. 365–86 in Andrew Pettegree, ed., *The Reformation World*. London: Routledge.

Turner, Bryan. 1974. *Weber and Islam*. London: Routledge & Kegan Paul.

Tuveson, Ernest. 1949. *Millennium and Utopia*. Berkeley: University of California Press.

——. 1968. *Redeemer Nation: The Idea of America's Millennial Role*. Chicago: University of Chicago Press.

Tyerman, Christopher. 2004. *Fighting for Christendom: Holy War and the Crusades*. Oxford: Oxford University Press.

U, Eddy. 2007. *Disorganizing China: Counter-bureaucracy and the Decline of Socialism*. Stanford, CA: Stanford University Press.

Urban, Hugh. 2007. *The Secrets of the Kingdom: Religion and Concealment in the Bush Administration*. Lanham, MD: Rowman & Littlefield.

Van Kley, Dale K. 1996. *The Religious Origins of the French Revolution*. New Haven, CT: Yale University Press.

Venturi, Franco. 2001 (1960). *Roots of Revolution*. London: Phoenix Press.

Vidich, Arthur, and Stanford Lyman. 1985. *American Sociology: Worldly Rejections of Religion and Their Directions*. New Haven, CT: Yale University Press.

Vogt, Peter. 2006. *Deuteronomic Theology and the Significance of Torah*. Winona Lake, IN: Eisenbrauns.

Wagner, Peter. 1994. *A Sociology of Modernity: Liberty and Discipline*. London: Routledge.

Wallace, Peter G. 2004. *The Long Reformation*. New York: Palgrave Macmillan.

Wallerstein, Immanuel. 1974. *The Modern World System I: Capitalist Agriculture and the Origins of the European World-Economy in the Sixteenth Century*. New York: Academic Press.

Walzer, Michael. 1963. "Puritanism as a revolutionary ideology." *History and Theory* 3: 59–90.

———. 1965. *The Revolution of the Saints: A Study into the Origins of Radical Politics.* Cambridge, MA: Harvard University Press.

Warfield, Benjamin B. 1909. "Calvin's doctrine of the knowledge of God." *Princeton Theological Review* 7: 219–325.

Watts, Pauline M. 1985. "Prophecy and discovery: On the spiritual origins of Christopher Columbus's 'Enterprise of the Indies'." *American Historical Review* 90: 73–102.

Weber, Max. 1946 (1915). "The social psychology of the world religions." Pp. 267–301 in H. H. Gerth and C. Wright Mills, eds., *From Max Weber: Essays in Sociology.* New York: Oxford University Press.

———. 1958 (1905). *The Protestant Ethic and the Spirit of Capitalism.* New York: Scribner's.

———. 1978 (1922). *Economy and Society.* Berkeley: University of California Press.

Weber, Timothy. 1979. *Living in the Shadow of the Second Coming: American Premillennialism 1875–1925.* New York: Oxford University Press.

Wechsler, William, and Lee Wolosky. 2002. *Terrorist Financing.* New York: Council on Foreign Relations.

Weigert, Stephen. 1996. *Traditional Religion and Guerrilla Warfare in Modern Africa.* New York: St. Martin's Press.

Weisman, Alan. 2007. *The World without Us.* New York: Thomas Dunne/ St. Martin's Press.

White, Hayden. 1987. *The Content of the Form: Narrative Discourse and Historical Representation.* Baltimore, MD: Johns Hopkins University Press.

White, Lynn, III. 1989. *Policies of Chaos: The Organizational Causes of Violence in China's Cultural Revolution.* Princeton, N.J.: Princeton University Press.

Whitrow, Gerald J. 1988. *Time in History.* Oxford: Oxford University Press.

Wilcox, Clyde. 1992. *God's Warriors: The Christian Right in Twentieth-Century America.* Baltimore, MD: Johns Hopkins University Press.

Williams, George H. 1962. *The Radical Reformation.* Philadelphia, PA: Westminster Press.

Williams, Sam K. 1975. *Jesus' Death as Saving Event.* Harvard Dissertations in Religion no. 2. Cambridge, MA: Harvard Theological Review.

Williamson, A. H. 2001. "Britain and the Beast: The apocalypse and the seventeenth-century debate about the creation of the British state." Pp. 15–27 in James Force and Richard Popkin, eds., *The Millenarian Turn: Millenarian Contexts of Science, Politics, and Everyday Anglo-American Life in the Seventeenth and Eighteenth Centuries.* Dordrecht: Kluwer Academic.

Wilson Bryan R. 1973. *Magic and the Millennium.* London: Heinemann.

Wilson, Robert R. 2002. "The Biblical roots of apocalyptic." Pp. 56–66 in Abbas Amanat and Magnus Bernhardsson, eds., *Imagining the End: Visions of Apocalypse from the Ancient Middle East to Modern America.* London: I. B. Tauris.

Wintrobe, Ronald. 2006. *Rational Extremism: The Political Economy of Radicalism.* Cambridge: Cambridge University Press.

Wojcik, Daniel. 1997. *The End of the World as We Know It*. New York: New York University Press.

Wong, Bin. 1997. *China Transformed: Historical Change and the Limits of European Experience*. Ithaca, N.Y.: Cornell University Press.

Wood, David. 1989. *The Deconstruction of Time*. Atlantic Highlands, N.J.: Humanities Press International.

Wood, Diana. 2002. "'Lesyng of tyme': Perceptions of idleness and usury in late medieval England." Pp. 107–16 in R. N. Swanson, ed., *The Use and Abuse of Time in Christian History*. Woodbridge, U.K.: Boydell Press.

Worsley, Peter. 1968. *The Trumpet Shall Sound: A Study of "Cargo" Cults in Melanesia*. New York: Schocken.

Wright, Lawrence. 2006. *Looming Tower: Al Qaeda and the Road to 9/11*. New York: Knopf.

Wright, Stuart. 2007. *Patriots, Politics, and the Oklahoma City Bombing*. Cambridge: Cambridge University Press.

Wuthnow, Robert. 1989. *Communities of Discourse: Ideology and Social Structure in the Reformation, the Enlightenment, and European Socialism*. Cambridge, MA: Harvard University Press.

Young, Katharine Galloway. 1987. *Taleworlds and Storyrealms*. Dordrecht: Martinus Nijhoff.

Young, Michael P. 2006. *Bearing Witness against Sin: The Evangelical Birth of the American Social Movement*. Chicago: University of Chicago Press.

Zakai, Avihu. 1992. *Exile and Kingdom: History and Apocalypse in the Puritan Migration to America*. Cambridge: Cambridge University Press.

Zamyatin, Yevgeny Ivanovich. 1993 (1921). *We*. New York: Penguin.

Zaret, David. 1985. *The Heavenly Contract*. Chicago: University of Chicago Press.

——. 2000. *Origins of Democratic Culture*. Princeton, N.J.: Princeton University Press.

Zarrow, Peter. 1990. *Anarchism and Chinese Political Culture*. New York: Columbia University Press.

Zerubavel, Eviatar. 1981. *Hidden Rhythms*. Chicago: University of Chicago Press.

Index